Democratic Development in East Asia

Democratic Development in East Asia explores an important but neglected topic in the literature on democratization in East Asia: the international dimension of democratization. It presents a coherent and comprehensive analysis of the impact of external political, economic and cultural factors on China, South Korea and Taiwan's political development since World War II. The author analyses the circumstances under which the international context affects domestic actors' choice of political institutions and actions, and concentrates on a selection of key international structures and actors that make up this complex picture. Shelley also examines the international political economy, aspects of the United Nations system, diffuse cultural factors and processes, democracy movements, and a number of international non-government organizations.

Becky Shelley is a Senior Analyst in the Department of Premier and Cabinet for the State Government of Tasmania, Australia, and an Honorary Associate in the School of Government at the University of Tasmania.

Politics in Asia series

Formerly edited by Michael Leifer
London School of Economics

Democratic Development in East Asia

Becky Shelley

LONDON AND NEW YORK

First published 2005
by Routledge
2 Park Square, Milton Park, Abingdon, Oxfordshire OX14 4RN

Simultaneously published in the USA and Canada
by Routledge
711 Third Avenue, New York, NY 10017

First issued in paperback 2015

Routledge is an imprint of the Taylor and Francis Group, an informa business

© 2005 Becky Shelley

Typeset in Baskerville by Taylor & Francis Books

British Library Cataloguing in Publication Data
A catalogue record for this book is available from the British Library

Library of Congress Cataloging in Publication Data
A catalog record for this book has been requested

ISBN 13: 978-0-415-64903-2 (pbk)
ISBN 13: 978-0-415-34250-6 (hbk)

**This book is dedicated to my grandparents,
whom I loved.**

Contents

Preface and acknowledgements

This book has its origins in a shorter piece I wrote about international non-government organizations' democracy promotion activities in China. This line of inquiry opened up broader questions about the nature and effects of the international dimensions of democratization in East Asia. I was surprised to discover that the literature on what I had, by then, decided was an important topic was limited. My supervisor, Baogang He, encouraged me to pursue the topic further and under his supervision I began to study the complex processes of interaction between international economic, cultural and political actors and processes and political development in South Korea, Taiwan and China. As the study progressed David Martin Jones also assumed a role guiding the research. I am deeply indebted to both Baogang and David. They encouraged me in every way and have played an invaluable role helping to develop and refine the arguments presented. I continue to benefit from the support and assistance of the School of Government at the University of Tasmania.

I am grateful for the generosity and enthusiasm with which scholars and the NGO community met requests for assistance with this research project. Thanks are due to Chung-si Ahn, Nora Chiang, Allen Choate, James Cotton, Han Do-Hyun, Ho Tung-Hao, Sunny Ho, Kanishka Jayasuriya, Daniel Kelliher, Byung-Kook Kim, Yawei Liu, Andrew Nathan, Kevin O'Brien, Paik Haksoon, Kie-duck Park, Park Tae-jin, Robert Pastor, Scott Snyder, Rex Wang, and Andrew Watson. The Carter Center and the East Asian Institute deserve special mention. The Carter Center allowed me to observe its activities during an election observation mission in Fujian Province in August 2000, and I had the privilege of researching and presenting a working paper at the East Asian Institute in 2001.

In acknowledging those who have helped me with this project I must also mention my family. Thanks are due to my sister, Abi, and her partner who generously fed and watered me in Hong Kong, my mother for (among many other things) reading an early draft, and Dad and Sue for ensuring I had enjoyable breaks in Sydney. Finally, thank you to my husband, Michael – for everything.

I thank the editors and publishers below for permitting me to reproduce the following materials and passages from my papers, which they originally published:

'Protest and Globalization: Media, Symbols and Audience in the Drama of Democratization', *Democratization*, 8, 4, Winter, 2001, pp. 155–174.

'Political Globalization and the Politics of International Non-governmental Organizations: The Case of Village Democracy in China', *Australian Journal of Political Science*, 35, 2, 2000, pp. 225–238, http://www.tandf.co.uk/journals/carfax/10361146.html

Abbreviations

AFIT	Asia Foundation in Taiwan
AFL-CIO	American Federation of Labor and Congress of Industrial Organizations
APEC	Asia-Pacific Economic Co-operation
ASEAN	Association of Southeast Asian Nations
BBC	British Broadcasting Corporation
CIA	Central Intelligence Agency
CROTC	China Rural Official Training Centre
GDP	Gross Domestic Product
IMF	International Monetary Fund
IRI	International Republican Institute
KMT	Kuomintang
NED	National Endowment for Democracy
NGO	Non-government Organization
UNDP	United Nations Development Programme

Introduction

Introduction

At the end of the twentieth century, democracy appeared the dominant trend in western and east-central Europe, in the Americas and increasingly in the Asia Pacific region.[1] Interest in the causes and patterns associated with this trend led several scholars to reconsider the international context of the phenomenon. A number of scholars undertook studies to assess the international dimension of democratization in Europe and the Americas.[2] This evolving body of literature suggests that the impact of the international context upon regime change is growing and is more significant than was formerly thought. As yet, however, comprehensive consideration of the international dimension of democratization has not been given to countries within East Asia.[3] This book attempts to remedy this deficit.[4]

Focus of the book

The book offers a comprehensive analysis of the international actors and processes that have influenced regime change in South Korea, Taiwan and China in the period since World War II. The book assesses what types of interaction between the international and domestic dimensions are significant. The central questions that shape this study consider: to what extent have changes in the external regional and global contexts – over time and across countries – imposed constraints or opportunities for democratization in East Asia? Further: how, why and when does the international context affect the choice of institutions and actions?[5]

The decision to exclude the case of Japan and to include China requires elaboration. The international dimension was, of course, a key factor in Japan's democratization. In fact, Japan is an extreme case where democracy was imposed by an external power, the Allied Occupation forces, as a consequence of losing the war in Pacific Asia.[6] Given this unique event, the case of Japan presents few opportunities to study the complex process of interaction between external and internal factors that shape the other cases we shall discuss.

By contrast, the study's inclusion of China is justified on several grounds.[7] Although China has been a one-party state throughout the period considered in this research, a 'creeping' process of democratization may be observed which merits analysis.[8] China is experiencing indirect and unanticipated consequences of international integration. This has resulted in several important, but incremental changes. Moreover, political developments within Taiwan and South Korea are crucially affected by their proximity to China. As such, studying China also illuminates certain features of those cases. Furthermore, China's regional and global influence is growing. Its international relations provide a good case study to demonstrate the international dimension of democratization's interactive processes. At the same time, literature examining the international dimension of democratization contains implicit assumptions about the democratizing effects of globalization. Consequently, this work contrasts South Korea and Taiwan's experiences of international integration with China's in order to reveal the impact of globalization upon liberalization and democratization in East Asia.

Methodology

An examination of the international dimension of democratization necessarily requires a multi-faceted approach. The study adopts a socio-historical, comparative approach. The comparative approach is a method to discover relationships among variables, not a method of measurement.[9] It is a broad-gauge, general method, not a specialized technique.[10]

Given that key texts in the international dimension of democratization field are edited volumes, their contributing authors' approach and focus varies. As a result, the potential to develop comprehensive comparative analysis of change over time, within and between countries and regions, is limited. Thus, in Laurence Whitehead's edited volume, *The International Dimensions of Democratization: Europe and the Americas*, Thomas Carothers and Kathryn Sikkink focus upon the Latin American region as a whole.[11] Meanwhile, other contributors, like Alan Angell, whose chapter considers political parties and exile politics in Chile, present country-specific studies with a narrower focus and considerable empirical detail.[12] These differences in approach make meaningful comparison difficult.

This research overcomes this problem by developing a detailed comparative analysis of the international dimension of democratization in each of the countries considered. It identifies patterns of interaction, as well as key features and differences between the cases. The research also evaluates the mediating effect of regional context and, in the concluding chapter, considers variations between Latin American, European and East Asian experiences.

The analysis is supported by interviews, observations and research conducted in South Korea, Taiwan and China between 2000 and 2002. It also reviews and assesses the print media, international non-government organization (NGO) reports, and theoretical and empirical literature.

Key concepts

The normative perspective underlying the book is that democratization is generally a positive development, and that democracy is the best form of government both thymotically and in terms of political and economic efficiency.[13] A distinction between democratization and liberalization should, of course, be made immediately. This distinction calls attention to the value of democracy as opposed simply to changes within authoritarian rule.[14] The process of liberalization, as compared to democratization, refers to the loosening of restrictions and expansion of individual or group rights within an authoritarian regime.[15] Democratization, by contrast, extends beyond the broadening of civil and political rights and constitutes a movement toward establishing a popularly elected, democratic political regime, which holds free elections regularly.[16] Liberalization can exist without democratization and, as the case of China demonstrates, can sometimes lead to renewed repression. In both theoretical and practical terms, contingency, ambiguity and reversibility shape the processes of liberalization and democratization.

Three conceptions of democracy underpin the analysis: minimal or electoral democracy, liberal democracy, and non-liberal democracy.[17] Minimalist conceptions of democracy define democracy as a civilian, constitutional system in which the legislative and chief executive offices are filled through regular, competitive, multi-party elections with universal suffrage.[18] In addition to the procedural features of a minimal democracy, a liberal democracy minimizes the power of groups not accountable to the electorate, such as the military, and seeks to ensure the horizontal accountability of office holders to one another. A liberal democracy provides for political and civic pluralism as well as individual and group freedoms. A fair and consistent system of the rule of law secures these freedoms.[19] Non-liberal democracies, by contrast, possess shallow democratic institutions. Although they may fulfil a minimal definition of democracy, elections in non-liberal democracies may not be competitive. Political parties may be weakly constituted and the integrity of democratic institutions may be undermined by a lack of accountability or rule of law.[20]

Core argument

The central argument of the book contends that analysing the patterns of interaction between the domestic and international dimensions of democratization must be given a higher priority by researchers, especially those interested in East Asia. This is because the region has been particularly and increasingly responsive to the international dimension of democratization. Moreover, in the context of the rapidly evolving impact of globalization and the growing importance of China internationally, the impact of the international dimension of democratization upon the Chinese regime should not be overlooked or underestimated.

The book argues that an approach which considers the international dimension of democratization is applicable beyond the Latin American and European contexts where it evolved to explain regime change between 1930 and 1990. Nonetheless, in accounting East Asia's experiences, it is evident that certain contingent features distinguish East Asia from other regions. Indeed, there are also important differences between South Korea, Taiwan and China's interactions with the international dimension of democratization. In particular, China's encounters with the international system distinguish it from other countries, and demonstrate the need for researchers to consider the multi-directional nature of influence when analysing the international dimension of democratization.

The country studies, taken together, underscore the relevance of different time periods to democratic outcomes. Both incremental and rapid changes in international relations have occurred since World War II. In the context of the cold war, international structures of power tended to put on hold democratic development in the region. The end of China's ostracism from the international order signified the end of the cold war in East Asia. This event coincided with changes in the international economy, and the expansion of an interest in human rights and democracy in international relations. These shifts in the international context facilitated a period of liberalization in each of the countries studied and, in South Korea and Taiwan, contributed to democratic transition.

Throughout the 1990s, liberal, internationalist objectives were in ascendance. A normative consensus emerged about the legitimacy of international action to promote human rights and democracy, as globalization facilitated complex and multi-level interactions between international and domestic actors. However, the case studies make evident the contingent nature of international actors' influence upon regime change in the region. They point to the fact that international actors are especially susceptible to shifts in the broader international context and within their own interest groupings.

The book demonstrates that, in East Asia, democratization has been dialectically related to the international context.

Structure of the book

The first chapter provides the conceptual context for the analysis that is to come. It reviews the alternative perspectives available for analysing the international dimension of democratization. Laurence Whitehead, in particular, has identified three critical international factors that bear upon the process: contagion, control and consent. Contagion refers to the indirect diffusion of democracy, control to its imposition, and consent refers to the development of the consent upon which a new democracy must be based.[21] These terms are referred to throughout the book. The book assumes that various combinations of these three factors have influenced regime change in East Asia, rather than any one in isolation. The analysis highlights that the impact of the international dimension upon democratization is mediated by the degree of permeability and mutability of the state concerned. The chapter then proposes a refinement of the conceptualization of the interactive process. This is done to avoid a dichotomous analysis in which either the domestic or the international dimension is assessed exclusively as an independent variable.

Chapter 2 analyses the role of the international political economy. It provides a good example of all three international factors in action: clearly demonstrating the effect of permeability; and highlighting the importance of different time contexts. The chapter focuses upon structural factors in the international political economy, and considers their impact upon development and democratization in each of the countries under study. The chapter demonstrates the significance of the United States to the region's political and economic development. Initially, during the 1950s–1970s, the international context had a negative effect upon democratic development in the region. However, after Sino-American rapprochement, the international context altered and began to support democratic change. This phase lasted from the 1970s until the Asian financial crisis in the mid-1990s. From the financial crisis onwards, multilateral institutions justified their expanded interest in good governance and democracy on economic as well as normative grounds. Given China's increased exposure to the international system, the consequences of these developments for China's political and economic development are considered.

Chapter 3 assesses the impact of the United Nations upon regime change in the region. This chapter argues that the United Nations has played a notably ambiguous role in democratization. The chapter traces the evolution of the United Nations' activity in promoting democracy, and identifies the salience of international factors in the establishment of the region's borders and institutional designs post-World War II. The chapter details how international factors have affected South Korea, Taiwan and China's membership status within the United Nations. The chapter then considers each case separately. The analysis shows how United Nations' interventions in Korea hindered its democratic development. It also reveals that the United Nations' recognition of the legitimacy of the Kuomintang regime inhibited the development of democracy on Taiwan. Indeed, it was Taiwan's eventual loss of status at the United Nations that triggered a domestic political crisis. In this sense, the United Nations indirectly assisted the transition to democracy in Taiwan. China's engagement with the United Nations is complex and multi-directional. The chapter's analysis of the human rights regime, and the United Nations Development Programme's democracy promotion activities in China, identifies an evolving dialectic between the United Nations regime and China. Scrutiny of each country's interactions with the United Nations demonstrates that the United Nations' impact upon regime change in East Asia cannot be reduced to a single pattern. The United Nations reflects major power interests, and as these interests have altered over time, so has the relationship between the United Nations and the region.

Chapter 4 examines how East Asia's political systems and political cultures respond to and engage with an emerging global culture. The chapter contrasts four competing perspectives of the relationship between the global culture of democracy and East Asian political practice. Subsequently, the chapter conducts a detailed examination of the character of the cultural encounter. The way in which four distinct political structures operate in South Korea, Taiwan and China is considered. The chapter maintains that a range of European and American political institutions and theories have influenced East Asia's political forms. Further, the chapter contends that a complex fusion of democratic forms with East Asian political practices is taking place. Paradoxically, although global culture has affected the choice of political institutions in each state, the domestic context mediates political behaviour and actions. The analysis explores this paradox in order to draw a distinction between the transfer of democratic institutions and the transfer of democratic norms. In effect, different hybrid models of democracy are evolving. Each hybrid blends elements of global culture with local, culturally derived practices, and politically determined state objectives.

The analysis then shifts to a more explicit focus on the role of international actors. Chapter 5 employs the metaphor of the drama of democratization to analyse the international dimension of democratic protest movements. It studies three democratic protest movements: the street protest in the southern port city of Kaohsiung in Taiwan on World Human Rights Day in 1979; the 1980 protest in Kwangju in South Korea in which over 200,000 people participated and took control of the city; and the student and worker protest in Tiananmen Square in 1989. Each of these protest movements ended violently. The analysis reveals the impact of the globalization of television news upon interactions between protestors and their international audience. It demonstrates that the international audience and the protestors were affected by the international news media's coverage of the events. The interactive function of the symbols used during the protest movements is traced, highlighting the way in which symbols unify both local and global actors in the course of protest movements. Finally, the chapter analyses the response of mass and international audiences to particular events. The chapter contends, in particular, that interactions between the international dimension and the democratic protest movement in Tiananmen served a democratizing function. Established democracies promoted this democratizing function and the experience clearly demonstrates the multi-directional nature of international and domestic interactions. Nevertheless, the democratic function was both contingent and transitory.

Chapter 6 assesses democracy promotion activities by prominent American-based non-government organizations (NGOs) in the region. It is informed by Philip Cerny's insight into the process of political globalization.[22] The chapter argues that NGO involvement in democracy promotion in East Asia exemplifies a process of political globalization that involves the intermingling of NGO, donor and political interests at the national and international level. A comparison of early NGO programs in the region with current programs in China reveals the evolution of NGO activities in the region. It is evident that when NGOs engage in democracy promotion, multi-level games spill over layers of power, involving an interplay of interests between local, national and international actors.

The conclusion summarizes the core argument of the book, identifies patterns within the international dimension of democratization in East Asia and accounts for differences in China's experiences. It then specifies the patterns of interaction the book has shown to be crucial to the democratization process. It contends that international economic and political factors are of far greater weight than cultural factors. Further, it argues that the role of international political actors is highly contingent. This is because international actors are especially susceptible to shifts in the broader international context and within their own regional and state interest groupings. The conclusion subsequently discusses the significance of the research for previous studies and theories on the theme of the international dimension of democratization. It emphasizes the importance of a complex conceptualization of interaction, especially given the effects of globalization. Finally, the book argues that, especially in view of the shifting international context after 11 September 2001, the international dimension of democratization requires even more attention from researchers interested in regime change.

1 Considering the international dimension of democratization

Introduction

The international dimension of democratization is an umbrella term for a range of external influences. Geoffrey Pridham, George Herring and Eric Sanford contend that the international dimension of democratization takes many forms, including unintentional and intentional effects, and direct and indirect forms of influence.[1] The international dimension of democratization also encompasses the effects of state and non-state actors, both unilateral and multilateral actions, and diffuse market and cultural forces.[2]

The international context has been described as the 'forgotten dimension' of regime transition.[3] Although acknowledging the importance of internal forces to the establishment and consolidation of democratic regimes, Laurence Whitehead urges consideration of the distinctive international contexts under which the majority of democracies became established or were re-established.[4] The purpose of such research, therefore, is not to determine whether the domestic or international context is more important for the transition to democracy, but rather to conceive and analyse the role of interactions between them.

The fact that the international dimension of democratization in East Asia has not been comprehensively studied points to a more general problem within transitions literature. These studies tend to develop generalizations based upon analysis of specific regional contexts, in particular Latin America. Guillermo O'Donnell and Philippe C. Schmitter's seminal contribution to the transitions field underlines the issue well.[5] Based upon their studies of Latin America, O'Donnell and Schmitter detail a process in which important divisions within the authoritarian regime create a context for transitional openings. They contend that liberalization assists the opposition to mobilize, assists the resurgence of civil society, and enables the negotiation of elite pacts. After a democratic breakthrough, in which a new government comes to power through national elections and the development of new political institutions, there is a period of consolidation.

Some political scientists regard the transition process outlined by O'Donnell and Schmitter as a universal model.[6] Yet Latin American experiences of the transition process differ from East Asia's in several respects.[7] Taiwan and South Korea's political evolutions were marked by the ambiguous role played by civil society, incremental liberalization, and the ongoing efforts of organized political opposition (not soft-liners within the regime) who pushed for change across successive local and national elections.[8] Most of the 'classics' of transition theory have neglected to address the Asian region. Their focus has been primarily on Latin American and European cases.

It is worth noting that there are two schools of transition theory: the structural school, which emphasizes the importance of environmental factors; and the process school, which stresses the role of actors and their strategic choices. A structural approach tends to use a diachronic approach, whereas a process approach usually analyses cases synchronically.

The structural approach identifies particular conditions that are regarded as facilitating the development of democracy. International structural factors, which are treated as significant, include economic conditions and integration into the global economy, the impact of international structures of power (including war and geo-political dependence), and cultural flows. According to this view, all political actors are regarded as working within a framework of structural restraints and opportunities. These structural conditions are thought to limit the range of alternatives open to political actors, and make it likely that certain courses of action will be more appealing than others.

The process approach focuses on the role of human agency in determining political outcomes. This approach emphasizes the autonomy of political actors and the importance of choice. It regards the indeterminacy of the potential outcome during transitional politics as creating a context in which the choices of strategic actors (rather than structural conditions) are the key elements. As a consequence of this emphasis, the process approach tends to focus attention upon elite politics.

As Jeff Haynes argues, however, while structures form the context within which political leaders act, individuals are not slavishly bound by structures: agency is also of great importance to political outcomes.[9] Thus, the analysis in this book focuses on the interaction of structural factors with political choice and action. Blending the structural and process approaches provides a more convincing account of the international dimension of democratization.

Categories of interaction

Whitehead identifies three perspectives that may be used to analyse international factors associated with the process of regime change. The categories are contagion, control and consent. There is significant overlap between the three. These perspectives were developed to explain the international dimension of regime change in Europe and the Americas, and their applicability to the East Asian context is generally untested.

Contagion

The first approach, contagion, does not require consideration of political actors. It refers to the diffusion of democracy through unintentional, voluntary channels and largely ignores the intentions of actors. A contagion analysis highlights the geographical distribution of countries classified as democratic and how they change over time.[10] Instruments of influence that might encourage countries to copy the political institutions of their neighbours include information transmitted neutrally from other democracies or countries in transition. Schmitter argues that the effects of contagion and consent are particularly relevant in the analysis of regime change in specific regional contexts.[11] Contagion is relevant to a consideration of the role of democracy movements in East Asia.

Control

The second interpretation, control, refers to deliberate acts involving the imposition of democracy or intervention by one country over another. A control explanation provides a better account than contagion for the speed, direction and limits of the democratization process.[12] The control approach is situated within a realist paradigm and focuses on the actions and imperatives of state powers, and the role of external agency. A control perspective may be used to account for Japan's democratization. Nevertheless, as the case of South Korea suggests, democratic institutions established first by the American military command, and then by the United Nations, can be readily undermined by domestic actors when domestic consent is absent.

Consent

The third and most complex explanation of the role of the international dimension concerns consent. The development of consent for regime transformation is often considered a domestic matter. Whitehead reviews this assumption, highlighting the ways in which international processes contribute to, or impede, the generation of the consent upon which new democracies must be based.[13] This book is primarily interested in this type of interaction.

Whitehead distinguishes between four aspects of consent. The first concerns the territorial limits, such as boundaries and/or national identities, to successive democratizations and their consequences for established alliance systems.[14] The process of defining territorial boundaries and forging national identities within East Asian states has been distinguished by its contested and unresolved character. International interest in the region's geo-strategic importance influenced the division of the Korean peninsula and the question of Taiwan's status internationally. This aspect of consent is relevant to the discussion in Chapter 3 of the United Nations' role in the region.

The second international aspect of consent refers to the main international structures that tend to generate consent for regime change, such as the creation or existence of regional blocs.[15] An example of this is the notion of democratic conditionality. Philippe Schmitter emphasizes the role of conditionality in regime change, and argues that it ought to be a category in itself.[16] Conditionality involves multilateral institutions deliberately using coercion by attaching specific conditions to the distribution of benefits to recipient countries.[17] Although membership of Asia's regional organizations is not conditional upon democratic status, the International Monetary Fund (IMF) imposed certain 'good governance' conditions upon South Korea after the Asian financial crisis.

The third aspect of consent concerns the ways in which authentic national democratic actors may be constituted from relatively diffuse transnational groupings.[18] Whitehead contends that a vital international dimension of many democratizations concerns the interactive process by which the external supporters of domestic political actors relinquish control over their protégés.[19] This contention is relevant to East Asia. For example, the decline of American support for South Korea's authoritarian leaders and the loss of international recognition of the Kuomintang (KMT) regime in Taiwan influenced the strategies of domestic political actors. Further, especially in the case of China, authentic national democratic actors may arise from relatively diffuse transnational groupings, such as overseas opposition groups or networks.

The final international dimension of consent proposed by Whitehead concerns international demonstration effects and their role affecting the underlying distribution of popular preferences and expectations.[20] Whitehead associates international demonstration effects with the almost universal wish to imitate a way of life identified with the liberal capitalist democracies. He highlights that international demonstration effects may serve to undermine any regime perceived as incompatible with these aspirations, or, alternatively, may serve to generate the support needed to sustain new democracies.[21] Two aspects of international demonstration effects are identified in this book: the first is pro-democratic and the second is anti-democratic. The first relates to the development and diffusion of a normative entitlement to democracy internationally. The second aspect involves the way in which demonstration effects are mediated by different regional settings. For example, the experiences of the former Soviet Union provided a clear example to the Chinese leadership of the dangers of political and economic liberalization.

It is contended that, notwithstanding their analytical utility, Whitehead's categories inadequately conceive of the interplay between the international and domestic dimensions of democratization. As a consequence, the relationship between the international and domestic spheres is primarily regarded in reactive terms.

Other research in the field also exhibits this tendency. For example, Geoffrey Pridham identifies two forms of linkage between the international and domestic dimensions of democratization, which he terms inner-directed linkages and outer-directed linkages.[22] For Pridham, inner-directed linkages are factors originating in the international context and which interact with domestic politics. Whereas, outer-directed linkages are those originating in the domestic system and interacting with external actors. Pridham 'unscrambles' outer-directed linkages and assesses background variables such as domestic attitudes to international actors, the structure of government and strategies of elite groups, and the role of wider societal influences.[23] Pridham's concern, thus conceived, is with how domestic attitudes and structures condition the response and strategies of domestic actors to the international context. Pridham does not develop further the full scope of these linkages.

This book broadens the scope of research into the international dimension of democratization beyond reactions. It considers the effects of *interactions*. To put it differently, during interactions between the domestic and international dimensions there is always the potential for a reciprocal effect. The process of interaction itself may have potential causative significance. Chapters 5 and 6 present cogent examples of the multi-directional effects of interactions between the international and domestic dimensions of democratization.

Actors and norms

A wide range of international actors and norms has the capacity to influence political systems in East Asia. The range includes multilateral organizations such as the United Nations, the World Trade Organization, the IMF, the World Bank and the Asian Development Bank; regional organizations such as the European Union, the Asia-Pacific Economic Co-operation (APEC) and the Association of Southeast Asian Nations (ASEAN); numerous international NGOs; and sovereign states, such as the United States, Great Britain and France among others. These international actors sometimes promote particular norms in the region, but not exclusively so, diffuse social and market processes are also important.

Schmitter hypothesizes that the international context surrounding democratization has shifted from a primary reliance on public inter-governmental channels of influence, towards an increased involvement of private, non-government organizations.[24] In recognition of the growing role of non-state actors in the international system, Schmitter develops a model to understand the functions different international actors serve (Table 1.1). Schmitter divides the international actors into two types: public, state actors, and private, non-state actors. Within these two broad categories he makes a further distinction between unilateral and multilateral actors. Schmitter identifies the categories of influence which state and private actors are commonly associated with.

Table 1.1 The 'sub-contexts' of the international context

		Basis for action	
		Coercion: backed by states	*Voluntary: supported by private actors*
Number of actors	Unilateral	Control	Contagion
	Multilateral	Conditionality	Consent

Source: Philippe C. Schmitter, 'The Influence of the International Context upon the Choice of National Institutions and Policies in Neo-Democracies', in Laurence Whitehead (ed.) *The International Dimensions of Democratization: Europe and the Americas*, New York: Oxford University Press, 1998, p. 29. Reprinted by permission of Oxford University Press.

Karen Dawisha and Michael Turner are critical of Schmitter's four-fold categorization. They argue that the distinctions drawn between these four types of agency create dichotomies between the state and private actors, and multilateral and bilateral linkages that are not useful.[25] This is because there is substantial cross-over between the types of interaction that state and private actors engage in. That is, states can and do perform a range of non-conditional, non-coercive activities; just as voluntary groups can condition their assistance, based on certain criteria, in order to encourage change in social and political structures within the recipient country.[26]

A further criticism may be levelled at the model. Distinguishing between state and private actors may be a more difficult process than is often assumed. For example, Chapter 6 reveals that funding and political ties between several international non-government organizations and the United States government undermine a clear separation between the public and private spheres of activity.

Forms and degrees of influence

The international dimension of democratization presents a particular difficulty in empirically establishing one efficient cause.[27] As a result, the book focuses on identifying general tendencies.

Dawisha and Turner develop an analytical model to comprehend the potential influence the international dimension may have.[28] Although the model is designed to understand post-communist transitions in Russia and the Eurasian states, it is also relevant to East Asia. Dawisha and Turner argue that the role of the international dimension is affected by what they term a state's mutability and permeability.

Mutability is the extent to which societies are capable of radical departures from existing social and cultural norms.[29] It concerns whether efforts at fostering democratic institutions and forms will be undermined by immutable pre-existing social, political and economic forces.[30] The book assumes that societies are, at least potentially, mutable.

The issue of permeability is particularly relevant when considering the effect of the international dimension upon political liberalization in China. States characterized by their impermeability may have extensive external relations, but their leaders may construct an isolationist approach, which enables them to seal off their countries from foreign encroachment.[31] Moreover, the political culture within such a society may also contain an isolationist current, which may resist the embedding of exogenous influences within the transitional society.[32]

In contrast to the idea of impermeability is the notion that all modern, advanced industrial societies are essentially permeable. This is largely due to the effects of globalization, advances in communications technology, the influence of international institutions, and the effects of a global economy. South Korea and Taiwan are essentially permeable societies, and although China is rapidly following suit, the legacy of China's previous international isolation remains. The assumption underlying this text is that the influence of the external forces has increased as a consequence of globalization.

Conclusion

The analytical perspectives described in this chapter were developed to consider the international dimension of democratization in Europe and the Americas. The applicability of these approaches to the East Asian context will be tested in the following chapters.

The literature on the international dimension of democratization discussed in this chapter tends to conceive the effects of the international dimension in reactive terms. This chapter argues that the reciprocal effects of interaction also need to be considered. The merit of this argument will become apparent in subsequent chapters, in particular those which consider the role of international actors.

2 Development, democracy and the international economy

Introduction

This chapter explores the relationship between the international context, development and democratic change through a consideration of three phases of political and economic development in East Asia. A structural, socio-historical analysis of factors associated with war, rapid regional change and economic crisis in East Asia is combined with an analysis of the effects of international incentives and constraints upon the formation of domestic coalitions and state structures. The impact of international structures of power upon democratization has varied over time, and includes factors such as economic integration, geo-political interests and transnational cultural flows.[1] This approach is consistent with Geoffrey Underhill's argument regarding international political economy. He states that there are:

> ... three fundamental premises of international political economy: i) that political and economic domains cannot be separated in any real sense, and even doing so for analytical purposes has its perils; ii) political interaction is a principal means through which the economic structures of the market are established and in turn transformed; and iii) that there is an intimate connection between the domestic and international levels of analysis, and that the two cannot meaningfully be separated off from one another.[2]

The concept of development and its relationship to democracy

Studies, such as this, that engage in broad comparison require the use of categories sensitive both to context and to change over time within cases. They also need to achieve the 'virtue of conceptual travelling' without committing the 'vice of conceptual stretching'.[3] The literature on development is large and definitions of development are diverse and contentious.[4] Two conceptions of development may be distinguished. One conception is concerned primarily with national economic growth, measured in terms of per capita gross domestic product (GDP).[5] The other develops a broadly defined notion of sustainable human development, in which the choices for all people in society are expanded.[6] Since China increased its engagement with the international political economy, the pursuit of sustainable human development came to be regarded as a goal by sections of the international community. However, when South Korea and Taiwan embarked on their high growth oriented development strategies, the narrower concept of growth of per capita GDP was the common measure of development.[7] This definitional shift from GDP to sustainable human development is important because it signifies the expanded criteria against which sections of the international community assess China's economic development.

The relationship between capitalist economic development and democracy has been the subject of detailed academic study.[8] Indeed, Rueschemeyer, Stephens and Stephens have observed that in some analyses 'democracy and capitalism are often seen as virtually identical'.[9] The East Asian region, at least until the mid-1980s, presented an exception to this view. South Korea and Taiwan experienced an extended period of economic growth and capitalist development without developing democracy. Clearly, democracy is 'no precondition for a capitalist market economy'.[10] China appears to want to follow this trajectory, development without (or at least prior to) democracy.

When democratic transition occurred in South Korea and Taiwan, a number of analysts regarded it as evidence in support of modernization theory.[11] The basic assumption of modernization theory is that there is one general process of development, of which democratization is the final stage. The model was developed in the post-war period and reached its height in the 1960s. As a means of addressing the parochialism and formalism of comparative research, modernization theorists widened their use of the term 'political system', so as to focus on performance, interaction and behaviour as well as political institutions.[12] Modernization theory focuses on specific domestic causal sequences linking economic development to democratization.

Flaws in modernization theory, relevant to this book, include a tendency to view change in societies as immanent and to direct attention too closely at internal processes of change. This focus leads to a failure to fully incorporate external sources of change. Bruce Cumings argues that modernization theory's tendency to examine single countries overlooks the systematic interaction of East Asian countries with each other and with the world at large.[13] Additionally, the roles and strategies of different actors are overlooked by modernization theory. Guillermo O'Donnell and Philippe Schmitter highlight that in the process of democratization 'unexpected events (*fortuna*), insufficient information, hurried and audacious choices, confusion about motives and interests, plasticity, and even indefinition of political identities, as well as the talents of specific individuals (*virtù*), are frequently decisive in determining the outcomes'.[14]

In the 1970s and early 1980s, bureaucratic authoritarian theory, world systems theory and dependency theories became popular and were used to account for Latin American development. Some scholars also applied the ideas to East Asia. They pointed to issues such as South Korea's high levels of international debt, around US$46 billion in the early 1980s, as evidence in support of this interpretation.[15] However, in light of East Asia's subsequent economic success, these interpretations were discredited.[16] Developmental state literature came to dominate analyses of East Asian development. Meta-theoretical concerns are of less interest to scholars in this area than for those working with systemic level theories.[17] Developmental state literature unmasks the roles played by the government and political systems in the economy. The literature contends that the active pursuit of strategic trade and industrial policies has been an integral element of East Asia's high growth economies. Key scholars in the area include Chalmers Johnson, Robert Wade and Alice Amsden.[18]

Authors of developmental state literature focus on explaining economic development and are less interested in the question of democracy. In addition to highlighting the adoption of strategic trade and industrial policies, the authors point out that this model of development contains certain undemocratic features. These features include political domination by one party combined with elements of authoritarian rule. Political legitimacy in this context derives from economic success. Chalmers Johnson regards the political economy of capitalism in South Korea and Taiwan as representative of a trade-off between 'greater performance but less political participation'.[19] Robert Wade develops 'governed market theory' in his study of Taiwan. Wade builds on the idea of the developmental state and development economics' understanding of the nature of the developmental problem.[20] Wade argues that the corporatist and authoritarian political arrangements in East Asia have provided the basis for market guidance.[21] Both modernization theory and developmental state literature accept that economic development precedes democracy. However, developmental state literature does not necessarily accept the *need* for democracy.

In 1997 the Asian financial crisis began in the Thai economy and spread to other economies in the region. One consequence of the crisis has been an increased interest among academics and international institutions, such as the IMF, in issues of good governance and democracy. The developmental state model consequently came under sustained criticism for features that had earlier drawn praise. Where previously developmental state policies and practices were praised for governing the market in a manner 'suggesting they have created a more competitive form of capitalism'[22], they were now admonished for the failure to ensure transparency, responsibility and democratic accountability.[23] This reappraisal of the developmental state model may have consequences for China's development path. The notion that political reform is necessary to sustain economic growth has become prevalent within sections of the international community, and at times international financial institutions have made their assistance packages conditional upon progressing political reform.

The cold war era: 1950s–1960s

International context

Between the 1950s and 1960s, international interest in the region focussed on cold war and economic issues. Development economics in this period reflected the concerns of modernization literature; economic growth was a priority. This focus dovetailed with the geo-strategic objectives of the competing powers. Unlike other regions, such as Latin America, East Asia was not traditionally dominated by a single state. Instead, there was substantial rivalry between several leading powers.[24] During the twentieth century, China, Japan, the former Soviet Union and the United States competed for power and influence in the region.

Japan's impact on the regional economic mode is considerable. Beginning with its attempts to foster the Greater East Asian Co-prosperity Sphere, Japan's emergence as the first non-Western industrial power was accompanied by imperial ambitions that radically re-oriented the political economy of East Asia.[25] The experience of Japanese colonialism in South Korea and Taiwan provided a model for state directed development.[26] After World War II, the United States played a central role in determining both the external framework and internal policy direction of Taiwan and South Korea's economies. The region was also influenced by Russian ideas. Leninist party structures influenced the Kuomintang which, in turn, influenced party structures on Taiwan.[27]

George Kennan articulated the 'Containment Policy' in 1947. Kennan argued that 'pressure against the free institutions of the Western world' would be 'contained by the adroit and vigilant application of counterforce at a series of constantly shifting geographical and political points'.[28] Kennan's comments were originally targeted at the Soviet Union. The sentiment was extended to include communism in Asia after the communist victory in China and the outbreak of war in Korea. The perceived power of the Chinese Communist Party and the region's close proximity to the Soviet Union influenced American foreign policy towards the Pacific. It resulted in America isolating China internationally, and integrating South Korea and Taiwan into the Western international economic order.

The success of the development strategies undertaken by South Korea and Taiwan has its roots in the Bretton Woods system. The Bretton Woods system was a product of American and British co-operation. The Bretton Woods system aimed to create a stable world economic order in which governments would have freedom to pursue national economic objectives within a monetary order based on fixed exchange rates and currency convertibility for account transactions. The International Monetary Fund was created to supervise the operation of the monetary system and to provide assistance to countries experiencing temporary balance of payments difficulties.[29] The establishment of the Bretton Woods system ushered in an era of unprecedented growth in international trade. Taiwan and South

Korea were beneficiaries of this environment. Thus, between the 1950s and 1960s the Americans supported a system that set as long-term goals the establishment of mechanisms for free trade, balance of payments, liberalization and free capital flows.

By contrast, China's engagement with the international political economy was not centred on the liberal trading order established at Bretton Woods; it centred on the Soviet bloc. Beijing's foreign economic policy during the Maoist period was not as self-reliant as its leaders claimed. China benefited from technology, military and capital equipment from Russia, and repaid these goods with raw materials. The close relationship between the two powers was neither as lasting nor as economically rewarding as Taiwan and South Korea's with the United States. Soviet assistance was eventually withdrawn from China, and by 1969 armed border clashes illustrated the widening Sino-Soviet split. This led China to a growing self-reliance with questionable political consequences.

Development effects

South Korea, Taiwan and China began their development projects from underdeveloped or crisis conditions. Each country underwent significant land reform and received tutelage from a major power. China adopted a planned economy strategy and a form of import substitution industrialization. After initially adopting an aid dependent import substitution industrialization strategy, South Korea and Taiwan shifted to an export orientation.

South Korea and Taiwan

In South Korea and Taiwan the incentive to develop rapidly was influenced by their precarious geo-political position. Their economic development was also assisted by the close relationship the countries developed with the United States and Japan, and by the outbreak of the Vietnam War.

The Korean War damaged the South Korean economy. In Taiwan the prospects for development were dismal. Natural resources were scarce, the island was heavily populated and, in the early 1950s, the government set aside more than 50 per cent of its national budget for defence spending to deter the armed threat from China.[30] The size of the trade deficit and shortfalls of food, crucial commodities and raw materials created a dependent economic environment. Under American advice, both South Korea and Taiwan adopted a model of import substitution industrialization. South Korea and Taiwan experienced growing trade deficits and aid dependence under this strategy.

John Lie argues that the benevolence of foreign aid to South Korea is frequently exaggerated.[31] Between 1953 and 1960 the United States and the United Nations largely financed the reconstruction and stabilization programs in South Korea. All major economic policy decisions, even those not directly involving aid funds, were made jointly by the South Korean government and the United States.[32] Aid provided capital investment, essential goods, technical assistance and modern machinery. Moreover, aid (especially under President Syngman Rhee's rule) encouraged existing unproductive commercial capitalism, high consumption, and led to imports competing with and discouraging domestic production.[33] Additionally, some assistance was carefully measured to ensure that South Korea did not compete with the donor.[34]

America was not prepared to provide aid to South Korea and Taiwan indefinitely, and American advisers urged a reorientation of their economic strategies. The advisers encouraged manufactured exports, foreign direct investment and, in South Korea's case, commercial borrowing. By the 1960s, South Korea and Taiwan had abandoned import substitution industrialization in favour of a policy of export-oriented economic growth. The policy encouraged the export of labour-intensive manufactured goods, based on comparative advantage. State-led incentives, an international economic environment underpinned by the Bretton Woods system, and South Korea and Taiwan's close alliance with, and access to, American markets were important elements in the growth of their economies. In addition, domestic protection from import competition coupled with strategic trade and investment policies assisted their development strategies.[35]

The resurgence of the Japanese economy and American intervention in Vietnam provided further stimuli to Taiwan and South Korea's economies. The Vietnam War was good for Taiwan's economy, helping to compensate for the termination of American economic aid. This was because the United States purchased large amounts of food and military equipment from Taiwan.[36] The Vietnam War generated demands for South Korean products and stimulated exports and industrialization.[37] The social costs of the Vietnam War for South Korea were high. South Korean soldiers comprised the largest allied force after the South Vietnamese themselves.[38] South Korean participation in the war was economically and politically attractive to the United States. The monthly pay of an American soldier was considerably higher than that of a South Korean soldier and South Korean casualties had virtually no effect on popular support for the war within the United States.[39]

Diaspora networks further facilitated the economic integration of South Korea and Taiwan into the expanding Japanese and American economies. By the mid-1960s, with the normalization of relations between Japan and South Korea, the regional economy became increasingly interdependent because of growing trade and foreign direct investment among them.[40] In effect, South Korea and Taiwan were integrated into Japan's growing economic networks and the international division of labour, as they followed Japanese companies in the product cycle.[41]

China

Previous experience of integration in the international economy had resulted in China lacking control over its own resources and experiencing economic atrophy and political impotence. After the 1949 communist revolution, Mao Zedong decided that, in order to address these problems, China needed to enhance its self-reliance and strengthen its position in the region. Mao's 'lean-to-one-side' statement allied China with the Soviet Union. The statement was born of a shared political ideology between the two states, but it also reflected Mao's view that China needed to strengthen its position against a potentially hostile America.[42] Soviet industrialization was initially China's development model. China's pre-war pattern of foreign trade was reversed, flowing to the Soviet bloc instead of to the West. Thousands of Chinese went to the former Soviet Union to study, and Russians provided technical advice and assistance on the ground in China.

The Chinese Communist Party emulated a range of Soviet economic forms. However, the collectivization of the economy did not actually increase the amount of agricultural product received by the Chinese government. By 1956, Soviets were criticizing Stalin and the Chinese Communist Party sought more indigenous ways to develop socialism. Ultimately, the Chinese Communist Party's departure from the Soviet developmental model, and deviation from Moscow's foreign policy line, was pronounced. 'The Great Leap Forward' was initiated in 1958. The Chinese government hoped that the mass mobilization of rural development (using the abundant labour supplies) would generate exports, which would then enable capital goods to be secured. Then, on 16 July 1960, Khrushchev suddenly announced that the Soviet government would be unilaterally terminating 600 inter-governmental contracts with China, and withdrawing all Soviet experts working in China.[43] The deterioration of relations between the Communist Party of the Soviet Union and the Chinese Communist Party also affected relations between China and other Soviet client states; China's trade with the Eastern bloc diminished.

In addition to the impact of the souring of relations with the Soviet Union, America's policy of containing Chinese communism, and its sway over its allies, affected China's development prospects. In April 1950 the National Security Council approved NSC–68. It proposed a dramatic increase in American expenditure and armed forces and called for American efforts to meet the communist threat anywhere it emerged. In line with the spirit of NSC–68 America's political and economic strategy toward China changed. For five years from September 1952, the United States succeeded in introducing the 'China differential' into the embargo lists imposed on the export of strategic items to communist countries.[44] The China Committee was established within the Paris Co-ordinating Committee for Exports of Strategic Materials to monitor this embargo. The embargo was acknowledged to be much more severe than that imposed on the Soviet Union and its Eastern European allies.[45] Although trade with Japan had expanded in the early 1960s 'autarky and a strict code of self-reliance had come to characterize China's external relations'.[46]

Thus, in the early 1960s, China's economy suffered as a result of poor economic policy, poor harvests, the withdrawal of Soviet technicians and aid, and its international isolation. China underwent several years of serious economic dislocation, malnutrition, high mortality rates and the stagnation of industry.[47] The human cost was extreme: over 30 million people are estimated to have perished. Domestic factors such as the Cultural Revolution further exacerbated China's development problems. Nonetheless, as Yongjin Zhang shows, during these two decades China developed extensive political and economic links with African and Asian countries.[48]

Democratizing effects

The democratizing effects of the international context during the 1950s–1960s differed between the cases. China and Taiwan did not experience any significant democratic opening, although South Korea did briefly. In Taiwan and South Korea, the international context of the cold war and the threatening external environment gave each state a rationale for repressing political opposition. The national importance of the export-oriented industrialization strategy was used to limit labour power and constrain the development of class coalitions. Rueschemeyer, Stephens and Stephens argue that capitalist development has historically led to the emergence of a denser civil society that can provide a counterpoint to state power, through enhancing the ability of subordinate classes to organize.[49] During this period, the state succeeded in co-opting and curtailing the development of a denser civil society in both South Korea and Taiwan. China experienced one of the most repressive periods of its history during this phase of international isolation, as it attempted to develop socialism with Chinese characteristics.

South Korea and Taiwan

In South Korea and Taiwan, external factors constrained development in a democratic direction, and reinforced authoritarianism. The threatening presence of North Korea and China was used by the regimes to justify political repression and martial law. South Korean President, Syngman Rhee, instituted the National Security Act to deal with the communist threat and launched a campaign against any perceived 'radicals'. By the spring of 1950, the campaign had filled South Korean prisons with over 60,000 prisoners.[50] In Taiwan, organized opposition against the Kuomintang was still reeling from the effects of the 28 February 1947 uprising on the island against the oppressive Chiang dynasty. During the month-long uprising, the Nationalist army killed about 20,000 of Taiwan's economic, political and social elite and entrenched deep suspicion, hatred and mistrust between the mainland

Chinese and the Taiwanese on the island.[51] When the KMT government retreated to Taiwan after being defeated by the Chinese communists on the mainland, Taiwan became a deeply divided society. The 'Temporary Provisions Effective During the Period of Mobilization for the Suppression of the Communist Rebellion' (the 'Temporary Provisions'), and martial law operated in Taiwan until 1987.

The United States helped to sustain the political systems in South Korea and Taiwan during the 1950s; it gave more civil and military aid to these two countries than any other two systems.[52] The United States assisted South Korea and Taiwan's economic development in order to underpin security arrangements and to provide a capitalist economic model to counter communism. Providing a democratic political model as an alternative to communism was less of a policy priority. Initially, the existence of martial law conditions in both South Korea and Taiwan was not an obstacle to international support of their regimes.

Ultimately, the excesses of Syngman Rhee's South Korean regime – electoral rigging, arbitrary and corrupt rule – contributed to a crisis in regime legitimacy. International commentators became critical of his rule. Rhee was described as a 'despot, a demagogue and a dangerous bluffer'.[53] Growing numbers of citizens demanded free and fair elections. Rhee's downfall in the Spring of 1960 was swift. American policy toward Rhee shifted from 'reluctant tolerance', to a public condemnation of the regime's repressive tactics and a simultaneous call for democratic reform.[54] Rhee resigned from his position as President and moved to the United States.

Following Rhee's resignation, democracy was in place in South Korea for a mere nine months. A range of restraints on political activity and freedom of speech were removed during this brief period, and social and ideological polarization between the conservative and radical groups came to the fore.[55] Acute ideological cleavages caused mounting social tensions and contributed to fears of instability. When General Park Chung Hee led a military *coup d'état* both the South Korean people and the international community were remarkably quiescent.

The South Korean military junta, the Supreme Council for National Reconstruction, ruled from 1961 to 1963. The military junta could not afford to jeopardize continued American support because, in the early 1960s, American aid programs accounted for fifty per cent of the national budget and military aid accounted for over seventy per cent of South Korean defence expenditures.[56] In the face of pressure from the United States and at home, the Council disbanded. The military leaders donned civilian clothes and held elections in 1963, which General Park won.[57] The elections signified a symbolic, rather than a substantive, shift toward civilian rule and democracy. Following the coup, the military played a pre-eminent role in South Korean politics for the next thirty years.

Integration into the international economy on favourable terms, and export-oriented strategies, had a number of social and political consequences in South Korea and Taiwan. Land reform in both South Korea and Taiwan contributed to making their development relatively egalitarian.[58] As their economies grew, both regimes continued to develop public welfare, and economic growth was not associated with increased income inequality. In both South Korea and Taiwan, the growth strategy resulted in a steady improvement of living standards that brought the government the acquiescence, if not support, of some segments of labour.[59]

In South Korea and Taiwan the shift to export-oriented industrialization altered the structure of the labour force. The countries emerged from predominantly rural societies to become dynamic, industrialized countries in the space of a generation. Urban manufacturing industries were the main site of proletarianization in South Korea and, simultaneously, a feminization of the workforce occurred.[60] In Taiwan, the geographic dispersal of the workforce was greater and the experience of urbanization somewhat different to that of South Korea.

Although the structure of labour relations in the two countries differs, in each case labour was politically excluded. This strategy enabled comparative advantages to be fully exploited. It also constrained the development of an organized, politicized labour movement. The regimes justified politically repressive laws and policies on the basis of the threatening external context.

In South Korea, a highly politicized labour movement had historical roots in opposition to Japanese colonialism.[61] President Rhee's anti-left campaign in the 1950s and the junta's decisions to freeze wages, ban strikes and dissolve all existing trade unions had undermined the labour movement's power and capacity to organize.[62] In 1963, the Park government amended the labour laws instituted by the American military command. The amendments imposed significant new constraints on labour autonomy and represented a step toward a corporatist system. Park, superficially following West German models, created a centralized body, the Federation of Korean Trade Unions.[63]

On Taiwan the Kuomintang enacted legislation that prohibited strikes, restricted wage bargaining and subjected all unions to local government supervision. These controls contributed to the early suppression of labour conflict and provided the basis for disciplined labour at the outset of export-oriented industrialization.[64] During the martial law period, the Kuomintang sought dominance over organized labour by drawing workers into a union federation, the Chinese Federation of Labour, which it sponsored and controlled.[65] An additional factor, enterprise level unionism, contributed to the nature of industrial relations in Taiwan. Taiwan followed aspects of the Japanese model, whereby unions operated at the enterprise level, and employers were required to provide welfare, housing, education and other forms of assistance to their employees.[66] Unions were small in scale and weak in power, playing the role of mediators for management better than the role of advocates for the workers.[67]

The relative weakness of labour movements in East Asia helps to explain the absence of leftist and nationalist coalitions which are usually hostile to market oriented policies.[68] The international environment and the economic strategy pursued, provided the regimes with a justification to repress labour and the left. In the process, they successfully weakened a potential base upon which organized opposition to the regime may have developed.

South Korea and Taiwan differ in terms of the relationship the state fostered with the private sector. American advisers were keen that a vigorous private sector be developed as a counter to communism. In South Korea, the Park regime encouraged Japanese-style trading companies. The regime sought to enhance South Korean global market power through vertical integration and the exploitation of economies of scale. This contributed to the emergence and consolidation of several concentrated industrial fiefdoms, known as *chaebol*.[69] The key economic position of the *chaebol* gave them political influence and also contributed to their dependence on the state. The close relationship that developed between business and the state was later regarded by some as an important aspect of South Korea's financial troubles in the mid-1990s.

State-owned enterprises played a key role in Taiwan's industrialization during the 1950s and 1960s. In 1952 state enterprises accounted for 57 per cent of total industrial production.[70] In addition to their direct control of state enterprises, the Kuomintang owned, wholly or partly, around 50 companies. This gave the Kuomintang significant power over domestic economic activities. As a consequence of the government's policies, the state-owned enterprises largely monopolized the domestic market. Local Taiwanese were encouraged to develop small to medium sized firms. These small and medium sized enterprises had to export to find a market for their product.[71] As a consequence, the local business class that developed in Taiwan was 'remarkable for its independence'; the individual enterprises were small, unorganized and beyond the influence of the Kuomintang.[72]

In South Korea and, to a lesser extent, in Taiwan the political subservience of the industrialists was supported by channelling foreign loan capital to local businesses through state-owned or state-controlled banks.[73] As domestic firms became increasingly internationalized, however, the cost to the government of pursuing policies that might reduce national competitiveness became both higher and more readily apparent to the domestic firms.[74] Businesses soon had more at stake in the role the government played. During the 1950s–1960s, external actors, local entrepreneurs, big businesses and workers seemed unwilling to disturb the authoritarian bargain. Thus, in South Korea and Taiwan, the regimes developed a form of performance-based legitimacy in a context in which their economies were highly dependent on a particular external trading environment.

China

During this time, for different but related reasons, China experienced one of its most politically repressive periods. The reliability of the 'lean-to-one-side' approach, the linchpin of communist China's early foreign policy, had been called into question during the Korean War after the Soviet Union reneged on an earlier commitment to provide air force support to China should it enter the Korean War.[75] Mao came to regard mass mobilization as an effective way to maintain and enhance China's security status.[76] A campaign encouraging intellectuals to criticize the cadres and bureaucrats began in May 1956 under the slogan, 'let a hundred flowers bloom together; let a hundred schools of thought contend'. The outpouring of dissatisfaction that ensued surprised the Chinese Communist Party, and was subsequently repressed. Popular dissatisfaction as a consequence of the failures of 'The Great Leap Forward', and the outcome of the 'hundred flowers' campaign contributed to the development of factional struggles within the Chinese Communist Party. During the Cultural Revolution the human rights of many Chinese citizens were abused. Purges and accusations began in 1965 and constrained political behaviour. Although this was not a period of democratic opening in China, a number of Chinese dissidents claim the experience of the Cultural Revolution influenced them to pursue the goals of democracy and freedom of speech later.[77]

Regional change 1970s–1996

The international context

During the period between the 1970s and the Asian financial crisis in the mid-1990s, the international political economy changed in three ways relevant to this chapter. Firstly, in the 1970s international relations radically altered with the end of China's diplomatic and economic isolation from the West. Secondly, during the 1980s the Bretton Woods system was undermined as economic competition deepened and regional trade blocs rose in prominence. Thirdly, in the 1990s, after the former Soviet Union collapsed, international interest in human rights democracy promotion gained status in international relations.

America's Nixon Doctrine, its retreat from Southeast Asia and rapprochement with China, as well as China's détente with the Soviet Union fundamentally altered regional power configurations. In the early 1970s Mao Zedong legitimized contact with foreign countries, and after 1978 and Deng Xiaoping's opening strategy, global exchanges became a key growth sector in the Chinese economy.[78] As China increased its interaction with the rest of the world, its vulnerability to international pressures increased. International derecognition of Taiwan and the termination of Taiwan's security treaty with the United States, together with the Carter administration's announcement of American troop withdrawal from South Korea, all contributed to a period of increased political repression in both South Korea and Taiwan. Some of the concerns among the political elite in Taiwan and South Korea were alleviated by America's implementation of the Taiwan Relations Act (1979) and the reversal of its decision to withdraw troops from South Korea. However, the signal to the South Korean and Taiwanese regimes that they could no longer rely so heavily on American support was obvious. After Jimmy Carter assumed the presidency, America's growing interest in human rights provided new incentives to the regimes in South Korea and Taiwan to appear to be liberalizing and democratizing their political systems.

With the waning of what has been termed the cold war, and in the spirit of détente, China's role in the region shifted. Changes in China's relations with the Soviet Union were swift and reflected realist diplomacy. China's foreign policy toward the Soviet Union was anchored by friendship, non-aggression and neutrality.[79] China began propagating the thesis of multi-polarity as a response to power realignments in global politics.[80] Governments in South Korea and Taiwan recognized that they needed to develop a new basis for their relationship with their communist neighbours.

As a result, South Korea changed its approach to international relations, relying less exclusively on its bilateral relationship with the United States. South Korea embarked on a diplomatic strategy, *Nordpolitik*, to normalize its relations with the Soviet Union, China, and Eastern Europe. It was hoped that this strategy would assist to bridge the gap between it and North Korea. In 1991, the two Koreas agreed to initiate a 'new détente' and to build a co-operative relationship. The resulting Agreement on Reconciliation, Non-aggression, and Exchanges and Co-operation between the two Korean states came into force on 19 February 1992. The agreement articulates a yearning within the Korean people for the peaceful unification of the divided land. In 1992, President George Bush Senior declared that 'the winds of change are with us now ... the day will come when this last wound of the cold war struggle will heal. Korea will be whole again'.[81] Nonetheless, in East Asia the remnants of cold war territorial disputes remain unsettled and highly contentious.

Both the issue of Taiwan's relations with China, and Korean reunification, are distinguished by their tinderbox character. During the early 1990s, concern about North Korea's nuclear capabilities flared. In 1991, North Korea refused an International Atomic Energy Agency inspection and, in March 1993, announced its intention of withdrawing from the Non-Proliferation Treaty. During negotiations to calm the crisis, the United States–South Korean military launched 'Team Spirit' military exercises, involving 120,000 troops. North Korea regarded these exercises as aggressive, and announced that it was going to a 'semi-war footing'.[82] In June 1993 North Korea announced it was suspending its decision to withdraw from the Non-Proliferation Treaty. However, tensions remained as the crisis continued into 1994. Washington needed Beijing's support to resolve the North Korea nuclear issue and, in order to improve its relations with China, in 1994 the Clinton administration de-linked China's human rights from the Most Favoured Nation issue.[83] Today, the situation on the Korean peninsula remains volatile, and continues to be affected by American foreign policy.

The question of Taiwan and China's unification is particularly vexed and is also affected by American foreign policy. From the signing of the Shanghai Communiqué (1972) until the mid-1990s, American policy on the Taiwan question was that a resolution needed to be achieved peacefully, and be acceptable to both sides. This policy was characterized by strategic ambiguity about the process to achieve this goal.[84] The Taiwan Relations Act (1979) states that it is the policy of the United States to resist the possible coercion of Taiwan by selling military defensive arms to Taiwan and by possible direct American involvement in any military crisis in the Taiwan Strait.

China retains a tough stance on unification and objects to American military sales to Taiwan. In Taiwan, the questions of independence, unification and national identity are politically contentious. The unresolved issue of sovereignty makes relations between the two entities extremely sensitive. This tension was exemplified in 1995–1996 when China launched a series of missile exercises over the Taiwan Straits during Taiwan's 1996 presidential election. As a consequence of China's actions, America dispatched two battle fleets to the waters near the Taiwan Strait.

Concomitant with the shifts in the region's power configurations, the effects of economic globalization were rapidly becoming apparent. The industrialized economies of Japan, South Korea and Taiwan emerged as serious international economic competitors. The international trading norms and the rule governing bodies established at Bretton Woods were being undermined by the growing power of regional trading blocs and protectionist policies. Within the American media, popular culture and successive administrations, the American trade deficit with the region was construed as a result of the unique and unfair characteristics of the Asian developmental model. Attempts were made to persuade Taiwan and South Korea to open their domestic markets and to deregulate their currencies. These issues were reflected in the 1985 Plaza Agreement and the 1987 Louvre Accord, which created the conditions for the globalization of financial markets and the rapid appreciation of the Taiwan dollar and the Korean won.[85]

The European Union and several of its member states increased their efforts to redress the weakness of Europe's economic ties in Asia compared with those of America. Before the onset of the Asian financial crisis, it seemed to many that the European Union was doomed to geo-economic marginalization in the then anticipated 'Pacific Century'.[86] European Union and member states' investment, finance and business networking links and strategic commercial presence were poorly positioned in contrast to the United States. This concern was heightened after the formation of APEC. European public and private sector leaders 'lamented their sluggishness in exploring the region's riches'.[87] Several European countries sought closer regional ties and reinvigorated their bilateral efforts. In July 1994 the European Commission established a new strategy for Asia that stressed the importance of modern Asia to Europe. Ultimately, an inter-regional frame-work, The Asia-Europe Meetings, was created and held its first summit meeting in 1996.

In addition to changes in the geo-political and economic context, a signif-icant expansion of human rights discourse influenced international perceptions of political practices within Asian states. International concern for human rights increased during the 1970s, and in the 1980s was extended to include an interest in promoting the development of democracy.

In the aftermath of the Vietnam War and the Watergate scandal, the American government sought new forms of foreign policy engagement that would bolster domestic support. A 1976 amendment to the Foreign Assistance Act required the Secretary of State to report to Congress on the human rights practices of all states receiving American military and economic aid. The newly elected Carter administration announced that it would link human rights issues to American foreign policy. In 1979 Congress passed a further requirement that the annual human rights review of countries receiving American aid should be extended to include all coun-tries, including China. International NGO reports on human rights practices in the region further focussed attention on the issue.[88]

Thus, China increased its interaction with the international community at a moment in time when human rights were gaining importance in interna-tional relations. Initially, China received mixed signals from the international community about the levels of human rights compliance required from it. The tacit anti-Soviet alliance between China and the Western states shielded China from scrutiny in the early 1970s.[89] Ironically, it was in the late 1970s, when China began to improve its domestic human rights situation and to increase its activity in human rights diplomacy, that it started to become a target of international human rights pressure.[90] In 1978, Amnesty International published its first report on China, which focussed on the treatment of political prisoners.[91]

Nevertheless, until the events at Tiananmen Square in 1989, human rights issues remained in the background of international relations with China. This reflected a pragmatic approach to human rights diplomacy by policy-makers, and the fact that, for many states, gaining access to China's market was a key foreign policy objective. The repression of the Tiananmen Square protest profoundly affected China's international relations. As a conse-quence of the events of 4 June 1989, China's human rights record became a matter of international concern. China experienced a two-year decline in its credit rating, foreign investment, export orders and tourism.[92] Some people argue that the event 'changed the character of US–China relations, possibly forever'.[93]

Since then China has sought to engage with the international community both politically and economically while emphasizing state sovereignty in relation to internal matters such as human rights. Such engagement, however, contains an inherent tension between the defence of state sovereignty and the effects of contagion and diffusion that occur as a consequence of interdependence with the rest of the world. Increased interaction, plus advances in technology, have meant that China is losing many of the instruments available to it to exercise sovereignty both domestically and externally.[94]

Development effects

The changes in the international context had a number of direct economic effects. During the period after the United Nations derecognized Taiwan, emigration and capital flight increased, foreign trade and investment slowed, and citizens began to voice dissent.[95] The South Korean economy suffered from the devaluation of the US dollar, the quadrupling of oil prices, rising trade deficits and inflation. In both South Korea and Taiwan, external political and economic shocks in the 1970s altered the relationship between capital and the state. The second oil shock, in 1979, contributed to Taiwan and South Korea embarking on a policy of structural adjustment and financial deregulation in order to make their economies more responsive to market signals.[96] Its cordial relations with the United States, and its new economic policies created a range of development opportunities for China.

South Korea and Taiwan

The deterioration of the Bretton Woods system and the changing role of the United States in the region created new challenges for countries pursuing export-oriented development strategies. Internationally, a new protectionism emerged during this period. The American Federation of Labor and Congress of Industrial Organizations (AFL–CIO) and other domestic groups urged an activist trade policy toward countries like South Korea and Taiwan, which had earlier benefited from preferential trade policies. Such organizations contributed to a change in American trade policy toward the region by focussing domestic attention on human rights abuses, poor labour and environmental standards, and the social consequences of domestic job losses. Trading states, such as America, became increasingly concerned with the defence of domestic jobs.[97]

The staff of the United States Trade Representative Office assumed a much higher profile internationally during this period. Intense international economic competition led to a tightening of quota restrictions on South Korean and Taiwanese exporters. This caused countries such as Japan, South Korea and Taiwan to open up new satellite factories in countries that had comparative advantage like China, Vietnam and Indonesia. China's gradual integration into the regional economy vastly expanded South Korea's and Taiwan's consumer market, natural resources and industrial potential.[98] The major determinants of the economic performance of individual economies shifted to a more regional level, and access to the

American market was no longer the key variable in the regional economic order.[99]

Rapid and sustained economic growth in the region contributed to a tendency to focus attention on regional, rather than national, economies. Kenichi Ohmae observed that on the 'global economic map the lines that now matter are those defining what may be called "region states"'.[100] Compared with the relatively hard and closed regionalism of the European Union and the North American Free Trade Agreement, regionalism in East Asia lacks formalism.[101] Natural economic zones played a key role in East Asian economic development, and contributed to the success of China's economic strategy. Gary Gereffi contends that rather than debate whether the market or the state provides the essential explanatory factor for East Asian economic growth, regional 'neighbourhood' effects offer a compelling alternative explanation.[102] East Asia came to be thought of in this period as an inter-related regional economy in which regionally specific factors such as overseas Chinese networks, similar business practices and the advantages of geographical proximity were key. Trade and investment flows were major forces pulling these economies together. During this period, despite continuing political tensions between the two entities, socio-economic exchanges between Taiwan and mainland China accelerated. Since contact commenced, the general trend in cross-Strait investment, trade and communications has been upward.[103]

China

From 1978 China gradually began to dismantle its web of administrative controls over trade and foreign investment. The economic reforms that China initiated, such as the 'Four Modernizations' and the 'open policy', greatly increased the scope and size of China's interaction with the international economy.[104] By the end of the 1970s, China was seeking long-term stability with its main trading partners. It signed agreements with Japan, the European Community, and several individual European countries, including Britain, France and Yugoslavia, as well as the United States.[105] A rapid increase in the transfer of technology and capital goods occurred.

In 1988 China announced a new policy of export-led growth, which was modelled on the experience of Taiwan and other newly industrialized Asian economies.[106] The new plan departed in several ways from previous policy. Under the 'open policy' Beijing had designated four Special Economic Zones, fourteen coastal cities, three delta areas and Hainan province as places with preferential conditions for foreign investment and as bases for exports. Under the new policy, China created a kind of gigantic export processing zone. It was not defined by geography, but by the juridical status of the enterprise involved.[107] China instituted this initiative notwithstanding the changes that had been wrought in the international economic environment since the 1960s, and the obvious differences between the other newly industrialized countries' economic and political structures and its own socialist based systems.

The institutional basis for foreign trade in China is quite different from that of South Korea or Taiwan. South Korea and Taiwan significantly restricted foreign investment inflows, whereas attracting foreign direct investment was a major part of China's development strategy. Huang Yasheng has identified a number of anomalous foreign direct investment patterns in China. Huang highlights that China's financial and economic institutions have created an environment in which domestic firms (particularly domestic private firms) experience systemic and pervasive discrimination in order to benefit inefficient state owned enterprises.[108] An inefficient political pecking order of firms has persisted throughout the reform era and has led to a high dependency on foreign direct investment.[109] In this context, Chinese joint foreign ventures, which are part of the rapidly growing 'non-state sector', have made a considerable contribution to China's fast economic growth.[110] Furthermore, South Korea and Taiwan maintained stable currencies, whereas China's real exchange rate has fluctuated. South Korea and Taiwan were able to protect some sectors that faced competition from imports, but China does not have sufficient control over either capital inflows or exchange rates to carry out policies designed for specific sectors in this way.[111]

Moreover, since 1992, a new type of joint venture has emerged in China, in which part of a state-owned enterprise forms a partnership with foreign investors. A proliferation of such ventures in the early 1990s triggered a process of corporatization and privatization of state-owned and collective enterprises.[112] The Chinese central government's decentralization policies, designed to separate ownership from management, gave each state enterprise increasing financial and administrative autonomy. Except for the required fiscal or production quotas, state enterprises and provinces were allowed to 'marketize' their production structures.[113] This process has created a unique dilemma for the Chinese central government. Foreign investment assists in the development of the Chinese economy and enhances the government's performance legitimacy. However, corporatization of China's state-owned enterprises erodes the system of state ownership, which is a central cornerstone of China's political system.[114] A fundamental tenet of socialist ideology is its commitment to state ownership, often not just for its 'instrumental value but also for its intrinsic one'.[115] The primacy of state ownership cannot be explicitly challenged in China and some prominent officials still choose to view private owners of capital as potential foes.[116] Comprehensive institutional reform of state owned enterprises remains a vexed issue for the Chinese government. Neither South Korea nor Taiwan needed to rely on foreign direct investment or negotiate this difficult issue during their pursuit of performance-based legitimacy in the 1960s and 1970s.

Furthermore, China's central government is not a monolithic bloc, and there is a range of competing organizations and interests. The central government's relations with the provinces – in particular the booming coastal areas and the under-developed western region – are increasingly complex.[117] The central government encounters escalating difficulties in ensuring policy compliance and the collection of taxes.[118] The erosion of central authority is undermining the capacity of the Chinese state to form the kinds of pacts that South Korea and Taiwan were able to develop with emerging business interests, civil society, and ethnic groups.

Also, reforms that have fostered economic growth have altered relations between the central Chinese authorities and the localities. For example, China succeeded in fostering the growth of collective rural industrial output on the basis of local government entrepreneurship.[119] Jean Oi characterizes this growth as indicative of a new institutional development – local state corporatism.[120] Oi argues that what has emerged in China is the coexistence of a strong local officialdom and public enterprise with a thriving market economy and a weakened central state.[121] Local state corporatism has potentially threatening consequences for centre–local relations when conflicts between the pursuit of local interests and central government interests need to be resolved. These complexities were absent from South Korea and Taiwan's export-oriented, rapid growth, performance-based strategies.

Nonetheless, China's strategy is yielding economic results. Perhaps no country other than China has so rapidly become one of the top ten trading countries and one of the largest recipients of foreign investment in the world.[122] Oi observes that China is arguably the most successful of the socialist states in implementing a program of economic reforms.[123] Chinese reforms have resulted in a transformation of socialism, not a transition to capitalism, and represent an alternative type of market reform that (so far) has avoided the social, political and economic turmoil experienced in Eastern Europe.[124]

Democratizing effects

Changes in the international context, together with the cumulative effects of economic growth, influenced state structures, the political elite, and opposition movements in South Korea, Taiwan and China in ways conducive to political liberalization. Between the 1970s and the mid-1990s two important movements seeking political reform, The Democracy Wall and the June 4 1989 movement, developed in China, while South Korea and Taiwan made the transition to democracy. South Korea and Taiwan's eventual transition to democracy was peaceful. Nevertheless, the intervening years were marked by increasing social tension and violent, repressive actions by the state, such as during events at the student led protest at Kwangju in South Korea during 1980 and during the human rights day protest at Kaohsiung in Taiwan in December 1979. Although China initiated some liberalizing reforms, it remains a one-party state.

South Korea and Taiwan

Changes in the international and regional context left the regimes in Taiwan and South Korea feeling increasingly isolated, threatened and insecure. These developments initially resulted in an increase in political constraints. President Park had imposed martial law in South Korea during October 1972, and the *Yushin* Constitution was promulgated two months later. Under this constitution South Korea was still officially a 'democracy'. Yet, authoritarian measures and controls were significantly increased. During this phase of Park's presidency, the international community came to hold South Korea in low esteem. *Time* reported that, as 'practised by President Park Chung Hee, "modern democracy" has become an Orwellian synonym for despotic one man rule'.[125] In Taiwan, the Kuomintang decided to postpone supplementary elections because of its loss of international recognition. This decision contributed to increased social unrest, as exemplified during the Kaohsiung protest.

Human rights and democracy issues were beginning to assume a greater position in international discourse. Yet, there was an ambiguity between the international community's professed interest in human rights and its response to democracy movements in the region. In 1979, during a visit to South Korea, United States President Jimmy Carter referred to 'the growing consensus among the international community about the fundamental value of human rights and individual dignity ... and the belief that this achievement [economic growth] can be matched by similar democratic progress through the realization of basic human aspirations in political and human rights'.[126] Nonetheless, as the Democracy Wall, Kwangju and Kaohsiung democracy movements show, in the late 1970s and early 1980s the international community's response to civilian led movements for democracy was not always coherent or consistent.

International concern for human rights and democracy expanded through the 1980s. The political elite in South Korea and Taiwan observed a shift in international attitudes during the Philippines' transition to democracy in 1986 and took note. The capacity of the political elite in Taiwan and South Korea to insulate themselves from domestic social forces seeking democratization, and international criticism of their authoritarian practices, had been reduced. External pressure was mounting for states in the region to move toward more substantive democracy.

The process of democratization in South Korea and Taiwan, which occurred in the same decade, has some similarities. The political elite, in response to domestic and external pressures, crafted the terms of the democratic transition. Both regimes initially succeeded in retaining power after the political and constitutional reforms were implemented. The Kuomintang was provided with keen incentives to democratize its political system by the tenuous international status of Taiwan, the existence of an increasingly assertive non-Kuomintang political movement, and a developing succession problem. In South Korea, international and domestic factors limited the feasibility of the use of force to repress domestic calls for democratization. These constraints stemmed from the political fall-out of the bloody suppression of the Kwangju democracy movement, widespread social support for democracy and concerns about the costs of further political repression given Seoul's role as the host of the 1988 Olympic Games. The Olympic Games were regarded as an opportunity to enhance the international image of South Korea, and the regime did not want the negative attention political unrest would create.

In addition, the cumulative effects of increased permeability and sustained economic growth were becoming apparent in Taiwan and South Korea. By the 1980s, performance-based legitimacy was no longer sufficient to ensure social acquiescence. Some scholars identify unusual features in the middle class and civil society in Taiwan and South Korea. David Martin Jones highlights the curious role played by the new middle class in East Asia. Jones argues that what has emerged is a peculiar form of illiberal democracy in which traditional values, such as order, have been fostered by the regimes to assist in their development projects.[127]

Jones argues that in both South Korea and Taiwan the middle class has been sensitive to the maintenance of a stable social order, which at times has led to them to operate as a democratizing agent and, at other times, has led them to support continuing authoritarian rule.[128] While it is evident that the middle classes in East Asia have played an ambiguous role during demo-cratic transition, the reasons for this are more complex than is often suggested. Jones argues that the customary values that he regards as modi-fying development in East Asia have 'largely been reinvented for the ideological purpose of channelling popular energy to collectively achievable economic targets'.[129] The newly modernized middle classes, which comprised a third of South Korea and Taiwan's societies, were thus incul-cated with national values by the state.[130] In this context, Jones maps the growing anxieties of the middle class who, in Taiwan, were 'largely unim-pressed by polymorphous joys of pluralism', and of the South Korean middle class in their 'search for order, certainty and security'.[131]

Although Jones critiques modernization theory, his analysis contains one of the same limitations as modernization theory itself, namely, too narrow a focus on internal processes of change. The 'plea for reassurance' that Jones identifies the middle classes in East Asia as seeking stems not only from a state-inculcated desire for Confucian harmony, but also from external factors. The experience of living in a divided country under the threat of war with their nearest neighbour for over thirty years affected the political culture of South Korea and Taiwan. Moreover, when South Korea and Taiwan began their tran-sition to democracy, the middle classes were less assured of the nature of their future relationship with their ally and mentor – the United States.

China

China has attempted to follow aspects of the so-called regional development model in which economic growth precedes democratization. Many of the economic conventions in the Asian mode seemed familiar to Chinese officials, who were used to a controlled and planned economic system.[132] Yet, by the time China decided to embark upon an Asian model of development strategy, this sequence of development was no longer palatable to the international community, which had become increasingly concerned with human rights and democratization.

International economic integration and the initiation of two economic policy programs, the 'Four Modernizations' and the export-oriented strategy, coincided with the emergence of democracy movements in Beijing. During the 1970s, the 'Four Modernizations' policy contributed to the emergence of the Democracy Wall movement, in which Wei Jingsheng called for the 'fifth modernization', democracy. In the late 1980s, economic reforms and international openness began to unhinge the stability of the Chinese regime, as citizens expressed their concern about rampant corruption, rising inflation, unequal distribution of economic growth and rising unemployment.[133] Consensus within the Chinese leadership about the economic strategy began to splinter. An attempt to address the problem of inflation was initiated with the price reform strategy. The strategy was a failure. By 1988 it had fuelled an emerging social crisis, culminating in the democracy movement in Beijing in 1989. Both the Democracy Wall and Tiananmen Square protests were eventually suppressed by the regime. Significantly, the Democracy Wall and the Tiananmen Square protests did not achieve widespread domestic support. Both movements were led by intellectuals and students, with weak connections with workers, and few with rural Chinese.[134]

Economic development is having a wide range of social effects that have potential implications for political reform. China is undergoing a rapid transformation from a predominately rural economy to a diversified one.[135] Labour force change is coinciding with demographic change. The growth of the working-age population has acted as a constraint on policy-makers, who are concerned about high unemployment levels. Additionally, the pattern of labour absorption moved from public enterprises in the 1980s, toward the private sector in the 1990s.[136] Changes in China's domestic economy have contributed to increasingly complex social tensions and issues. As yet, these tensions have not led to democratization. The benefits and costs of industrialization, economic development and international integration vary across provinces and between the centre and localities. At the village level, rural China has experienced a political opening, and the opportunity for a limited form of electoral participation has emerged. In urban areas the experience differs, and social tensions associated with economic development are unsettled. Within the western region, in which the majority of China's minority groups live, economic development is slow and uneven, and the prospects for further political liberalization are slim because the Chinese government regards minority group interests as threatening national unity and stability.

The Chinese government observed the implosive effects of political and economic reforms in the former Soviet Union. It provided a powerful example to the Chinese Communist Party of the dangers of the liberalization of economic and political life. National unity has become a key motivating and unifying symbol in post-Tiananmen China. Political, ethnic or religious movements, which are regarded as challenging Chinese unity, are not tolerated. Notwithstanding significant economic reforms, and China's rapid integration into the global economy, political reforms lag well behind.

The Asian financial crisis and beyond

International context

More recent changes in the international political economy that may affect China's development and democratization trajectory are analysed in this final section. These developments include the effects of globalization, the widening of the concept of development from a measurement of the growth of per capita GDP to the notion of sustainable human development, and the emergence of an international focus on the issue of good governance.

A paradigm shift has occurred. It is no longer regarded as acceptable for states, such as China, to develop economically without also adopting the institutions of democracy in the long term. This has been a key feature of the period post-Tiananmen, and has heightened since the Asian financial crisis. It is contended that a new normative framework and expanded interest in governance prevails in the international system. This standard has come to be regarded as persuasive not only on normative grounds, but also on economic ones.

Globalization has meant that the central process in the development of the modern capitalist nation state involves a complex and interdependent shift of both political and economic structures to a broader scale.[137] This has resulted in the emergence of 'new circuits of power' which overlap, cut across, and fragment the state.[138] These circuits of power are regarded by some as resulting in a 'retreat of the state', and by others as creating a 'myth of a powerless state'.[139] The implications of these developments for state sovereignty, development and democratization are complex.

Questions about the continued advisability of the Asian model of export-oriented growth have arisen.[140] These derive from a concern, internationally, about the extent to which late adopters of an export-oriented development strategy will be able to replicate the successes of early developers, especially given the growth of more protectionist policies; and whether it is acceptable to the international community for developing countries to derive their comparative advantage through exploitative industrial relations, and lax environmental standards. Thus, the opportunities to prosper economically on the basis of the kind of neo-mercantilist policies of South Korea and Taiwan in the current international environment may have been reduced.

Moreover, the communications revolution has made the transfer of both money and ideas easier than ever before. There is a 'new kind of vulnerability for China in a world in which ideas are of growing importance in interstate relations and penetrate with increasing ease across borders'.[141] Economic globalization, including the internationalization of production and finance, has resulted in regimes in the region becoming more vulnerable to external economic and political pressures. The volume of capital flows has increased considerably, and has been influenced by new electronic technologies.

Judged by trade volumes, the world economy has become increasingly integrated. Membership of the World Trade Organization may further alter China's investment landscape by encouraging more foreign investment and diminishing the importance of overseas Chinese business networks.[142] The World Trade Organization basically consists of an elaborate set of multilateral agreements concerning international trade in goods and services, and a dispute settlement procedure. Many of China's domestic interest groups, in particular state-owned enterprises and provincial governments, will be losers due to World Trade Organization accession. Compensating these interest groups without violating World Trade Organization rules will be difficult.

Development effects

The Asian financial crisis highlighted the downside of regional economic integration. China, South Korea and Taiwan were among the world's top thirty exporters in 1997.[143] As regional trade accounted for almost a quarter of the total trade of these export-oriented economies, lower consumer confidence in each state affected the export performance of its neighbour.[144] The negative effects of economic integration were experienced in South Korea, when massive capital flight contributed to the crisis that occurred in their economy. US Federal Reserve Chairman, Alan Greenspan, observed that the Asian financial crisis shows that the global financial system facilitates 'the transmission of financial disturbances more effectively than ever before'.[145]

By virtue of its strict control over currency transactions, China was not as damaged as South Korea by the financial crisis. However, China's accumulation of public debt is clearly unsustainable and its banking system is at least as fragile as those systems which triggered the Asian financial crisis.[146] By the mid-1990s, after a decade of sustained growth, foreign trade and investment had become sufficiently large, relative to the rest of the Chinese economy, that for perhaps the first time in its post-1949 history, China faced an external macro-economic shock that was having a destabilizing impact on its domestic economy.[147]

The decisive decision-making units that addressed the crisis were embedded in pre-globalization institutions, such as the IMF, with the United States playing the key role. IMF prescriptions for South Korean economic recovery went far beyond the original ambit of interest envisaged in the Bretton Woods system. The IMF, World Bank, Asian Development Bank and several European countries promised credit to South Korea totalling US$57 billion. In return, the South Korean government agreed to a list of economic, institutional and labour reforms, including financial sector restructuring, tight money policies, dismantling of ties among government, banks and businesses, a program of trade and capital account liberalization, and labour market reforms.[148] President Kim Dae Jung seized the opportunity to use the reforms to limit some of the power of the *chaebol*.

The crisis presented an opportunity for the European Union, through the Asia–Europe Meetings, to develop more substantive ties with the region, but it largely failed to deliver.[149] Beyond statements about the need for greater market and policy reform, the European Union offered to establish an Asia–Europe Trust Fund at the World Bank whereby a mere 30.9 million euros would help resource the provision of some technical assistance.[150]

Consensus emerged within multilateral development agencies that a cause of the financial instability could be found in the state institutions and structures within the Asian developmental state model. Ironically, this new stance came after the pronouncement on the good economic health of the Asian mode by multilateral development banks only a few months earlier.[151] The degree of economic liberalization and democratization present in South Korea was viewed as insufficient to ensure the level of transparency and accountability necessary for sustained economic growth. It was concluded by some academics that the 'root cause of the crisis was the institutional pattern of paternalism and authoritarianism practised in almost all the Asian states for decades,' which had contributed to the development of a form of 'crony capitalism'.[152]

The IMF and the World Bank broadened the scope of their activities in the region to include an interest in the notion of 'good governance'. The idea that it is impossible and, indeed counterproductive, to separate completely political reform from economic reform, both of which were regarded as mutually reinforcing, became orthodoxy.[153] Policy-makers and academics broadened their view on the fundamentals of economic growth to include the concept of good governance. For example, Dani Rodrik argues that developing countries:

> ... need to create an environment that is conducive to private investment ... They need to improve their institutions of conflict management – legally guaranteed civil liberties and political freedoms, social partnerships and social insurance – so that they can maintain macro-economic stability and adjust to rapid changes in external circumstances. In the absence of these complements to a strategy of external liberalization, openness will not yield much. At worst, it will cause instability, widening inequalities and social conflict.[154]

Rodrik, based on his analysis of the economic shocks of the late 1970s and early 1980s, concludes that the countries that fell apart did so because their 'social and political institutions were inadequate to bring about the bargains required for macro-economic adjustment – they were societies with weak institutions of conflict management'.[155]

Notwithstanding its developmental state traits, South Korea was also praised for the degree of democracy it had developed. Former United States Secretary of State, Madeleine Albright, was among those who regarded South Korea as better able than other economies in crisis in the region to adjudicate the distributional conflicts associated with the IMF-imposed macro-economic adjustment strategies. This was because South Korea's democratic institutions provided better mechanisms to reduce conflict than authoritarian regimes such as Indonesia. She said this was 'in part because ... people were able to elect new governments, which started work in a climate of openness and trust, and with the moral legitimacy to call for shared sacrifice'.[156]

If such a view is correct, and good governance is important for both economic stability and adjusting to economic crises, it does not augur well for China, where the rule of law and the institutions to manage conflict are weak. Indeed, some argue that unless Beijing's rulers go ahead with major reforms, such as fostering a climate of law and the free flow of information, 'the day is coming in which the Middle Kingdom will hit the skids'.[157]

There are many critics of the IMF bailout of South Korea with its stress on good governance and neo-liberal reforms. A number of critics identify the role America played in foisting its own policy preferences and business interests upon South Korea in the name of good governance.[158] The issue of IMF banking reforms is interesting because, theoretically, the fund is not supposed to intrude on private sector contracts when drawing up reform proposals.[159] Cumings identifies the 'deep meaning' of the crisis as evidence of an American attempt to shut off the Asian model of development before it spread to China.[160] Others point out that the IMF 'grossly exceeded its mandate, as laid out in its articles of Agreement, and has shown itself both arrogant and far too close to the interests of its principle shareholder, the USA'.[161]

Democratizing effects

The leading role of the United States in the international political economy was clearly exemplified during the Asian financial crisis. Evidence of America's expanded global strategy was clear during former President Bill Clinton's first term of office. Clinton stated that 'economy, security and democracy' would be the three pillars of American foreign policy.[162] This was a shift from the security first containment strategy that had previously characterized American foreign policy.[163] This policy focus was symbolized in the 'engagement and enlargement' strategy. Under Clinton's presidency American foreign policy sought to bring countries into a more open trade order, with the expectation that such involvement would have 'socializing' effects on the countries.[164] This was evident in the Clinton administration's approach toward China. The Clinton administration aimed to integrate China into the international economic order with the hope of promoting reform, encouraging the development of the rule of law and socializing China into the prevailing order.[165] Influential voices in or close to President George W. Bush's administration have called for a mixed engagement/ containment strategy.[166] This hedging strategy is regarded by many analysts in Beijing as quite sinister.[167]

Chinese scholars have identified that the United States is adept at using international law and international institutions to achieve its goals, and that this is quite different from the traditional use of power.[168] Some people in China are questioning the liberal nature of globalization, and caution that China must be vigilant about the 'strategic trap' of a globalization ideology propounded by the hegemonic power of the United States.[169] Popular books such as *China Can Say No* criticize the United States and advocate the defence of China's interests and sovereignty.[170] Economic problems associated with rapid liberalization have reinforced political sentiments such as nationalism.

The Chinese government hopes to derive the benefits of economic globalization through its membership of multilateral organizations such as the World Trade Organization. Yet, World Trade Organization membership may increase the tensions and pressures between the centre and the provinces. The bilateral agreements that China has signed include opening up many service sectors to foreign investment, reducing subsidies to agricultural production, and a significant general tariff reduction.[171] The World Trade Organization is integrating the Chinese economy into the global economy with an unprecedented depth, thus changing the internal and external balance of the Chinese economy. David Zweig argues that the China case shows that local communities and new corporate organizations that benefit from transnational linkages can undermine even strong authoritarian states that try to control their global exchanges as they open to the outside world.[172] This is because although keeping control is easy when domestic actors do not know their interests, once leaders allow transnational flows and global communications to penetrate the domestic economy, the demands for exchanges increase as those with comparative advantage in transnational exchanges seek to expand their linkages.[173]

The international context, which contributed to the success of the development strategies of Taiwan and South Korea, was indifferent to the question of democracy. All that mattered to the Western international trading order was that they were not communist. By contrast, China's development has occurred in an international environment that is quite attentive to issues of democracy and good governance. Throughout the 1990s, international incentives to democratize increased, and were based on both a normative and an economic logic. The Asian financial crisis demonstrated, that in a globalized international economic order, the economic costs of systems of government that do not ensure accountability have grown.

In addition to the effects of economic globalization, the terrorist attacks on the World Trade Center and the Pentagon on 11 September 2001, and the United States decision to enter into conflict in Afghanistan and Iraq have altered the international context in which China develops. Security issues have resumed their pre-eminent position in international relations. These events appear to have strengthened Chinese sensitivity about issues of national security and national sovereignty. As a consequence, there is a growing desire within China for a resolution of the Taiwan question and for unrest in places such as Tibet and Xinjiang to be dealt with swiftly and firmly. China may become even less responsive to external pressure to improve political and human rights.

Conclusion

This chapter has considered the relationship between the international context, economic development and democratic change. It has provided a socio-historical analysis of three phases of East Asian development. These three phases broadly encompassed factors associated with war, rapid regional change and economic crisis. In considering these factors several international incentives and constraints affecting the choice of political institutions and actions were identified and analysed.

During the cold war, factors arising from the geo-political environment affected the character and form of South Korea's and Taiwan's political institutions and political behaviour in ways that favoured authoritarianism. In this period, factors arising from the geo-political environment affected the character and form of South Korea, Taiwan and China's state structures. In South Korea and Taiwan a range of international incentives and constraints indirectly influenced the development model, the organization of labour, and opposition movements in ways that supported authoritarianism. China's relationship with the international order was contentious during this period, and contributed to its isolation.

Between the 1970s and the Asian financial crisis, regional economic inter-actions increased in importance. Regional as well as international factors affected development outcomes. The Taiwan–China relationship emerged as a complex one and is not amenable to a simple reduction: as China and Taiwan became more economically integrated, politically they moved further apart.

Shifts in the international context arising from China's international economic integration, the end of the cold war and a growing interest in human rights, placed new pressures upon authoritarian regimes in the region. In South Korea and Taiwan these international factors combined with the cumulative effects of economic growth to influence state structures and opposition movements in ways that favoured democratization.

Governments in South Korea and in Taiwan began to feel internationally isolated and vulnerable as a consequence of changes in regional power configurations, coupled with the emerging international concern for human rights and democracy. These international factors combined with the cumulative effect of sustained levels of economic growth to influence state structures and opposition movements in ways that favoured democratization.

During the cold war, Taiwan and South Korea participated in the international political economy while repressing political opposition at home. Their pursuit of economic growth first and democracy second was not criticized. This sequence of development is no longer acceptable to the international community. During the 1990s development, democracy and human rights became hegemonic political ideals. It has been in this international environment that China sought to emulate aspects of the development model (but not necessarily the democratizing outcomes of South Korea and Taiwan). However, this chapter has revealed that shifts in the international economic system and normative change in the international community may impinge upon China's strategy. Additionally, due to the particularities of its domestic context, the government in China faces several difficult and particular challenges which may affect its capacity to sustain performance-based legitimacy.

In the next chapter, the focus shifts from an examination of economic regimes and processes to the role of political regimes. This chapter has revealed the prominent role played by the United States in regional economic development, and in the following discussion of the United Nations another aspect of America's influence is revealed.

3 International regimes
The role of the United Nations

Introduction

The impact of the United Nations upon democratization in East Asia has been notably ambiguous. The United Nations is responsive to changes in the international order and global context, and as such, the role of the United Nations in inhibiting or promoting democratization has been mediated by different time contexts. During the cold war, interactions between the United Nations and the region functioned to constrain the development of democracy. United Nations intervention in South Korea, and recognition of the legitimacy of the Kuomintang regime in Taiwan, affected domestic actors' choice of political institutions and actions. During this period, the United Nations' stance toward the region facilitated the development of certain authoritarian political forms in South Korea and Taiwan. Moreover, its isolation of China internationally strengthened China's totalitarian tendency.

The United Nations' eventual decision to recognize China had significant consequences within China and throughout the region. China's assumption of a place at the United Nations Security Council had the (unintentional) effect of creating new opportunities for democratization in Taiwan. China's participation in the United Nations regime has been multi-layered and complex. China uses a power paradigm to challenge the legitimacy of several tenets of the United Nations system, particularly as they relate to democracy, human rights and self-determination.

Although South Korea, Taiwan and China have each been affected by their engagement with the United Nations international regime, their interaction is not reducible to a single pattern. Moreover, the evolving relationship between the United Nations and China demonstrates that China is not a passive participant in the international system. China's interactions with the United Nations are proving to be of potential causative significance, not only to China, but also to the regime itself.

Sovereignty, international regimes and democratization

The concept of state sovereignty is a foundation principle of the United Nations. The sovereign state system was established in Europe with the

Peace of Westphalia in 1648 and the Treaty of Utrecht in 1713.[1] This system recognizes the rights of states with defined territory to have their own forms of government, free from intervention, and to conduct relations with one another on the basis of sovereign equality.[2] The spread of the sovereign state system internationally has been characterized by both hierarchy and unevenness, which has made the question of sovereign equality problematic.[3] Notwithstanding the United Nations' adherence to the notion of state sovereignty and sovereign equality, the regime has been particularly responsive to the interests of its most powerful members.

Shifts in the sites of power, technological change, increased economic integration, and a range of problems that are global in scope have affected other aspects of the principle of state sovereignty. Globalization refers to a universal set of processes which generate a multiplicity of linkages which transcend the states and societies that make up the world system.[4] One consequence of globalization is that power structures spill over the territorial limits that indicate the authority of one state as opposed to another.[5] The erosion of territoriality is evident in matters of environmental protection, nuclear and security vulnerability, and economic viability.[6] As a consequence, the practice of state sovereignty has become more complex.

In response to these international developments, some states have agreed to place less emphasis on sovereignty in exchange for the benefits derived from membership of international organizations. This is particularly evident in economic regimes such as the World Trade Organization. Revisions to the principle of state sovereignty and non-intervention are also apparent in international security regimes. Events in Bosnia, Iraq, Rwanda and elsewhere created a context in which a connection between violations of human rights and threats to international peace could be drawn. In accordance with this rationale, the North Atlantic Treaty Organization overrode the principle of non-interference in the interests of humanitarian concerns in Kosovo.

The expansion of the role and functions of international regimes causes consternation among a number of states. China is highly sceptical about this form of intervention by international regimes. Chen Weixiong, from China's Ministry of Foreign Affairs, argues that state sovereignty ought to be the guideline in international life. Chen contends that any weakening of this concept will lead to 'very uncertain, even dangerous, consequences'.[7] Chen questions the effects of intervention in the name of humanitarianism. He states:

> In 1999, one regional military bloc carried out intensive and successive bombing over Yugoslavia for 78 days. Even depleted uranium projectiles were used. The reason: to free the region from a humanitarian crisis. The result: 1,800 deaths, 100,000 people wounded and 1,000,000 homeless.[8]

Robert Cooper argues that there are different conceptions of sovereignty within the international system of states.[9] Cooper posits that 'modern states' are primarily concerned with non-intervention and state sovereignty.[10] China and several other states in Asia may be characterized as modern states. By contrast, '"post-modern states" do not emphasize sovereignty or the separation of domestic and foreign affairs'.[11] Within some international regimes, like the European Union, a post-modern conception of sovereignty is developing. Within the United Nations there are tensions between states that assert the right to the exclusive practice of state sovereignty and states that adopt a more flexible, or 'post-modern' view. These differences of opinion are particularly evident in the United Nations human rights regime. Nonetheless, the modern conception of sovereignty remains predominant within the United Nations system. This reflects the origins of the United Nations international regime.

International regimes and democratization

The term 'international regime' refers to networks of rules, norms and procedures that regulate the behaviour of states or other actors in a given area and control its effects.[12] Following World War II the role of international regimes expanded. The United Nations regime was designed with the aim of resolving the tension between the sovereign autonomy of states and international stability.[13] The main purpose for which the United Nations was set up was to ensure peace. Executive power in maintaining peace was vested in the United Nations Security Council. The five Permanent Members of the Security Council – the United States, the Soviet Union, China, Britain and France – reflected the balance of powers existing at the time of its creation. During the cold war, the achievement of a collective security system enshrined in the United Nations Charter was especially difficult. The United Nations peacekeeping operations were barred from use in internal conflicts, a permanent United Nations force was never created, budgetary provisions were provided on a voluntary basis, and the exercise of veto powers by the Permanent Members of the Security Council undermined the principle of sovereign equality. Many of these problems with the United Nations regime remain, and a number of agreements outside of the United Nations have further weakened its role.

International regimes undergo continuous transformation in response to their own inner dynamics, as well as to change in their political, economic and social environments.[14] Clearly, the United Nations and other international regimes have undergone a process of transformation since their establishment. One area where such change is evident is democracy promotion. An interest in democracy has its roots in the United Nations human rights regime. In 1945, the United Nations Charter codified a commitment to human rights prior to clarifying what human rights were and, in 1948, the General Assembly endorsed the Universal Declaration of Human Rights. During the 1970s, a number of Western states gave human rights a greater priority on their foreign policy agenda. The rights proclaimed in the

Universal Declaration were elaborated in the International Human Rights Covenants. The International Covenant on Civil and Political Rights and the International Covenant on Economic, Social and Cultural Rights were completed in 1966 and came into force in 1976. A variety of single-issue treaties and declarations on a range of specific topics were also developed during this period.

The United Nations has been providing electoral assistance since its founding; its Charter enshrines the principle of self-determination. Historically, this principle was targeted at the development of self-government and decolonization. In 1991, the General Assembly passed resolution 46/137, which emphasized the 'significance of the Universal Declaration of Human Rights and the International Covenant on Civil and Political Rights, which establish that the authority to govern shall be based on the will of the people, as expressed in genuine and periodic elections'.[15] It further stressed its 'conviction that periodic and genuine elections are a necessary and indispensable element of sustained efforts to protect the rights and interests of the governed', and declared 'that determining the will of the people requires an electoral process that provides an equal opportunity for all citizens to become candidates and put forward their political views, individually and in co-operation with others, as provided in national constitutions and laws'.[16] To this end, the Electoral Assistance Unit (later called the Electoral Assistance Division) was established. In addition, within the United Nations Development Programme (UNDP), a Management Development and Governance Division was established to respond to the increasing demand for technical assistance in governance and management development.[17]

The influence of international regimes upon democratic change has varied. There is a tendency in the literature to focus upon the role of regional regimes during democratic transitions. For example, Whitehead observes that a distinguishable feature of European and South American democratization is the influence of regional rather than global processes.[18] Certainly, the European Community has played a role encouraging and supporting transitions to democracy. In Europe a decision was made to offer full membership of the Community to certain European states, provided they comply with a number of conditions, including the establishment of democratic institutions.[19] It set in motion a complex and profound set of mutual adjustment processes, both within the nascent democracy and in its interactions with the rest of the Community, nearly all of which tended to favour democratization.[20] Requiring members to be democratic as a condition of membership is a new phenomenon, and may be a peculiarly European innovation.[21]

Vikram K. Chand attributes international regimes' growing support for democracy, particularly free elections, to five factors.[22] First, as a consequence of the wave of democratization that began in the 1970s, there were changes in the composition of the world's main international organizations. Second, America generally supported attempts to strengthen the commitment of international organizations to democracy. This was a result of the end of the cold war, and the renewal of interest in Immanuel Kant's democratic peace hypothesis among policy-makers.[23] Third, domestic democratic activists had a growing capacity to appeal directly to the international community. Fourth, changes within the global normative climate underpinned the growing involvement of international organizations in democracy promotion activities. Fifth, the erosion of traditional state sovereignty made states more vulnerable to outside influences, including the pressures to democratize.

Since the end of the cold war, states face a widening range of pressures from international regimes to comply and conform to the human rights and democratic standards the regimes articulate. In response to these pressures China asserts a 'modern' conception of state sovereignty, in which the principle of non-interference is sacrosanct. During the cold war, authoritarian regimes in South Korea and Taiwan did not experience this kind of international pressure, as United Nations internationalism was deployed to contain the spread of communism rather than to promote democracy.

China, Taiwan and the Koreas: United Nations membership

Whitehead highlights that the establishment of national boundaries is an 'eminently international act'.[24] External factors influenced the territorial boundaries, sovereign status, and position within the United Nations of each country under study. The ideological conflicts that characterized international relations during the cold war had a decisive impact on territorial disputes within the region. Both Korea and Taiwan were subjects of disputed sovereignty claims. The United Nations response to these problems reveals the prevalence of power politics within the organization. In dealing with these matters it is evident that major powers have the capacity to wield disproportionate influence within the United Nations regime. Indeed, power rather than the norm of democracy seems to be the prevailing principle in interstate relationships.[25] Paradoxically, the United Nations regime is concerned with norms, but responds to power.

In the first eight years of operation the United Nations was frequently characterized as an instrument of the United States. The United States could rely on 34 out of the original 51 General Assembly member states votes, and on a majority in the Security Council (with the exception of the Soviet Union's veto powers).[26] America's dominance in the United Nations and the development of the cold war influenced the international community's response to the competing sovereignty claims of the Kuomintang and the Chinese Communist Party.

During the civil war of 1945–1949, the Kuomintang government had full diplomatic recognition, even by the Soviet Union.[27] After their defeat on the mainland and retreat to Taiwan, representatives of the Kuomintang government continued to hold seats in virtually all United Nations bodies and organizations. The new communist government in Beijing challenged the legitimacy of ongoing Kuomintang representation in international organizations, and sought to replace them with their own representatives. The United Nations was captive to cold war ideological division and rejected the Chinese Communist Party's requests for representation.

International developments, such as the division of Europe in the wake of the Berlin crisis, influenced America's and, in turn, the United Nations' decision to maintain the status quo and continue to deny the People's Republic of China a place in the United Nations. The direct military clash between China and United Nations Command forces during the Korean War further deepened America's resolve to isolate China from international bodies.

Throughout the 1950s and 1960s, the United Nations continued to deny membership to the communist government in Beijing. Initially, the United States succeeded in securing this outcome because it could influence a majority of the member states votes. Subsequently, in the 1960s, the United States employed a range of parliamentary tactics in order to continue to preserve the Kuomintang government in Taipei's position.[28] Over time, achieving this outcome was increasingly difficult. The Kuomintang's claim to be the legitimate representative of China became more spurious as the years passed. In 1964 France became the first Western power since 1949 to recognize the Chinese Communist Party government; six years later Canada and Italy followed suit.[29]

During the 1960s and 1970s, decolonization transformed the United Nations General Assembly. Throughout this period (despite its isolation from the Western international order) China had developed strategic connections with a number of decolonized states. China was a key actor in the Non Aligned Movement. Ultimately, these relationships proved useful to China for achieving United Nations member status. As the number of Asian and African states joining the United Nations increased, the United States gradually lost the numbers in the United Nations General Assembly. This changed context facilitated China's admission to the United Nations. At the 26th General Assembly in 1971 the United States ceased its lobbying activities and resolution 2758 passed. The United Nations now recognized the People's Republic of China as the 'sole legitimate government of China'; thus transferring membership and the recognition of sovereign authority from the government in Taipei to the government in Beijing. The impact of the United Nations decision was twofold; while the regime in China was legitimized, the Kuomintang regime lost its legitimacy internationally. Taiwan was reduced to (and remains) an 'entity'.

After resolution 2758 was passed, the Kuomintang leadership, adhering to a 'one China' policy, rejected proposals that would have given the Security Council seat to the People's Republic of China, while admitting the Republic of China government as a separate member of the General Assembly.[30] Since then the government in Taiwan has revised its position, and from 1993 onwards has sought General Assembly membership.

Taiwan's campaign to join the United Nations is symbolic of the impact of democratization upon Taiwan's politics and foreign policy.[31] Taiwan's strategy to gain support for its membership bid has focussed on developing bilateral relations with individual states. In general, Taiwan has not succeeded in gaining diplomatic recognition from powerful countries. Still, with the support of some of these states, Taiwan has attempted to join the United Nations eight times.

Paradoxically, the Chinese government relies upon power-based strategies (similar to those used by the United States to block its own entry to the United Nations during the cold war) against Taiwan. China manoeuvred to stop Taiwan's membership bid on the basis that it is recognized internationally as having exclusive sovereign authority over all China, and Taiwan is a part of China. Indeed, the United States now pressures Taiwan to negotiate with the mainland regarding unification. International politics restricts Taiwan from what some people in Taiwan see as its right to claim an independent identity in international bodies. A local paper, the *China Times*, noted in 1999 that, 'only support from the United States can guarantee Taiwan a safe future'.[32] During Taiwan's attempt to join the United Nations in 1999, the number of countries opposing its bid increased, and even included the United States, the United Kingdom and France. Pakistan's representative, speaking against the initiative at the United Nations in 2000, argued that the issue had become a wasteful yearly debate.

That the exercise should prove to be a waste of time is interesting because there are precedents which would appear to support Taiwan's case for member status. Previously, the concept of state sovereignty has been represented in the United Nations by more than one seat.[33] In 1945 the United States conceded two extra votes in the United Nations General Assembly for the Soviet Union – one for the 'sovereign' republic of the Ukraine and the other for Belarus.[34] In 1973, the Federal Republic of Germany and the German Democratic Republic were admitted to the United Nations, and, through the accession of the German Democratic Republic to the Federal Republic of Germany during 1990, the two states united to form one sovereign state.[35]

Furthermore, the Korean case represents an example of United Nations flexibility. The two Koreas both claim to be the exclusive, legitimate rulers of the entire Korean peninsula. When the Korean War ended in an impasse, each entity pursued *de jure* recognition from other countries and, since the goal was to have their claims of exclusive legitimacy confirmed, neither would accept dual recognition.[36] At the end of two decades of diplomatic manoeuvring, the governments in Seoul and Pyongyang were each recognized by a similar number of states. Indeed, over time, they were each recognized by the same states; by 1976 a total of 49 countries simultaneously recognized both regimes.[37]

Notwithstanding the opposition of South Korea and its allies, Pyongyang joined the World Health Organization, which conferred upon it the customary privilege of applying for observer status in the General Assembly. In 1973, the United Nations General Assembly extended an unconditional invitation to North Korea to send observers to its deliberations on the Korea question. Prior to this, North Korea had ignored invitations due to its view that the United Nations, as a co-belligerent in the Korean War, had no right to act as an impartial arbiter on the Korean question.[38] The entry of the North Koreans unsettled South Korean power in the United Nations and the usefulness of United Nations support for its legitimacy claims was weakened. Finally, in September 1991, both Korean states became full members of the United Nations.

Interestingly, the situation in Korea has some similarities with Taiwan and China. The common attributes of sovereignty have not been in evidence in China's relations with Taiwan for over 50 years. Taiwan has undergone a process of democratization (a fact that states supporting Taiwan's membership bid refer to). Denial of United Nations membership to Taiwan is primarily due to China's exercise of power. It suggests the failure of the United Nations to uphold the principles of national sovereignty and autonomy. Some people thought that the prevalence of power politics in international organizations would diminish with the end of the cold war. An expectation grew that the United Nations would become a more effective agency of global governance.[39] Indeed, as detailed in the last chapter, several international bodies put good governance on the agenda at the end of the cold war when they began to urge governments to develop and improve standards of democratic representation, accountability and transparency.[40] However, international interest in China's power rather than Taiwan's democracy has been decisive in determining the outcome of Taiwan's bids for United Nations membership. The importance of power politics to the regime was made apparent during the United Nations' early activities in the region.

United Nations intervention in Korea

At the end of World War II, the United Nations' role in Korea reflected the changing nature of the international system. Although self-determination and the establishment of democracy in Korea were of concern to the United Nations, key international actors sought to influence and control the timing and nature of the Korean decolonization process.

International negotiations concerning the future of Korea began during World War II. The Cairo Declaration of 1943 and the Potsdam Declaration of 1945 resolved that Korea would become free and independent in 'due course'. The President of the United States of America, Franklin D. Roosevelt, proposed the establishment of a multilateral trusteeship that would assist postcolonial peoples toward independence.[41] This proposal did not reflect the will of the Korean people. After Japanese Emperor Hirohito surrendered to the Allied powers, most Koreans anticipated an independent and unified government would be established on the peninsula.[42] Within Korea concern developed about the implications of the proviso 'in due course', and a nationwide movement opposing the trusteeship proposal and seeking autonomy was launched.[43] The Allied powers largely ignored these domestic developments.

Due to military considerations, the Allies agreed that Soviet forces would accept the surrender of Japanese troops north of the 38th parallel and the Americans would be responsible for those south of the parallel. This expedient measure contributed to problems later when the relationship between the United States and the Soviet Union deteriorated. Soon geo-political rivalry, rather than internationalist ideals, prevailed in matters regarding the Korean peninsula.

The United States–Soviet Union Joint Commission had its first meeting in 1946; this and subsequent meetings were mired in disagreement about interpretations of the provisions of the trusteeship and the Soviet proposal for the withdrawal of all foreign troops. The United States changed tack and, in 1947, submitted all problems concerning Korean independence to the second United Nations General Assembly.

The United Nations General Assembly, in keeping with the principle of self-determination, established the United Nations Temporary Commission on Korea to help Korea establish a national government. Regarding the attainment of independence, it recommended that elections be held no later than March 1948. However, this recommendation was never fully implemented. The Soviet Union refused the Commission entry north of the 38th parallel.[44] The Temporary Commission sought further instruction and, following General Assembly directions, proceeded to observe elections in the south. Full political participation in the election was not only undermined by the Soviet Union's stance. This was because, since 1946, the anti-communist policies of the American military government in the south had forced sections of the worker and left-wing political parties to go underground.[45]

The first Korean National Assembly was founded through the 10 May General Election in 1948, which the United Nations observed. One hundred seats were left vacant for representatives from the north. The National Assembly drafted the first constitution. The constitution instituted an American type of presidential system, with some parliamentary features, such as a prime minister, cabinet council, executive legislation and a ministerial report to the National Assembly.[46] As a result of the election, Syngman Rhee and the Korean Democratic Party emerged as the central force in South Korean politics.

South Korea's first President, Syngman Rhee, formally notified the United Nations Commission of the establishment of the Republic of Korea. The government was inaugurated and independence proclaimed on 15 August 1948. On 25 August 1948, North Korea held its own independent elections for a Soviet-style political system, and, on 9 September of the same year, proclaimed the establishment of the Democratic People's Republic of

Korea. By the end of June 1949, American troops were almost completely withdrawn from South Korea. However, a small number of advisory personnel were retained who influenced the development of the South Korean army. In particular, they advised on the creation of the Korean Military Academy along the lines of the program at West Point.[47] Several graduates of the academy were to become powerful figures in Korean political life.

In June 1950, North Korea launched a southern invasion with the intention of reunifying the peninsula. The United Nations' response reflects international relations at that time, and the prevailing views of Washington.[48] The United States political elite was adhering to a new internationalism, which was essentially a rationale for the role of the United States as 'world policeman'.[49] According to Cecilia Lynch, the Americans exercised this role through unilateral and multilateral methods which were explicitly carried out in Korea.[50]

The 'loss of China' to communism, and the Spring crises in Czechoslovakia and Berlin suggested to American policy-makers that the Soviet Union was expanding its sphere of influence. In the United States, Secretary of State, Dean Acheson, thought that a North Korean victory would precipitate a Chinese invasion of Taiwan, and hence would alter the balance of power in the region. However, the United States was reluctant to rely solely upon its own resources to contain the spread of communism in East Asia.

The United States referred the matter to the United Nations Security Council, which established that North Korean actions 'constituted a breach of the peace'. Soviet representative, Joseph Malik, was absent from this Security Council meeting. The Soviet Union had boycotted the meeting because of the Kuomintang's ongoing status as the Permanent Member of the Security Council representing China. In the absence of a Soviet Union veto, America was able to get the United Nations to assist it to limit the expansion of communism in East Asia, which it regarded as emanating from the 'loss of China'. The United Nations Security Council established a United Nations Command invoking collective security against a breach of the peace. The then President of the United States, Harry S. Truman, wrote to Secretary of State Dean Acheson:

> Regarding June 24–25: Your initiative in immediately calling the Security Council of the U.N. on Saturday night and notifying me was the key to what followed afterwards. Had you not acted promptly in that direction we would have had to go into Korea alone.[51]

Most of the United States' allies were reluctant to commit troops to the conflict in Korea. The British Foreign Office and India separately initiated negotiations on compromise solutions. These included India's proposal to restore the status quo in exchange for the transfer of the United Nations seat from the government in Taipei to the government in Beijing.[52] These proposals were rejected by Acheson. Acheson was able to use the United Nations to promote what he saw as a 'free world' agenda, but which might also be regarded as serving American geo-political interests.

On 29 July 1950 the Soviet Union indicated it would resume participation in the United Nations Security Council. Thus, the Soviet Union had veto power over any further Security Council resolutions concerning Korea. In response, the United States referred subsequent matters to the General Assembly where it could influence a majority of the votes.

As the war drew on, policy-makers in the United States were divided on the question of crossing the 38th parallel. South Korean President, Syngman Rhee, announced that South Korean forces would not stop at the parallel and would strive to unify the peninsula. The United States wanted to clarify China's attitude toward the conflict in Korea. Through the Indian Ambassador, China indicated that it would join the war if the 38th parallel were breached. On 30 September 1950, a resolution restating an earlier United Nations policy on Korea was introduced in the General Assembly. The resolution referred back to the 1947 plan, which called for the establishment of a 'unified, independent, and democratic government of Korea'.[53] The United Nations command in Korea, led by General Douglas MacArthur, interpreted the resolution as empowering the military forces to drive beyond the 38th parallel and unify the peninsula.

Concern among the allies, in particular the British, increased following General MacArthur's northward sweep. The Indian ambassador to China consistently warned that the Chinese would not tolerate a march to the Yalu.[54] Interestingly, Mao had led the government in Beijing to make extensive preparations to assist North Korea in the conflict even before the United Nations forces pushed north. Chen Jian argues that Beijing's reaction to the Korean crisis needs to be understood in the context of the increasing confrontation between China and the United States in East Asia in 1949 and 1950, Mao's desire to use the crisis to mobilize both the Chinese Communist Party and the nation, and the Chinese Communist Party's intention to revitalize China's great power status through the promotion revolutions (following the Chinese model) in East Asia and the world.[55] The Soviet Union did not honour an earlier commitment to provide the Chinese forces with air support and, as a consequence, the Chinese People's Volunteers initially entered into the conflict alone. China's decision to enter the conflict, even without Soviet assistance, reflects the Chinese leadership's view that the result of the conflict would influence the fate of the entire East, including Taiwan.[56] Once China became engaged in the Korean conflict the United States succeeded in labelling China an aggressor in a resolution passed by the General Assembly on 1 February 1951.[57]

The Soviet Union proposed a cease-fire during an address to the United Nations on 23 June 1951. On 10 July 1951, the first conference of the full armistice delegations was convened. South Korean President Rhee opposed an armistice which left the nation divided. He warned a truce would mean a 'national death sentence'.[58] Rancorous negotiations proceeded over the next two years concerning the armistice and the repatriation of prisoners of war. Finally, on 27 July 1953, an armistice was concluded between the United Nations Commander, the commanders of the (North) Korean People's Army and the Chinese People's Volunteers. The South Korean government has never signed the armistice and attempted to derail the negotiation process by unilaterally releasing prisoners of war. The Armistice Agreement created an uneasy truce. An American military presence remains near the heavily militarized 'demilitarized zone', and all except token representatives of other nations have withdrawn.[59]

Implications for democracy

United Nations activity in Korea had a multi-layered impact. The United Nations intervention in the conflict influenced both the South Korean political system and the regional geo-political landscape. The Chinese Communist Party leadership re-examined China's alliance with the Soviet Union. The 'lean-to-one-side' approach was called into question and the leadership emphasized 'self-reliance' as a fundamental principle.[60] The conflict helped to sanction the implementation of NSC-68, served as a basis and justification for American military containment of communism in Asia, and enabled the United States to discredit China among other nations.

The broader economic impact of the Korean War and its relationship to political development were discussed in the previous chapter. President Rhee used the Armistice Agreement to gain important economic and security concessions from America. The United States agreed to a mutual defence treaty with South Korea, delivered over US$1billion in economic aid over three years and provided equipment to enable the expansion of the South Korean army to twenty divisions (about 700,000 soldiers).[61]

United Nations intervention further contributed to the development of structural conditions in South Korea that made the political system susceptible to various forms of military involvement in politics. The political capability of the military increased considerably, as did the military's inclination toward political activism.[62] After the armistice, the South Korean army emerged as one of the largest in the world in absolute numbers, and the military were 'absolutely and relatively more important to the society than they had been previously'.[63] This development was looked on favourably by both the United States and the United Nations.

Korean politics swung to the right after the war. Political opposition was constrained, and left wing politics denounced. President Rhee's political tactics involved using the military for partisan purposes. Resentment grew among citizens when Rhee planned to establish a lifetime dictatorship through constitutional amendment. In March 1960 student-led protests against the corruption of the electoral process ousted the Rhee regime.[64] A period of brief democratic opening followed. But it was brought to an abrupt end in April 1961, when military leaders, General Park Chung Hee and Lieutenant Colonel Kim Jong Pil, led a *coup d'état*.

General Park argued that the military revolution was not 'intended to strangle democracy', but rather was designed 'to suspend it temporarily while it is undergoing medical treatment. In other words, the military revolution assumes a nature of controlled or remedial democracy'.[65] After the coup, the military were to dominate South Korean political life and deny democracy for the next thirty years. It was not until 1993 that a civilian government began to purge members of the military elite from Korean politics. The United Nations paid little attention to these authoritarian developments in South Korea, as the United States acted as a 'protector' of the South Korean state.

The impact of the United Nations intervention upon South Korean political culture was also significant. The volatility of the situation at the 38th parallel contributed to the development of garrison nationalism in South Korea. David Brown argues that when uncertainty about national unity is combined with the presence of an external threat, it generates the perception of a society in crisis that 'can only survive on the basis of unquestioning allegiance to the incumbent authoritarian regime and leader'.[66] Brown develops the concept of 'the nation as garrison under siege' to explain this phenomenon.[67] In this scenario, authoritarian leaders define the nation in 'reactive' terms and the existence of an external enemy provides the basis for national unity.[68] In the process, democracy is delayed. In South Korea garrison nationalism legitimized certain instruments of authoritarianism, such as the National Security Act and the Korean Central Intelligence Agency, which were employed by the state to ensure that the threat from North Korea and communist insurgents was limited. In the process, political opponents were systematically repressed.

Over time, as the external and domestic context altered, it became increasingly difficult for the South Korean state to justify continuing with such authoritarian practices. This was due to the erosion of the credibility of the communist threats assumed by garrison nationalism, the cumulative effects of socio-economic development, and the evolving problems of leadership succession.[69] Once the transition to democracy was underway, the South Korean foreign policy agenda began to alter. President Roh Tae Woo placed settling relations with North Korea on the national agenda. Progressing this goal has proved difficult.

In October 1988, President Roh Tae Woo addressed the United Nations General Assembly on his initiative, *Nordpolitik*. He appealed to the United Nations to assist his government to resolve the problem of Korean unification.[70] Evgeny Afanasiev highlights the stagnancy of the mechanism for maintaining peace in Korea, and the saturation of the peninsula with conventional armaments and weapons of mass destruction.[71] These factors ought to suggest finding a peaceful resolution to the situation are a matter of international importance. Yet, the United Nations has been less than proactive in assisting with this goal. Although United Nations agencies play a significant role in matters relating to North Korean nuclear capabilities, questions regarding Korean unification are primarily the province of bilateral relations among the major powers and the governments in Pyongyang and Seoul.

Since 1994, South Korea and the United States have pursued a policy of engagement with North Korea. It is designed to coax the regime in Pyongyang toward the beginnings of confidence building, while containing the North Korean nuclear program and simultaneously offering the country a form of development assistance.[72] More recently, South Korean President Kim Dae Jung has embarked on a policy of 'constructive engagement' with North Korea, commonly referred to as the 'Sunshine Policy'. The policy provides the broad framework and operating principles through which Seoul manages its relations with Pyongyang. It is a long-term comprehensive strategy, which clearly states that South Korea does 'not intend to absorb North Korea', and that it will 'actively promote exchanges and co-operation between South and North Korea'.[73] The initiation of the 'Sunshine Policy' was facilitated by the new post-cold war international relations, changes in the North Korean regime, and Kim Dae Jung's personal decision to pursue the issue during his presidency.

Fierce debates and criticisms of Kim Dae Jung's approach emerged within South Korea due to the discrepancy between making good progress on negotiations regarding economic issues and slow progress on security issues.[74] President Roh Moo-hyun, Kim's successor, has put building a firm foundation for peace on the Korean peninsula as his first policy goal. Yet, clearly, resolving matters on the peninsula cannot depend upon South Korean policy leadership alone.

The 'Sunshine Policy' was adversely affected by the Asian financial crisis, and by United States President George W. Bush's global 'war on terror'. During his State of the Union address, President George W. Bush included North Korea within the so-called 'axis of evil'. This has had an adverse impact on North Korea's relations not only with South Korea, but also with the international community generally. Even prior to these events, however, external support for settling the Korean question was weak. The major regional powers – Russia, China, Japan, and the United States – benefit from maintaining the status quo.[75] An isolated North Korea is in China's diplomatic interest; as the only country that has diplomatic relations with all the parties to the conflict, China has been serving as an important communication hub linking North Korea and its neighbours.[76] Peaceful reunification would have an impact on the United States, whose bases in South Korea form part of its overall security configuration in the Pacific.

More important, however, is North Korea's nuclear weapons program, which is a key driver of American foreign policy toward the region. The Six-Party Talks between both Koreas, China, Japan, Russia and the United

States are making little progress toward the goal of eliminating North Korea's nuclear weapons programs. It seems that, as was the case during the division of Korea, inter-Korean relations continue to be crucially affected by external factors.

The Kuomintang and the United Nations

The influence of United Nations upon the development of democracy in Taiwan falls within two phases. The first phase, when the Kuomintang government was a Permanent Member of the Security Council, was not conducive to the development of democracy in Taiwan. The United Nations' decision to continue to recognize the Kuomintang regime as the legitimate rulers of China inhibited the development of democracy. The inadequacy of the United Nations position contributed to ongoing tensions in the Taiwan Straits, and affected the development of Taiwan's political institutions and political culture. The Kuomintang used the threatening external environment to justify the retention of a range of extra-constitutional measures which stifled democracy and contributed to garrison nationalism. Taiwan's loss of the Security Council seat marks the beginning of the second phase. In this phase United Nations actions assisted democratization. However, as will be shown, this was an unanticipated, unintentional and indirect consequence. Taiwan's loss of status in the United Nations was the catalyst for a crisis of legitimacy within the Kuomintang regime. It stimulated the politicization of identity politics and reinvigorated democratic activists in Taiwan.

Yun-han Chu argues that the character of the state in Taiwan was influenced by the dubious constitution of the regime at both the international and domestic level.[77] These anomalies combined to place constraints on the development of democracy. The unresolved and contentious question of sovereignty influenced (and indeed continues to influence) many dimensions of island politics, including its political institutions and political culture.

Until the late 1970s the Kuomintang used its status within the United Nations to justify its claim to represent all of China. Consequently, the regime instituted a constitutional order that reflected this claim. This resulted in the political dominance of the mainlander elite – founded on the principle that there is only one China, Taiwan is part of China, and the Republic of China government should be the sole legitimate government representing all of China.[78] United Nations recognition gave authority to the political system established by the Kuomintang on Taiwan. It contained a five-branch national government. A functioning legislature claimed to represent all the provinces of China. Its life-term members had been elected in 1948 on the mainland, and continued in power (unchallenged) until constitutional reforms were instituted in 1991 and 1992.

The Kuomintang fostered national cohesion by asserting the imperative of national unity against communist China. For the Chiang Kai-shek regime, keeping Chinese nationalism alive involved maintaining the claim over the mainland. Thus, the idea of a regime representing the whole of China was fostered by the notion of a Chinese community which, in turn, was nurtured by a process of cultural invention in order to nationalize traditional Chinese culture, and discourage the public expression of Taiwanese identity.[79] In the context of the garrison state, the Kuomintang regime attempted to construct a strongly Chinese national identity. Government institutions, popular culture, and the media stressed mainland Chinese roots and the importance of history and life on the Chinese mainland not in Taiwan itself.[80] For a time this process was assisted by the legitimacy bestowed by the United Nations upon the Kuomintang's claims.

In keeping with its founder Sun Yat-sen's ideas of tutelary democracy, the Kuomintang tried to make nominal progress away from party dictatorship toward constitutional democracy.[81] In October 1952, Party Chairman and President of the Republic of China, Chiang Kai-shek, stated that 'Sun Yat-sen's highest goal was to build a political system in which sovereignty resided with the people', and that 'in order to oppose communism and recover our nation, the primary task of our Party is to carry out local elections, build our nation's political system, and establish the solid foundations for our people to practice democracy'.[82] However, what developed in Taiwan was a form of democratic façade, analogous to President Park's 'remedial' or 'controlled' democracy in South Korea.

In reality, the Kuomintang initiated reforms that gave the Party apparatus on Taiwan a high degree of organizational capacity within a corporatist structure.[83] In addition to the enhanced powers of control these actions created, the uncertain international context was used to justify the retention of extra-constitutional measures promulgated during the civil war. The 'Temporary Provisions' extended the emergency powers already given to the President and permitted his tenure in office to be indefinite.[84] Chiang Kai-shek was unchallenged as leader of the Kuomintang regime, and held the position of President until his death in 1974. Initially he was succeeded by his Vice President, then in 1978 Chiang Kai-shek's son, Chiang Ching-kuo, was appointed to the presidency for life. The 'Temporary Provisions' inhibited the development of opposition politics on the island. Political parties were banned and opponents of the Kuomintang regime were frequently labelled communist agitators and detained. Moreover, those attempting to assert a Taiwanese identity separate from the Kuomintang's 'Chinese' identity were harshly dealt with. Chiang Kai-shek and Chiang Ching-kuo treated people who sought Taiwan's independence with the same vigour they used in dealing with communists in Taiwan.[85]

The problem with deriving legitimacy for the constitutional order from external sources was twofold. Firstly, as time passed it became evident that the likelihood of the Kuomintang retaking China was small. Secondly, United Nations recognition of the Kuomintang's claim was not indefinitely assured.

These problems were apparent immediately after the Kuomintang's arrival in Taiwan. Prior to the Korean War, it had seemed unlikely the

Kuomintang would continue to hold the United Nations Security Council seat. After the People's Republic of China was established on 1 October 1949, the Soviet Union, most Eastern European countries and Burma recognized the new government. India and Pakistan followed a few months later. For a time during the early part of 1950, it appeared that even American faith in the Kuomintang was wavering.[86] The British government, having been unable to reach any agreement with Australia or the United States, declared on 6 January 1950 that they would recognize the communist regime; Israel, Afghanistan and the Scandinavian countries followed suit.[87] However, the British government did not establish diplomatic relations and maintained *de facto* recognition of the Kuomintang government in Taiwan. After the Korean War, the British government shifted from their (albeit weak) support of Chinese communist government to support of American proposals that consideration of the question of China's United Nations membership be deferred. Thus, from early on, it was apparent that the position of the Kuomintang regime would be vulnerable to revisions in the foreign policies of United Nations Security Council members.

The loss of legitimacy

The loss of the United Nations seat to mainland China in 1971 and subsequent derecongition by its major allies undermined the Kuomintang's claim to be the sole legitimate government of all of China. In turn, these events eroded the Kuomintang's domestic legitimacy. In this sense, the United Nations and the international community indirectly assisted the development of democracy in Taiwan. The vexed nature of the sovereignty question had influenced the development of identity politics on the island and contributed to increased demands by local Taiwanese for political inclusion. The question, 'who are the people – Taiwanese or Chinese', became a pressing domestic issue, which was increasingly being politicized by an emergent opposition movement.

The existence of a constitution, the design of which was consistent with democracy, provided democratic activists with a basis for demanding a return to the constitution and the removal of the extra-constitutional provisions.[88] Thus, the changes in the external environment triggered a 'political awakening' which provided opportunities for the growth of political opposition.[89] The non-Party or *tangwai* (outside the party) political candidates began to enjoy success in local elections in the late 1970s.

The changed external environment crucially affected the internal legitimacy of the Kuomintang regime. The Kuomintang's institutional capacity for mobilization and control was eroding. This was due to the impact of derecognition, the effects of sustained economic growth, and the looming succession crisis. Speculation about the possibility of a continuation of the 'Chiang dynasty' or a military take-over and disputes between various power centres within the government and the Party about a successor undermined regime credibility.[90] Preoccupation with internal power struggles momentarily weakened the social control of the ruling authorities, resulting in reduced risks in confronting the regime.[91] As a consequence, non-Party political candidates became increasingly bold in their endeavours.

In response, Chiang Ching-kuo began to change the regime's legitimization strategy and commenced a gradual process of liberalization. The ban on non-official contacts with mainland China was lifted and a gradual process of Taiwanization of the Kuomintang was initiated. By 1984, a more lenient view toward opposition politics began to be accepted by some Kuomintang factions. In early 1986, President Chiang Ching-kuo announced that the Kuomintang would launch major political reforms to democratize the polity. Then, in 1986, a group of non-Kuomintang candidates boldly announced the creation of the Democratic Progressive Party and pushed to accelerate the process of political reform.[92] In 1987, martial law was finally lifted, and national electoral processes became more democratic. During the 1989 election, agreement was reached for the compulsory retirement of the life-long members of the national representative bodies. By the 1990s, democratization was well underway.

The United Nations may be said to have played a role in the development and reform of political structures on Taiwan. Firstly, it indirectly influenced the form of performance-based legitimacy the Kuomintang developed. Secondly, after derecognition, it provided a trigger and a political space for opposition forces in Taiwan to reshape the relationship between the state and society. Internationally isolated, the Kuomintang regime was more responsive to domestic demands for political reform. The consolidation of democracy in Taiwan remains a complicated process. More than fifty years after the United Nations first deliberated on the question of the relationship between Taiwan and China, the matter continues to be debated at the United Nations and to define many aspects of the island's politics. The way in which United Nations decisions have influenced political life in Taiwan reveals the indirect (and at times ironic) effects of the international dimension of democratization.

Integrating China into the regime

After China became a member state, its relationship with the United Nations evolved to become complex and multi-faceted. During this period, the regime itself was undergoing a process of normative change. Interest in human rights and democracy increased, if not among the Chinese Communist Party apparatus, at least within sections of the wider international society and among the overseas Chinese community.

Since the end of the cold war and the events in Tiananmen Square in 1989, China's exposure to international pressures to democratize has increased. United Nations pressures on China to democratize came indirectly via universal human rights principles and norms.[93] More direct forms of influence are also evident as United Nations democracy promotion programs in China, such as those by the UNDP, begin to take effect. At the same time, China has engaged in a realist strategy to limit external human rights and democratization pressures. China seeks, at times quite autocratically, to assert its sovereign authority over all its domestic affairs. China uses international regimes to advance its claims and objectives internationally, while denying the legitimacy of international human rights regimes' criticisms of its domestic practices.

In the immediate period after it joined the United Nations, China familiarized itself with international norms and conventions and learnt the rules of the game. Samuel S. Kim provides a detailed empirical analysis of China's participation in the United Nations during the first five years of its membership.[94] Kim argues that the most immediate impact of China's entry was largely symbolic.[95] As a Security Council and General Assembly member, China adopted a 'low-profile and apprentice-like posture'.[96] As a consequence of having been excluded from the United Nations for so long, once Beijing did enter the organization, countries and non-government bodies appeared prepared to give it time to adjust. As a result, concerns about human rights abuses in China were slow coming onto the agenda.[97]

China's initial role in the United Nations was marked by its passivity. In part this was because China was becoming familiar with the regime, but it was also because China did not regard the United Nations as a significant aspect of its foreign policy, or an important independent actor in its own right.[98] During much of the 1970s China's behaviour in international organizations was generally marked by the 'discrepancy between normative activism and participatory aloofness'.[99]

By the 1980s China had changed tack. Robert Keohane contends that decisions about joining international regimes will be affected by changes in the characteristics of the international system, which alter the opportunities and costs to actors of various courses of action.[100] In late 1978, China began to seek multilateral aid and technical assistance from the United Nations and its specialized agencies. In October 1978, the Chinese government formally asked the UNDP for technical assistance. In September 1979, the Representative Office of the UNDP in Beijing was opened. Of particular interest to this study is the UNDP China Rural Official Training Centre program (CROTC).

Prior to 1979, China had not signed any United Nations sponsored human rights conventions, or participated in the work of any United Nations human rights organs. By 1982, China seemed to have accepted that human rights were an important component of world politics. China played a key role in propounding the right to economic, social and cultural rights.

Table 3.1 demonstrates China's increased activity in the human rights regimes in the 1980s, in particular the specialist conventions. China did not ratify either the International Covenant on Economic Social and Cultural Rights or the International Covenant on Civil and Political Rights, although it has signed both. It is also evident that China's participation in listed treaties is not strikingly different from other permanent members of the Security Council. Moreover, China has signed treaties in which individual

Table 3.1 Ratification of United Nations human rights treaties by Security Council permanent members (entry into force date as at 28 March 2001)

UN Treaty	China	France	Russian Federation	United Kingdom	United States
International Covenant on Civil and Political Rights	—	4/2/1981	23/3/1976	20/8/1976	8/9/1992
International Covenant on Economic, Social and Cultural Rights	—	4/2/1981	3/1/1976	20/8/1976	—
Convention Against Torture and other Cruel, Inhuman or Degrading Treatments or Punishments	3/11/1988	26/6/1987	26/6/1987	7/1/1989	20/11/1994
Convention on the Rights of the Child	1/4/1992	6/9/1990	15/9/1990	15/1/1992	—
Convention on the Elimination of All Forms of Discrimination Against Women	3/9/1981	13/11/1984	3/9/1981	7/5/1986	—
Convention on the Elimination of All Forms of Racial Discrimination	28/1/1982	27/8/1971	6/3/1969	6/4/1969	20/11/1994
Refugees	24/9/1982	23/6/1954	2/2/1993	11/3/1954	—
Genocide	18/4/1983	14/10/1950	3/5/1954	30/1/1970	25/11/1988
1st ICCPR Protocol	—	17/5/1984	1/1/1992	—	—
2nd ICCPR Protocol	—	—	—	10/12/1999	—

Source: Philip J. Eldridge, *The Politics of Human Rights in South East Asia*, London: Routledge, 2002, p. 64.

rights are explicitly recognized, such as the Convention against Torture and Other Cruel and Inhuman or Degrading Treatment or Punishment.

Thomas Franck argues that a normative entitlement to democracy in international law has gone through both a normative and a customary evolution.[101] He identifies three phases: firstly, the normative entitlement to self-determination; secondly, to free expression as a human right; and finally, the entitlement to a participatory electoral process. The right to democracy has been bundled under the umbrella of the human rights regime. The Universal Declaration of Human Rights asserts democratic principles such as the right to take part in government and the right to universal suffrage. In the International Covenant on Civil and Political Rights democratic principles such as these are articulated as a legal obligation.

The idea of human rights has its roots in European political theory. Jack Donnelley stresses that there is nothing natural, let alone inevitable, about ordering social and political life around the idea of human rights.[102] The idea of universal human rights is based on a metaphysical notion of the individual as an autonomous being, and is predicated on a concept of basic human nature in which rights are independent of time, place, culture, ideology or value positions. By contrast, China's theory of human rights is based on the argument that social actions should be understood and evaluated by norms and rules that are internal to the culture.

For many people there is a very significant difference between the formal status of human rights and democracy: human rights are international legal norms, whereas democracy is a political ideology.[103] Political socialization, particularly post-cold war, conveys the impression that states are moving toward 'homogeneity' of domestic values and organization.[104] Yet, consensus on existing rules, norms and values within the international system does not exist. During its participation within the United Nations regime, China has played a key role in challenging and questioning the apparent 'normative consensus' on the priority of individual human rights and democracy.

From the 1980s onwards, information about human rights abuses within China was being gathered with greater ease by international non-government organizations and other bodies. Improved access to Tibet and the activities of the Dalai Lama stimulated international interest in Tibetan issues. At its March meetings in 1986 and 1989, the United Nations Commission for Human Rights criticized Chinese actions in Tibet, but these did not represent the formal start of systematic attention.[105] Then, the events in Tiananmen Square during June 1989 occurred. By this time, international society's sensitivity to human rights and democracy issues had become much more acute. The 'hugely increased' normative ambitions of international society were nowhere more visible than in the field of human rights and democracy.[106] This did not mean that human rights abuses diminished in this era of more acute awareness; in fact, if anything, they may have increased. Nonetheless, the United Nations focussed its attention on human rights conditions in China and, in response, China altered its diplomatic strategy toward the United Nations. Thus, it is evident that the Chinese government's interaction with the United Nations firstly, came late, and secondly, evolved as force which challenged aspects of the regime thereafter.

In this context, during August 1989, the United Nations Sub-Commission on the Prevention of Discrimination and Protection of Minorities, a subsidiary expert body of the Commission on Human Rights, passed by a secret vote 15:9, the first ever resolution in United Nations history censoring a Permanent Member of the Security Council, for human rights abuses. In response to such international criticism, China has increased its engagement with the international community on questions of human rights.

For example, in 1991 the Chinese government published a human rights white paper. According to China's theory of human rights, there is no such thing as 'natural human rights', entitlements that inhere in persons, but only citizens' rights as defined and extended by the state.[107] In a notable innovation, the white paper establishes a hierarchy of rights.[108] Nonetheless, it is important to emphasize that the white paper does not refute or challenge the idea of human rights in principle. Five points underpin China's official stance on human rights: China's priority is to provide basic living conditions for its people, incremental change should take precedence over rapid change, political stability is of paramount importance, Chinese Communist Party survival is crucial for the country, and intervention in China's internal affairs will not be tolerated.[109] These fundamental principles take priority over human rights when there is a conflict or contradiction.

Beijing also embarked on a pro-active diplomatic strategy in response to Western states' criticisms of its human rights record. As a result, an unprecedented Asian regional human rights conference was held in Bangkok in March 1993. A number of conference participants developed the Bangkok Declaration in preparation for the second United Nations World Conference on Human Rights to be held in Vienna that year. The Bangkok Declaration stipulates that universal standards should not override Asian regional and cultural values, the requirements of development, or state sovereignty.[110] There was a great deal of debate and disagreement between participants about the universalism versus relativism of human rights. Ultimately, the universality of human rights was reaffirmed at the Vienna Conference.

In addition, in order to deflect international criticism of its human rights practices, China has succeeded in developing a 'linkage *realpolitik*'; that is, China has been practising a form of linkage sanctions diplomacy.[111] China threatens to withhold commercial contracts to industrialized countries and promises aid to developing countries – provided they do not introduce or pass resolutions critical of China's human rights record.

Clearly, the Chinese government is concerned about its international image, reputation and legitimacy. Thus it is, at least potentially, capable of being shamed for non-adherence to international standards.[112] China's active role in deterring condemnatory resolutions at the annual meetings of the United Nations Commission for Human Rights and engagement in human rights discourse is evidence of its desire to enhance its international reputation and standing.

China's search for a 'pathway from the periphery' in the world order represents a struggle for power and a quest for prestige.[113] China's leaders want China to be accepted as a major player in the international community, and as such they are vulnerable to international criticism. Thus, although there is a clear dominance of the realist paradigm in Chinese foreign policy, power is not the sole concern. Moreover, China's economic reform policies require it to be fully integrated into international society.[114] Yet, China's strong stance on sovereignty and non-intervention limits China's flexibility in the international arena.[115] Balancing these competing interests is difficult. It requires China's engagement with international human rights regimes and discourse, the very legitimacy of which it questions. It is evident that China's interactions with the United Nations are proving to be of potential causative significance, not only to China, but also to the evolution of the regime itself.

China and UN democracy assistance

In the context of China's evolving engagement with the United Nations, one area where United Nations agencies have influenced political reform in China is the UNDP village self-governance training program. In 1987 the National People's Congress introduced the Organic Law of Villagers' Committees on a provisional basis. The law introduced a form of electoral democracy into village level governance. It provides for the direct election of villagers' committees by village residents. By 1992 most of China's provinces had completed at least one round of elections for villagers' committees. In 1998 a revised law was promulgated which entrenched the legal status of village elections. China has sought international assistance for its village self-governance program from a range of international sources, including the UNDP. The Chinese government recognizes the benefits of engaging sections of the international community in projects such as this. As will be discussed in Chapter 6, the village self-governance initiative has garnered a good deal of positive press in the American media for the Chinese government on the sensitive issue of political rights.

The UNDP launched a three year China Rural Official Training Centre Program in 1996. The project's development objectives were broad and ambitious:

> ... [t]o improve the standard of living of China's 900 million rural residents and to promote sustainable economic growth in China's countryside by improving the implementation of grassroots self-government and by providing training in public and economic management for

elected village committee members. The project is designed to assist the China Rural Official Training Centre of the Ministry of Civil Affairs in: a) curriculum and teaching materials development; b) implementation of pilot programs; and c) capacity building.[116]

The program has created significant training opportunities in China. It has also played a role mobilizing support for villagers' committee elections among the international donor community. In May 1995, the UNDP hosted a presentation on the CROTC to over twenty potential donors. Target beneficiaries of the UNDP project included the national staff of the CROTC and Ministry of Civil Affairs. It was hoped that 60,000 provincial, prefecture and township level government officials would benefit from the development of curricula and training methodologies, which would then enable them to conduct their work more effectively. In turn this would assist four million villagers' committee members to manage village affairs more efficiently.

An independent evaluation report was conducted at the conclusion of the program. It highlights several advantages of UNDP involvement. UNDP funding met with less criticism than programs by other international donors in the context of domestic sensitivity to 'peaceful evolution'. This is because the UNDP is widely regarded as representative of 'world government'.[117] In assessing the impact of the project, the report concludes that the three sets of training texts developed for officials at the county, township and village level are contributing to the creation of a democratic culture, and assisting in the consolidation of village self-governance. Nearly 2,000 officials, trained during 2000–2001, then conducted training sessions themselves, creating a multiplier effect. The training methods used in the sessions emphasized equality, free discussion and participation, and thus were a departure from more traditional pedagogy.

Kim argues that the United Nations human rights regime has exerted influence in the gradual evolution of China's theory and practice of human rights, and is thus 'improving long-term prospects of transition to democracy'.[118] China's engagement with the United Nations agencies, such as the UNDP, exhibits a similar tendency. The UNDP CROTC program has facilitated the context for a gradual improvement in village self-governance in China.

Conclusion

It is evident that the United Nations has had an ambiguous impact on the development of democracy in East Asia. Although the United Nations contributed to the complexities of sovereignty issues in the region it has played a marginal role assisting in the resolution of these issues. The United Nations intervention in Korea facilitated the development of garrison nationalism and the military's dominance of political life. In Taiwan the role of the United Nations falls within two phases. Initially, it served to support

Kuomintang rule; subsequently however, the United Nations indirectly assisted in democratization. Since China joined the United Nations it has faced a range of pressures to reform its political system and improve the human rights of its citizens. Although China, Taiwan and South Korea have each been affected by their engagement with the United Nations, their inter-actions are not reducible to a single pattern.

Some people argue that, post-cold war, a fundamental political cleavage has developed between those in the international system who stand for 'internationalist, Europeanist, democratic values, including human rights', and those, such as China, who pragmatically remain 'wedded to national or exclusivist thinking'.[119] Yet, such a dichotomy cannot be maintained completely. China is more integrated into and co-operative within interna-tional institutions than ever before.[120] Such engagement and interaction creates the potential for change within China's borders. The Chinese govern-ment works hard to develop its role within the United Nations and to secure its place in international society. China is concerned to stymie negative condemnations of its domestic practices at the United Nations. In order to do this China has had to engage more fully in international human rights discourse and the United Nations regime. Thus, although the Chinese government may 'reject' Europeanist criticisms of its human rights practice, it does accept the idea of rights. The next chapter, which considers the global culture of democracy, details other interesting features of East Asia's interactions with liberal ideas.

4 Global and local cultural interactions

Fusing democratic institutions with domestic ideas

Introduction

The concept of democracy is diffused across a range of cross-cutting discourses, including cultural ones. This chapter contends that a commitment to democracy has become one aspect of global culture. The chapter argues that the emerging consensus, internationally, on the merit of democracy is based upon a minimal conception of democracy, rather than a liberal conception of democracy. Thus, consensus is emerging internationally about the centrality of the institution of elections to a fully developed political arrangement.

The analysis in this chapter demonstrates that the transfer of democratic institutions needs to be distinguished from the transfer of democratic norms. This distinction is important because although the spread of global culture is evident in the choice of domestic political arrangements in East Asia, the strategic choices and actions by domestic political actors suggests that the impact of global culture has not been homogenizing in its effects. Rather, the operative model of democracy developing in East Asian states is a hybrid. Within each hybrid, electoral democracy is being synthesized with local political praxis. This suggests that East Asian states are working out their own distinctive practice of democracy.

A normative entitlement to democracy?

In 1979 John Dunn wrote, 'we are all democrats today'.[1] The idea is no longer novel. Rather, the questions are what does it mean to be a democrat in East Asia, and what kind of democracy do we more generally agree about?

The dynamics of continuity and change have long been in evidence in East Asia's political systems. Historically, a range of foreign political institutions and theories has influenced East Asian political forms. Sun Yat-sen blended elements of liberal democratic and socialist ideas with institutions from China's past. The communist leadership in China subsequently adopted aspects of socialist theory and institutional structures. British,

American and European models have influenced constitutional design in both South Korea and Taiwan. Generally, political leaders from East Asia have created and ordered local political life in a pragmatic, creative and instrumental manner.

As discussed previously, three conceptions of democracy are relevant to this book: minimal, liberal, and non-liberal. Minimalist conceptions of democracy define democracy as an institutional arrangement for arriving at political decisions in which individuals acquire power by means of a competitive struggle for the people's vote.[2] In order to qualify as democratic, the elections must also be free and fair, meaning suffrage is universal and equal, campaigning is open, the ballot is secret, and a neutral authority administers the counting. A liberal conception of democracy contains elements in addition to those within the minimal conception. It requires horizontal accountability, constrains executive power, upholds constitutional rule, provides extensive individual and group freedoms, and maintains rule of law, based on an independent judiciary and civilian control of the military.[3] Non-liberal democracies may contain some of the features of a liberal democracy, but they are weakly embedded. In non-liberal democracies democratic institutions are 'grafted' onto societies with 'an alternative cultural baggage', and democracy may be put to use for a set of illiberal purposes.[4]

Francis Fukuyama's book, *The End of History and the Last Man*, argues that, throughout the world, a remarkable consensus has emerged concerning the legitimacy of liberal democracy as a system of government.[5] Yet, clearly, there is no consensus about the merit of liberal democracy in all contexts. China's leaders reject the applicability of liberal formulations of democracy to China, as do a number of other states. The argument that a normative entitlement to democracy is developing in the international system can only be supported if a minimal conception of democracy is adopted.

The notion of polling the whole nation has a relatively short history. Indeed in 1703, Charles Leslie mocked Locke when he asked, 'would they send men about to poll the whole nation?'[6] In the mid-eighteenth century, there was a general consensus within academic political theory and the political elite that democracy was not a viable form of regime; between 1776 and 1850 this consensus gradually began to disappear in Europe and North America.[7] The transition in political language toward democracy reflected a broad shift in human culture from pre-modern to modern; the new political idiom, at face value, was rational, universal, and unsuperstitious.[8] The most important aspect of the shift in the legitimizing beliefs definitive of the modern era, was the belief that the source of political authority lies in the people.[9]

Thus when Thomas Franck argues that democracy is 'on the way to becoming a global entitlement', he is referring to the evolution of a democratic entitlement from a moral prescription to an international obligation, that began gradually from at least 1918 onwards.[10] Nonetheless, the idea remained only loosely developed by the community of states until the post-cold war era. Despite the references to 'democratic rights' in the United Nations Declaration of Human Rights, the conditions of the cold war meant that formal incorporation was politically impossible.[11] During the cold war, the United States and the Soviet Union supported elections primarily when they went their way, and a number of governments and intellectuals were contemptuous of the claim that open and fair elections were a central source of international political legitimacy.[12] The fall of the Berlin Wall and the spread of democracy to parts of Eastern and Southern Europe weakened these constraints. These shifts in the international context meant that non-democracies, like China, seemed less admirable than before.[13] Such countries were criticized for their authoritarian practices and lack of democracy.

Throughout the 1980s and 1990s the international interest in democracy extended beyond rhetoric. In addition to indirect, diffuse processes of contagion, a significant number of projects to promote democratic transition were initiated. International enthusiasm about the prospect of encouraging the development of democracy is apparent in the programs of international institutions, regional organizations, non-government organizations, bilateral efforts and academic transition literature.

Nevertheless, criticisms of international democracy promotion activity have been mounting. During the 1980s the idea of democracy was often linked explicitly with the idea of human rights. The idea of human rights, however, preceded the idea of democracy in the West, and it is obvious they were not necessarily regarded as being related.[14] Some members of the human rights community are concerned with the emergence of a dual approach to democracy promotion and human rights protection, and argue that human rights alone, and not democracy, should be the main concern of the international community.[15] Also, there is the criticism that democracy is too often conceived by such actors in narrowly procedural rather than substantive terms, and thus fails to get beyond the most tangible level of political activity, elections, in complex transitional societies.[16] Other matters of institutional design have not received the same attention as elections.

Clearly, human rights and a concern for democracy now constitute a part of an evolving global culture. This is sometimes referred to as the development of a 'new international standard of civilization'.[17] Today, only a few states publicly justify denying democracy. Yet, the meaning of the term 'democracy' is simultaneously contested and unclear. As Dunn states, only a 'complete imbecile' would be likely to take the 'public cant' of democracy at its face value.[18] The actual institutional relationships implied when referring to democracy vary a great deal. Nonetheless, a degree of consensus has emerged internationally on the role of participatory elections as a legitimizing norm.[19] In this sense global culture may be regarded as concerned with democracy in the minimal sense.

Elections are mechanisms for ascertaining the will of the people. As a consequence, pure procedural democracy can easily degenerate into non-democratic, or even anti-democratic, formalism.[20] Electoral, or minimal democracy does not assure rationality or representation, or equality.[21] Why then do sections of the international community stress the importance of electoral democracy? Adam Przeworski argues that although a minimal conception of democracy does not assure representation or equality, electing rulers is a practice 'nothing short of miraculous'.[22] This is because the mere possibility of being able to change governments can avoid violence, and because conflicting political forces obey the results of voting.[23]

Strategies to understand global culture and democratization in East Asia

The global culture of rights and democracy impacts upon Asian political development in an interesting and under-theorized way. Historically, comparatively little attention has been given to the mechanics of the intricate processes of cultural contact, intrusion, fusion and disjunction.[24] Culture affects when, and in what ways, people become involved in political life and also influence the way in which formal institutions operate.[25] As identified in Chapter 1, in the context of an increasingly globalized world, a society's political culture is essentially permeable, that is, capable of being influenced by exogenous ideas and norms, and is also potentially mutable, that is, capable of radical departures from existing cultural norms.[26] Culture is not something people inherit as an undifferentiated bloc of knowledge from their ancestors.[27] Rather, culture is a set of ideas, reactions and expectations that is constantly changing as people and groups themselves change.[28] Moreover, political development is not a process in which there is simply a decline of local modes of behaviour and a rise of rationality and impersonal efficiency.[29]

Clearly, modes of global and local cultural interactions are diffuse and diverse, and the interpretative frames with which to analyse such processes also differ. Four strategies for linking global ideas with local practices can be identified, which this chapter terms the Conflict, Congruent, Convergent, and Cross-cultural arguments. Although there are disadvantages and advantages within each approach, each assists in the development of an understanding of the different aspects of complex cultural interactions.

Conflict

Samuel P. Huntington expounded the civilizational conflict argument in an article in 1993 and subsequently expanded the thesis in the book, *The Clash of Civilizations and the Remaking of World Order*.[30] In the international context since 11 September 2001 the rhetoric of civilizational conflict has become particularly pertinent. Huntington argues that countries are divided along civilizational lines, and that the great divisions and sources of conflict among humankind are cultural.[31] He contends that Western universalism (the belief that people throughout the world should embrace Western values, institutions and culture because they embody the highest, most enlightened, most liberal, most rational, most modern, and most civilized thinking) is dangerous to the world, because it could lead to major inter-civilizational war and the defeat of the West.[32] In sum, 'clashes of civilizations are the greatest threat to world peace, and an international order based on civilizations is the surest safeguard against war'.[33] Adherents to Huntington's thesis would reject the idea that a normative consensus about democracy is developing in global culture, and would argue against efforts to promote democracy across civilizational divides.

Huntington's thesis has a number of weaknesses. He develops fixed conceptions of both the West and the rest, in which culture(s) are viewed as immutable and incommensurable. Further, he assumes a degree of consensus within what he terms 'kin' cultures that may not exist. Alfred Stepan warns against assuming that any of the world's major religious–civilizational traditions are univocally either pro-democratic or anti-democratic.[34] Stepan argues that cultures may contain multi-vocal components that are useable for (or at least compatible with) democratic political constructions.[35] The attempt by the former President of Singapore, Lee Kuan Yew, to define Asian values in opposition to liberal democratic notions was contradicted by South Korean political leader, Kim Dae Jung. This public exchange highlights the ongoing struggles over meaning within so-called 'kin' cultures.[36] Notwithstanding these limitations, the Conflict approach does alert researchers and policy-makers to the danger of uncritically presuming that a Western liberal view is the 'world view'.

Congruent

Contrary to Huntington's depiction, which presupposes immutable cultural differences, the Congruent approach regards liberal democratic ideas as consonant with historical East Asian practice. Some academics argue that in many Confucian societies liberal ideas are not an intrinsically alien ideology, and suggest there is an indigenous liberal, and even social democratic tradition.[37] They identify values and visions of life which can stand as precursors to freedom, and a range of ways in which the modern system of concepts was unpacked and reworked in local contexts.[38]

Several Chinese scholars have emphasized aspects of compatibility between Confucianism and liberalism. Liang Shuming claims both Confucianism and liberalism recognize and respect the self, individual rights and human dignity.[39] Former President of Taiwan, Lee Teng-hui, identifies within Taiwan's cultural heritage precepts that he believes could also serve as succinct statements of the essence of modern democracy.[40] For example, in the third century BC Mencius said, 'give the people what they desire; never force upon them that which they abhor', by so doing, one can win the support of the people, and thus the opportunity to rule.[41] Lee Teng-hui regards this ancient Chinese wisdom as one of a range of reminders to rulers to always pay close attention to the will of the people and to comply with the popular will, 'which leads to the realization of the concept of popular sovereignty'.[42]

Kim Dae Jung argues that Asia has democratic philosophies as profound as those of the West, and identifies within the teachings of Confucianism, Buddhism and the native religion of Korea, *Tonghak*, ideas fundamental to democracy.[43] Further, Kim Dae Jung highlights that although the invention of the electoral system is 'Europe's greatest accomplishment', China and Korea had sustained county prefecture systems for about 2,000 years when European societies were being 'ruled by a succession of feudal lords'.[44] It is worth also noting that, until the late 1980s, the Chinese authorities did not refer to cultural factors as a reason to reject the human rights or liberal democracy.[45]

At times some of these arguments engage in a degree of conceptual stretching in their attempts to find proto-democratic ideas within Asia's traditions. Bilahari Kausikan cautions that most Asian societies have such long histories and rich cultures that it is possible to 'prove' nearly anything about them.[46] Whereas it is difficult to deny the humanistic character of Confucianism, Confucian philosophy is a long way short of implying an advocacy for the full extent of the liberal tradition. Nonetheless, recognition of the ways in which local cultures contribute to democratization is significant.[47] The Congruent approach eschews the stark depiction of cultural dissonance presented by the Conflict approach. Moreover, the Congruent approach may contribute to the development of 'unforced international consensus', in which agreement may be reached on the norms that ought to govern human behaviour, notwithstanding disagreement about why they are the right norms.[48]

Convergent

Those who adopt the Convergent approach think East Asia becoming modern without becoming Western unlikely. Such analysts argue there are no viable alternatives to liberal democracy. In this scenario, East Asian political forms will eventually resemble liberal democracies. Francis Fukuyama's analysis of modernity holds that 'history leads us in one way or another to liberal democracy'.[49] Fukuyama posits that in economic, political and social areas 'there are good reasons for thinking that the distinctive institutions and practices fostered by Asia's cultural systems will converge over time with the patterns seen in the West'.[50] As such, the idea of a universal and directional history leading up to liberal democracy may become more plausible to people, and issues of cultural relativism will resolve themselves as more and more societies with diverse cultures and histories exhibit similar long-term patterns of development.[51]

By contrast, David Held is critical of Fukuyama's evolutionary, linear conception of historical progress. Held objects to Fukuyama's:

... complacency about the triumph of capitalism and liberal democracy, his neglect of systematic sources of conflict and schism (from feminism to issues of transnational justice facing the international economic order), and his naïve belief that the most urgent problems to be faced in a "post-historical world" will be boredom.[52]

Central to Fukuyama's thesis is the global power of the liberal democratic idea. Fukuyama presumes a liberal–Marxist dichotomy, which (after the collapse of communist regimes in Europe) leaves liberal democracy as the only remaining option.[53] The diffusion of the idea of democracy has been extensive, but it is not necessarily the liberal version Fukuyama identifies that is spreading. By privileging and preferring liberal democracy Fukuyama overextends his argument. Indeed, it seems that illiberal democracy is a 'growth industry', and that only a small number of transitional countries are consolidating a liberal version of democracy.[54] Several Asian political leaders have highlighted this fact. They advocate a third alternative to the liberal–Marxist dichotomy, the 'Asian way', in which economic modernization occurs without political modernization.[55]

Cross-cultural

The final approach discussed is termed the Cross-cultural. Cross-cultural analysis rejects the assumption that states are culture bound, assuming instead that complex processes of cultural hybridization define modernity. Further, it accepts that centuries of 'contamination' have characterized the history of the Asian region.[56] As such, it does not assume that an autochthonous Asian political system is being influenced by global culture. Rather, the approach argues that Asian political systems have long been permeated by other cultures in an ongoing process of interaction and exchange. The modernizing process, in this view, can occur without sacrificing particularistic cultural roots. In this sense, East Asia's experience as the first non-Western region to become modernized suggests the authentic possibility of 'multiple modernities'.[57] Bhikhu Parekh contends that there is no obvious reason why a political system may not combine liberalism and democracy differently to the West.[58] That is, there is no reason to assume the political 'end point' for East Asia entails a convergence with liberal democratic political practices.

The Cross-cultural approach is supported by historical evidence. Historically, East Asia has experienced cross-cutting cultural influences from Japan, China, the United States and Europe. Confucianism and Buddhism, imported from China, influenced Korean philosophy, and liberal philosophies have begun to heavily influence many educational, socio-economic and political structures.[59] Christianity has been the fastest growing religion in Korea since its introduction about 200 years ago, and has played a role in contributing to the development of the value of individualism, the spirit of free enterprise and democracy in South Korea.[60] External values and assumptions have long penetrated Taiwan.[61] The 28 February 1947 uprising and massacre led some Taiwanese people to turn from mainland Chinese culture toward Japan, the United States and other Western capitalist democratic countries in search of political emancipation and cultural enlightenment.[62] In China, which escaped foreign colonization, the possibility of it was enough to provoke some leaders into perceiving that power might be put to new, essentially Western, goals.[63] A tension emerged in China over the relative importance of values and techniques; between a belief that power was derived from the intensity of people's commitments to established values and the (more Western) belief that power would come from the pragmatic use of science and technology.[64] As a consequence of these influences, it is small wonder, then, that East Asia's choice of political models has been both diverse and uncertain.[65]

Kishore Mahbubani argues that an unprecedented historical phenomenon is being witnessed: a fusion of Western and East Asian cultures.[66] Thus, in the post-cold war era, the task is not to demarcate civilizations but to mix and meld them.[67]

Each of the four strategies discussed helps us to understand aspects of local and global cultural interactions. Interestingly, they tend to overlook the potential for reciprocal effects during such interactions. Some members of the political elite within Asian states regard the emphasis on democracy and human rights within global culture as problematic, and question its legitimacy. Historically, Western countries defined all of the terms of the human rights discourse, and also used their positions of economic and political superiority to pressure weaker parties to comply.[68] Several of the region's political leaders have challenged the assumptions underpinning the 'new international standard of civilization'. This was exemplified during the region's first human rights conference in 1993, which resulted in the Bangkok Declaration. The Bangkok Declaration articulated the concern, among some of the region's political elite, about the predominance of liberal cultural values within the international system. While South Korea and Taiwan were not signatories to the Bangkok Declaration, China was.[69] The Declaration was an attempt to re-orient human rights discourse in recognition of the value and importance of cultural difference. The Declaration emphasized that human rights should be considered in the context of national and regional particularities and various historical, religious and cultural backgrounds.[70]

The ways in which global culture might incorporate aspects of non-Western culture are rarely considered. The 'Asian way' discourse generally, and the Bangkok Declaration specifically, highlight the potential for reciprocal effects during local and global interactions. They demonstrate the growing need to think about how the West might reinterpret some of its own beliefs in light of its interactions with other cultures.[71] The leaders of several Asian states have questioned the discourse of modernity, and are inviting Western states, scholars, NGOs and international bodies to critically analyse their assumptions about rights, democracy and development. In the process, the international community's bias toward civil and political rights as opposed to economic, social and cultural rights has been underscored and critiqued.

Both within Asia and in other regions, it appears many people are working out their own path to modernity and political forms. The degree to which cultures converge during the process of modernization is significant, since they are all participating in the spread of a world culture based on advanced technology, yet it seems political cultures will always have a strongly parochial dimension, because political systems are anchored in their history.[72]

Democratic political structures and domestic political cultures

Are states in East Asia synthesizing global norms with local cultural practices? If so, what are the terms of the mixture? It is important to note the ways in which hegemony is not merely reproduced but is reconfigured in the hybridization process.[73] These questions are explored in this section, which uses the approaches considered above to analyse the evolution of elections, political parties, the media, and rule of law in South Korea, Taiwan and China.

Some significant qualifications need to be made concerning the applicability of the term 'democracy' in relation to developments in China. China does not fulfil the basic criteria of minimal democracy at the national level. Yet, as discussed in the previous chapter, a limited form of democracy is developing in rural China, where direct elections for villagers' committees are now widespread.

Electoral procedures and the transfer of power

Some academics concur with Fukuyama's argument that Asia's political practices will converge with those of established liberal democracies. For example, Larry Diamond and Ramon H. Myers regard Taiwan and South Korea as approximating liberal democracies.[74] The prevalence of elections in East Asia does provide limited evidence in support of this argument. By contrast, other scholars accept that Taiwan and South Korea have been democratizing, if by '"democracy" we mean nothing more (or less) than a political procedure for "the filling of offices through contested elections"'.[75] They contend that in Asia competitive elections may be put to use for a set of non-liberal purposes – even where elections allow for an alteration of ruling parties. Further, they argue that a political language rooted in traditional, non-liberal concepts of hierarchy, familial order, and the desirability of harmonizing conflicting interests, renders unlikely the emergence of liberal democracy in Asia.[76] A range of modifications to the practice of democracy suggests that political systems in East Asia converge with a liberal model of democracy in a very limited sense. Although regular elections are contested and conducted by secret ballot on the basis of universal suffrage, the norms, which underpin liberal democracy, are less evident.

Even in those instances, such as in South Korea, where the political institutions of liberal democracies were adopted, it was not until the late 1980s that elections met even the requirements of minimal democracy. Paternalistic authority permeated South Korean political practice. Paternalistic authority often operates through institutions that can be bent to the convenience of power-holders.[77] South Korea's political leaders revised the constitution nine times in forty years; all nine revisions concerned the system of government, the term of the President and the procedures for presidential election.

As a result, South Korea's constitutions functioned more 'in accord with traditional political norms than with the Western concepts expressed in the successive constitutions.'[78] Although some elements of South Korea's formal political system were similar to those in liberal democracies (popular sovereignty, representative government, and the separation of government powers), the sudden expansion of mass participation occurred at a time when the political elite were not inclined to respect the idea of a legitimate opposition, public debate, or power sharing.[79] During the First Republic (1948–1960) there was a lack of consent, among the domestic political elite, for the norms associated with democracy. The Second Republic (1960–1961) adopted a parliamentary constitution in which the President was elected by the National Assembly. A military coup ended this brief period of democracy, and General Park Chung Hee installed the Third Republic (1963–1972). Park reintroduced a presidential system in which the President was to be elected directly by the people for a maximum of two terms. During the 1971 presidential election Park Chung Hee was nearly defeated by opposition candidate Kim Dae Jung. Soon after, President Park established a more authoritarian political system, with the *Yushin* reforms. The electoral system during the Fourth Republic (1972–1979) did not provide for a direct presidential election; presidential elections were the result of an election, without debate, by the concurrence of the National Council for Unification.[80] A murderous coup ended Park's rule, and General Chun Doo Hwan assumed power. During the Fifth Republic (1980–1987), Chun retained much of Park's electoral system, although the President was elected by a presidential electoral college, rather than by the National Council for Unification, for a term of seven years.

When President Chun decided to extend his term beyond seven years, widespread political protests ensued. Not only were there domestic criticisms of Chun's decision, the United States urged Chun to reconsider. Ultimately, Chun stepped aside and the ruling coalition, led by Roh Tae Woo, outlined several democratizing measures in the 'June 29 1987 Declaration'. Roh Tae Woo's announcement of the institution of direct presidential elections has been described as 'shrewd', indicating that he carefully considered the opinion of the United States administration and Congress.[81]

This brief overview of South Korea's electoral democracy suggests that although South Korea's political institutions derived from liberal democratic models, elections were susceptible to manipulation by various domestic actors for authoritarian purposes. The adoption of democratic political models in South Korea did not necessarily entail the diffusion of liberal democratic norms. Real political choice did not eventuate until 1988. Byung-Kook Kim highlights that during the years of authoritarian rule Korea embraced democracy as its state ideology not because of a belief in the 'intrinsic ideological superiority of democracy, but because of an acute sense of military insecurity and political vulnerability.'[82] Rejecting democracy outright would have cost South Korea its foreign patron, the United States. As a result, a concept that had no substantive philosophical meaning to the Korean people was 'suddenly placed on an alter', and criticizing democracy or capitalism was decried as subversive by the state and repressed.[83]

By contrast, the impact of global norms upon electoral processes in Taiwan differs from that of South Korea. Schmitter observes that hybrid regimes combine elements of autocracy and democracy.[84] The Kuomintang regime attempted to combine these elements from the moment it retreated to Taiwan. The Kuomintang enabled popular participation in local elections, while excluding participation in national elections. This was based upon the claim that the Legislative Yuan represented all of China's provinces, not simply Taiwan Province. Between August and December 1947, the Republic of China government had conducted national elections to select national representatives throughout mainland China and Taiwan. After the Kuomintang retreated to Taiwan, further elections within China's provinces could no longer be held.[85]

Thus, Taiwan's electoral system was crucially affected by the Kuomintang's sovereignty claim over mainland China. The Council of Grand Justices (made up of President Chiang Kai-shek appointees) made a ruling which enabled representatives elected on the mainland to continue to hold office on Taiwan until such time as the Kuomintang resumed control over the mainland, and a national election could be conducted.[86] Although, in 1969, a popular election at the national level took place in Taiwan, the election was for a limited number of seats in the Legislative Yuan, in order to replace those representatives elected in 1947 that had died or resigned. The majority of national representatives elected in 1947 retained their power until national elections in Taiwan during late 1991 and 1992 replaced them.

Nonetheless, local elections commenced in Taiwan during the 1950s and, as in South Korea, universal suffrage was instituted. As early as 1951, elections were conducted for provincial, township, city and county councils, and for the chiefs or leaders of villages, townships and Taiwan's 21 counties and major cities.[87] The elections reflected Sun Yat-sen's ideology which combined Western and Chinese ideas about power and authority with the 'Three Principles'.

In the mid-1950s, after the completion of land reform, the character of local elections changed as younger and more capable candidates began contesting local seats.[88] Non-Party politicians learned from their experiences in local elections. Bearing a heavy Confucian scholar-official tradition, the Kuomintang were reluctant to persecute and imprison elected officials and election times became 'democratic holidays', meaning that non-Party candidates could ignore some of the restrictions of martial law and (if elected) could escape persecution over their election campaigns.[89] Thus, the Kuomintang's particular blend of autocracy and democracy enabled non-Party candidates to participate in local elections, while denying them the opportunity to form political parties or to compete for power in the national bodies. Nonetheless, this experience of electoral participation and campaigning was to prove influential during the subsequent democratization of national electoral processes.

The response of voters in South Korea and Taiwan to democratization has been interesting. Both South Korea and Taiwan are notable for the fact that, during the first opportunity to elect an opposition government, the electorate chose not to do so; there was no 'founding election' so to speak. In both cases ten years passed before competitive elections resulted in the transfer of presidential power to an opposition candidate. In South Korea, rival opposition leaders Kim Dae Jung and Kim Young Sam failed to co-operate and unite. Thus, in the first post-reform presidential election, both Kims stood, the opposition vote was split and the South Korean population was denied the chance to unseat the ruling regime. It was not until 1997 that the power of the presidential office was transferred to the opposition when, on his fourth attempt, Kim Dae Jung was elected President. In Taiwan, during 1989, the first election following the legalization of the political parties did little to unseat Kuomintang control. The 1992 Legislative Yuan election, the first comprehensive election of its kind in Taiwan, also failed to produce any stunning political upsets.[90] It was not until 18 March 2000, during Taiwan's second direct election for President and Vice President, that an opposition member, Chen Shui-bian, won the office of President and power was transferred from the Kuomintang to the Democratic Progressive Party. Even so, Chen Shui-bian's victory is widely regarded as being due to the fact that the traditional Kuomintang vote was split between the Kuomintang nominee, Lien Chan, and a former member of the Kuomintang, James Soong.[91] These interesting features of South Korea's and Taiwan's political life are indicative of the prevalence of personality politics in East Asian political processes.

Differently again, global norms have had less of an impact upon political liberalization in China. The diffusion of liberal democratic ideas has been limited in China. This is due to China's relative isolation from the international system, and also because the Chinese leadership has attempted to develop its own political forms. The Chinese leadership has designed a Chinese-style polity, governed by a single ruling party, which combines socialism and a limited conception of democracy, with Chinese customs and philosophy. Presently, the Chinese Communist Party selects candidates for indirect election as representatives in city and provincial congresses, and the National People's Congress. Under the supervision of the Chinese Communist Party, functional constituencies elect representatives to township, city and county congresses. These bodies (as well as commissions in the Chinese Communist Party) primarily monitor, review and recommend their findings to leading Chinese Communist Party and state authorities.

A limited electoral democracy has emerged in China's villages. By law all candidates for villagers' committees must be directly nominated by villagers, there must be competition (that is, there must be more candidates than positions), and voting must be done in secret. Village self-governance developed autonomously in a number of rural areas as a consequence of the changes occurring in rural life due to Deng Xioaping's economic reforms. The abolition of the communes and shift to a contract-based system transformed the relationship between rural Chinese and the Chinese Communist Party. In a number of areas administrative atrophy had set in, and the government was facing increasing difficulties in ensuring policy compliance. The provisional introduction of the Organic Law of Villagers' Committees was designed to serve an instrumental function – to ensure tax and grain procurements and to avoid mobilized rural unrest. Nonetheless, once the law was implemented international factors came into play. The efforts of a range of international NGOs contributed to the decision to include the right to a secret ballot in a revised version of the law. The role played by NGOs will be expanded upon in Chapter 6.

The relationship between the villagers' committee and the village Party Secretary remains one of the most contentious issues. The revised Organic Law of Villagers' Committees stipulates that the Party branch is the village's 'leadership core', therefore, villagers' committees do not have final say over village political life. Kevin O'Brien and Lianjiang Li argue that a rethinking of the Chinese Communist Party's role must occur before there is real electoral democracy in China's villages.[92] O'Brien and Li's contention has been questioned by Baogang He. His case study of Zhejiang reveals that when the Party branch in the village has tight control over the village's economic resources, the nomination procedure and other electoral processes, electoral competition tends to be low.[93] However, when there is another force to counteract the Party's power, be it an economic one, such as village businesses, the existing villagers' committee, or kinship and factional relationships, competition tends to be high.[94]

There is some evidence to suggest that the experience of village elections has fostered the emergence of a concept of public accountability and contributed to more transparent political processes, this is evident in the more open accounting of village spending.[95] It is increasingly common for a financial audit of villagers' committee expenses to be publicized. For example, during an election in a village in Xianyou County, Fujian Province, large blackboards at the number one polling station detailed the village finances, including money spent on the Villager Representative Assembly, taxes, office expenses, banquets, and the village Chairperson's electricity subsidy. Thus, village elections are facilitating the transfer of power within the villages and contributing to behavioural learning in democratic procedures.

Since the transition to democracy commenced, elections in Taiwan and South Korea have facilitated the peaceful transfer of political power. Prior to that, however, the institutionalization of electoral procedures in East Asia did not necessarily have democratic consequences. The international community's normative commitment to democracy, and emphasis on the transfer of democratic institutions, such as elections, downplays the importance of a normative commitment to democracy on the part of the domestic political elite. Clearly, the transmission of the global culture of democracy has not necessarily entailed the homogenization of domestic political processes in East Asia.

It is important to consider the ways in which aspects of autocracy have been reproduced in the process of hybridization. What is developing in China's villages is a model of governance which utilizes the mechanics of elections to achieve state proscribed goals. The South Korean case demonstrates that even where the institutions of democracy are created, the ruling elite may use them in ways that sustain and protect their rule. This is true not only of East Asia, it appears many countries are settling into a form of government that mixes a substantial degree of liberal democracy with a substantial degree of illiberalism.[96] Nonetheless, as was the case in Taiwan, limited, non-liberal elections may develop into a force of transformation within the political system itself. It is (at least potentially) possible for democratic norms to be learned by operation of the political process itself.

Political parties and securing the vote

Taiwan, South Korea and China's political systems are evolving in a manner that suggests the development of hybrid models of democracy. It seems that locally derived ideas about power and authority have been reinvented in the process of hybridization, and contribute to the distinctive character of East Asian political practice. This is particularly evident in the relationship between electoral competition and political parties. A history of single party rule has facilitated an electoral propensity for East Asia's citizens to be influenced more by personality than by policy when casting the ballot.

South Korea's constitutions have recognized the role of political parties in elections and legislative activity, and the role of political parties in the proceedings of the National Assembly has been well established since the early 1950s.[97] Nonetheless, political parties functioned in South Korea under a range of highly authoritarian constraints. Twice in South Korea's history (1961 and 1980) all political parties were dissolved and their leaders arrested or banned from political activity.[98] There was no formal independent opposition party in Taiwan until 1986.[99] Although efforts to create an opposition party began in 1960 with the attempt to form the Chinese Democratic Party, it was not until the late 1970s that an organized (although still illegal) opposition began to emerge in Taiwan.[100] Within China, opposition parties are banned; however, overseas opposition movements have been active for some time.

The transition to democracy in South Korea has resulted in the expansion of public space and the growth of civil society. Nonetheless, the development of a more pluralistic political system has been constrained by the nature of South Korean political parties. In 1987, democratic reforms provoked an extensive realignment of South Korea's political and social forces around regional sentiments.[101] Even after a decade of democratic elections, South Korean political parties remain firmly entrenched in regionalism.[102] Historical and cultural factors contributed to the development of South Korea's two regional patronage networks, however, it was during Park Chung Hee's period of rule that regional patronage networks took on an institutionalized character, as they fostered factionalism within the political parties.[103] As a consequence, all of the political parties nurture regionalist networks for support, yet, interestingly, none defend it as a legitimate principle of political organization.[104]

Regionalism is inhibiting the development of an attitudinal commitment to democratic norms in South Korea because public officials selected on the basis of patronage are more responsive to the leaders of their patronage network than to the law or the general public; the continuance of the networks marginalizes sections of the population, and the networks are contributing to political cynicism.[105] Another consequence of the prevalence of regionalism in South Korean politics is that South Korea's party structures are not designed to recruit members from the population, and do not create ideologically alternative policies. The political parties 'usually limit themselves to the discussion of the allocation of ministerial posts and regional distribution of investment resources'.[106]

Moreover, since the transition to democracy, South Korean opposition politics have been highly changeable and capricious. In the 1997 election, South Korean political parties not only lacked cohesion but were barely discernible, with fluid platforms and borders.[107] Political parties readily change their names to suit the public mood and splinter groups are common.[108] Of the four major parties that competed in the 1987 election, all have since changed their names. However, notwithstanding the fragmentation of party politics, there is a profound continuity of personalities.[109] Both before and after the transition to democracy, a small number individual personalities have thoroughly dominated South Korea's political institutions.[110]

Corruption has also been a feature of South Korea's party politics. President Roh Tae Woo (purportedly) attempted to reduce nepotism and corruption in Korean politics during his term. Yet, during 1995 it was revealed that Roh collected massive sums of money from leading *chaebol*, which enabled him to buy off political opponents and foster the political merger of Kim Young Sam with his party.[111] Roh Tae Woo was charged and briefly imprisoned for corrupting Korean politics. During his presidency, Kim Young Sam also attempted to diminish corruption in politics. He introduced a real name financial transaction system and set limits on the amount allowed to be spent per candidate on election campaigns. These measures have been only marginally successful. The real name initiative was subsequently weakened and the limit on campaign spending is largely ignored. Indeed, one worrying consequence of Kim Young Sam's initiatives, was the revelation that opposition faction leaders such as Kim Dae Jung and Kim Young Sam were on the government payroll during the 1980s.[112] Money politics stains the upper echelons of South Korean politics. By contrast, money politics percolated from the lower levels of politics to the top in Taiwan.

Party politics in Taiwan is embedded in the historical and political-cultural legacy of Kuomintang authoritarian rule. Taiwan's political parties are differentiated by the existence of a cleavage between the Taiwanese who lived on Taiwan prior to the Kuomintang's arrival and the mainlander Chinese who came after 1948.[113] The organizing strategies of the major political parties also differ. The Kuomintang tends to rely heavily on local faction-based mobilization; whereas, the Democratic Progressive Party relies upon ideology-based mobilization.[114] A local faction is a set of interpersonal networks that function for political purposes in the local, as opposed to the national, arena.[115] Prior to the formation of opposition parties, local factions developed without challenging the political legitimacy and domination of the Kuomintang. The local factions monopolized the privileges of access to local political power and economic interest through patron–client relations with the authoritarian government.[116] Under this system, the Kuomintang fostered at least two factions in most localities, these factions relied on institutionalized vote buying mechanisms to secure electoral outcomes, and, in return, they received various forms of economic gain.[117] Thus, money politics emerged in Taiwan during the authoritarian years, when co-opting the local factions was an important component of the Kuomintang strategy for controlling the limited electoral process.[118]

Sun Yat-sen's modification of Western democratic ideas and institutions fused with lineage and other cultural ties to produce a hybrid political model in Taiwan. Taiwan's local factions are primarily based on lineage, marriage, geographic, and academic ties. Prior to Chiang Ching-kuo's death in 1988, all the local factions at the county and city levels operated under the restrictions prescribed by the Kuomintang and could not expand into island-wide alliances.[119]

In Taiwan vote buying is a key aspect of faction mobilization, and two types are identifiable: gift and true purchase.[120] In several Confucian societies money is the standard form of gift at weddings and is the customary religious offering to gods and ancestors. It does not buy undecided votes, but reinforces the loyalty of supporters and is an expression of an ongoing factional relationship or *guanxi* between the voter and the candidate.[121] The art of *guanxi* exchange lies in the skilful mobilization of moral and cultural imperatives, such as obligation and reciprocity, in pursuit of both diffuse social ends and calculated instrumental ends.[122] The second type is true vote buying, where a candidate solicits votes in areas where they would otherwise receive no support. According to newspaper accounts during 1989 and 1990, several electoral successes are attributable to vote buying.[123]

Corruption and factionalism quickly transmitted to national representative bodies as a consequence of democratic electoral reforms.[124] At present, influence buying and power peddling are rife, with representative bodies increasingly affiliated with criminal groups. These criminal groups are recruited by local Kuomintang factions to safeguard their electoral strongholds. There is no more serious blot on Taiwan's democracy than the penetration of organized crime into politics, and the presence of organized crime figures in legislative bodies at various levels.[125] As the nature of electoral politics has become more local and idiosyncratic, middle class voters have been turned off by the electoral process.[126] Consequently, the role of money politics, vote buying, factions and crime in Taiwan compromises the free and fair status of the electoral process.

Interestingly, a similar practice of vote buying and coercion has developed in China's villagers' committee elections. Open campaigning is generally frowned upon, and the night before an election the village dogs bark through the night as people visit houses seeking support. Through vote buying, candidates advertise themselves and make voters aware that they are running for elections.[127] Candidates influence voters by giving out packets of cigarettes, inviting people to dinners, or offering money. The Organic Law of Villagers' Committees includes provisions to counter threats, bribes, forged ballots or other improper practices through lodging reports with local governments, People's Congresses and other relevant departments. In elections in Fujian Province brightly coloured comic strips depict bribery and vote buying. They clearly demonstrate that the practice is officially illegal. The National People's Congress' Director of the Division of Internal Affairs Committee on Internal and Legislative Affairs argued against implementing harsher sanctions against vote buyers at a conference on standardizing village election procedures. He stated that the Organic Law, like the Marriage Law, is a 'soft' law concerning citizens rather than civil servants, who receive subsidies rather than salaries. As such, the aim should be to educate rather than punish malfeasants.[128]

In fact, debate within China about village elections focuses more on the dangers of populism than of corruption. Børge Bakken argues that there is a Chinese cultural aversion towards imperfection.[129] Within Chinese intellectual debate about village elections there is a concern that electoral democracy cannot ensure that the 'best' person is elected. Jin Rong suggests that when the ballot box is used, people vote according to *guanxi*, familial ties, or their own likes or dislikes, instead of selecting on a principle of moral goodness or perfection.[130] Elections may, thus, become unprincipled and chaotic without any moorings in the correct and principled social norm.[131] This concern is expressed within sections of the Chinese bureaucracy as well. A member of the Division of Rural Affairs, Department of Basic-level Governance and Community Development in Heilongjiang Province highlighted that in the poor areas of the province most of the capable people have left to work outside the village. As a consequence, in his view, there are too few people 'skilled and qualified' for the office.[132] In China, the value and merit of popular sovereignty, even where legally enshrined, is frequently questioned, because it cannot ensure rule by virtuous men who embody the 'best' moral values.

Both in China's village elections and nationally, open opposition organizations are not allowed. Opposition organizing takes place primarily outside China. The Chinese overseas opposition movement existed prior to events in Tiananmen Square in 1989; however, following this dramatic event several new organizations were created. Andrew J. Nathan describes the overseas democracy movement as congeries of individuals and organizations who have been trying to promote Chinese democracy from locations outside China.[133] The largest groups are 'The Front for a Democratic China', launched in the campus of the Sorbonne in September 1989, and the 'Chinese Alliance for Democracy', established during 1983 in New York. The main support base of the overseas democracy movement is among Chinese scholars and students in the United States, Taiwan, Hong Kong, Europe, Australia and Japan.[134] These organizations draw upon global norms and use the discourse of democracy and human rights to highlight their cause internationally.

The extent to which these organizations can be characterized as political parties is limited. At its launch, The Front for a Democratic China was led by exiled student leaders Wuer Kaixi, Yan Jiaqi, Chen Yizhi and Wan Runnan. The organization was soon confronted by a number of internal troubles stemming from the undemocratic manner in which the leadership selected delegates and developed strategies. The leadership core found developing power-sharing arrangements and ensuring accountability and transparency difficult. Some supporters began to compare the organization to the Chinese Communist Party.[135] Factional infighting and the misuse of finances began to undermine The Front for a Democratic China's credibility.

Notwithstanding international interest in encouraging democratic development in China, it has been difficult for several of these organizations to sustain the external support upon which they depend. For example, in 1990, after the events in Tiananmen Square, the Sydney branch of the Chinese Alliance for Democracy boasted more than 1,500 active members.[136] Six years later, the combined Australian membership of the Chinese Alliance for Democracy, The Front for a Democratic China, and United Alliance for Democracy and Chinese Liberal Democratic Party totalled fewer than 40.[137]

Learning and adapting

Thus far, the discussion has highlighted that although international factors have influenced the choice of political institutions in East Asian states, the choice of political actions has been primarily influenced by local norms and practices. To what degree do the political elite's actions reflect local precepts about power? And as such, to what extent do these cultural or civilizational factors conflict or converge with democratic norms?

The responsiveness of East Asia's political elite and mass society to the norms of international society has not been uniform. Political cultures are learned by non-political experiences and by the operation of the political process.[138] In the process of operating electoral democracy, East Asian states have adapted the political process in accordance with local and instrumental ideas about power and authority.[139]

Political power in South Korea, Taiwan and China is highly personalized. As a consequence, a heavy emphasis is placed on power, prestige, patronage and paternalism. Members of political parties in South Korea follow the party bosses who, like the fathers in traditional Korean families, alone make all the important decisions.[140] The cohesion of the Kuomintang was founded on a centralization of power in the paramount leader who, in addition to the formal power of his offices (head of state, leader of the party, executive head of the government, and the active commander in chief of the military), was supported by a complex web of client networks which infiltrated the hierarchy of the party, bureaucracy and other state sanctioned auxiliary organizations.[141] Within China and among the Chinese overseas opposition movement, there is a concern that leadership be by a person who embodies the best moral qualities. In South Korea, Taiwan and China power is personified, and elite recruitment is often based on *guanxi* and family ties. The political culture is affected by the principles of Confucianism, which emphasizes the personal qualities of individual leaders. Power, in this context, is highly personalized and hierarchical. As a consequence of paternalistic authority, the 'social distance' between the state and the individual is narrow.[142] Nonetheless, this does not necessarily imply a conflict with liberal democratic norms. Both East Asia and the West have relied to varying degrees on consensual norms of social behaviour.[143] In East Asia, however, the emphasis has been placed on the primacy of moral culture and the power of the virtuous example, not legal enforcement.[144]

Vote buying and gift giving have historical and cultural roots in East Asia, but the issue of corruption is also difficult to account for from a cultural perspective. Money politics is also a feature of countries making the transition to democracy without a Confucian heritage. In Thailand, the Philippines, Eastern Europe, and also in long-standing liberal democracies such as the United States, there is evidence of political corruption. This suggests that political corruption may have its own autonomous status, which is not dependent on the level of development or cultural history of a particular country.

The media

Finally, this chapter considers the role of the media and rule of law, particularly since democratization commenced. The notions of press freedom and free speech are closely linked to a liberal conception of democracy. The idea of the press as the Fourth Estate in a liberal democracy is an informal, but central, element in the system of checks. In East Asia, the media has evolved a different social and political purpose. Lee Jae-kyoung, Professor of Journalism at Ehwa Women's University in Seoul observes:

> While the notion of the freedom of the press and of democracy have literally evolved hand in hand in the West, the South Korean media have lacked such an institutional foundation ... Simply put, the idea of the free press in South Korea was nothing more than a superficial imposition of a foreign idea which completely lacks indigenous institutional support.[145]

Despite the removal of most of the formal restrictions on press freedom, the political elite employ notions of moral responsibility and personal networks in a manner which undermines the independence and freedom of the media. South Korean President, Roh Tae Woo, repealed the Basic Press Law in 1987 and (with the notable exception of the National Security Act) there are few remaining limitations on the dissemination of information in South Korea. With the abolition of authoritarian means of media control, political pressure upon the media has become more personal.

According to Roger du Mars, the government is finding more sophisticated ways of managing editorial directions, these include employing personal relationships to apply pressure and initiating a series of aggressive tax audits against executives of newspapers critical of the President.[146] Government officials 'hint', 'request', 'entreat' or even 'cajole' editors into self-censoring sensitive articles.[147] Government ministries are covered by a core group of reporters who are placed under intense pressure to conform. The 'spin' that is sought on political stories in South Korea implies that the story ought to always contain a moral element in keeping with the government template of moral governance and authority.[148]

Corruption in the media was endemic during the period of authoritarianism in South Korea and has continued (although to a lesser degree) since democratization commenced. In a survey of 700 journalists, conducted in 1989, 93 per cent of respondents said they had received bribes from their news sources; five years later, another survey indicated that this figure had dropped to less than 30 per cent.[149] Not only do journalists receive bribes from the government, some journalists have extorted money from businesses on the condition that they will not publish scandalous or derogatory material.

In Taiwan, as in South Korea, the ruling elite promoted the idea that all forms of mass communication had identifiable social responsibilities. For the Kuomintang, this involved making a positive contribution to social control and national reconstruction; the media were thus politically 'guided' on what stories to cover and how.[150] Although there were strict limitations placed upon the issuing of radio, newspaper and television licenses under martial law, there was no official limit on the number of magazine licenses. Some magazines provided a forum for intellectual debate and criticism of the Kuomintang regime. However, this should not be construed as suggesting that the Kuomintang was prepared to tolerate a degree of press freedom. The Chinese intellectual elite has a long history of remonstrating with the political centre against injustice, this practice has a cultural logic with antecedents that are thousands of years old.[151] Thus, the Kuomintang's attitude toward intellectual magazines supports aspects of the Congruent argument, in which Confucian precepts are regarded as consonant with aspects of the liberal democratic tradition. However, this point should not be overstated. There were severe penalties for pushing the limits of the regime's tolerance too far. Beginning with the *Free China* magazine and continuing with the journal *Formosa*, advocating the ideas of freedom and democracy could result in heavy punishment. These issues are discussed further in the next chapter.

Since the lifting of the restrictions which inhibited media freedom, the media industry in Taiwan is booming. The last of the press laws, the Publication Law, was repealed in 1999. In March 1999, the American-based Committee for the Protection of Journalists concluded that, within Asia, Taiwan has the most freedom of the press.[152] This means that anyone in Taiwan can own or publish newspapers or magazines.

The lifting of martial law led to a dramatic growth in all sectors of the media as new private owners entered the media industry.[153] In the process, individual newspapers have aligned themselves with factions within the Kuomintang or the Democratic Progressive Party and, as a consequence, reporting has little pretence to balance.[154] Moreover, a survey conducted by the Association for Taiwan Journalists showed that corruption among the journalists, although petty, reveals a culture of co-option, in which journalists are seen as 'agents of propaganda, not impartial reporters of facts'.[155] Vicious and often uncorroborated personal attacks on political opponents suggest that Taiwan's political culture has yet to negotiate the fine line between freedom of speech and the responsibilities that accompany democracy.[156]

Although the Chinese media remain an instrument of the state, Yuezhi Zhao argues that China has reached a stage in which market forces have penetrated every aspect of media operations, and that a mix of 'Party logic and market logic' are the defining features of the media system.[157] During the process of media commercialization, corruption has become entrenched and is now an endemic problem.

In the late 1970s and early 1980s, the Chinese Communist Party's view of the media as instruments of class struggle was officially dropped. Instead, the media were promoted as instruments of economic and cultural construction.[158] However, the Chinese Communist Party still insists that the media are a tool of propaganda and persuasion, and continues to exert censorship powers.[159] Although there have been moments of increased media freedom, such as those witnessed during Spring in 1989, they have proved short-lived.

The regime in China continues to limit external media sources; however, the globalization of communications is impinging upon the effectiveness of this strategy. The availability of the internet, email, international paging systems and mobile phones is facilitating the breakdown of the government's media controls. Some Chinese citizens are succeeding in breaking through the firewalls constructed by the government and are regularly accessing independent media reports via the internet.

The idea of the media as the Fourth Estate does not appear to have developed in East Asian states under study. Even since democratic transition in South Korea, the domestic media continue to be influenced by state-defined moral and political purposes. The state exerts this influence through informal mechanisms and more coercive tactics, such as tax audits of media executives and owners. In the process, the state creates a context in which journalists self-censor. Indeed, at times the journalists themselves use their position of influence for personal gain. In Taiwan, a boom in the media industry has resulted in polarized and sensationalized media reporting. Thus it appears that even where institutional constraints have been lifted, the development of the concept of the media as a check against the abuse of power is weakly developed in East Asian states.

Rule by law and virtue

Finally, the impact of global norms upon the way in which South Korea, Taiwan and China instrumentalize rule of law is assessed. The rise of a law-based political system requires certain attitudinal and institutional supports, such as the idea that the constitution is the highest form of law, an independent judiciary, and laws regulating electoral and political processes.[160] Whether these attitudes and institutions exist, and whether they are deployed in an effective manner, depends upon political, as well as institutional arrangements.[161]

Jianfu Chen identifies that, for developing countries, the globalization of law predominantly means the transplantation of Western laws.[162] However, as Kanishka Jayasuriya argues, in East Asia notions of rule of law need to be 'understood in the context of notions of political authority and rule embedded in the very interstices of the state'.[163] Thus, again, there is evidence of hybridity in East Asia's political forms.

Since the First Republic, South Korea has had provision for a law-based political system and a judicial review system. The system, like the constitution, has undergone revision, and has varied between an American, European and a mixed system. During the years of authoritarianism, rule of law was weakly instituted. Since democratization commenced, this is gradually changing. The 1987 constitution introduced a European type of constitutional court. Despite initial scepticism among many jurists, this court has been able to play a significant role in the governmental process.[164]

Kun Yang argues that changes in the political climate, coupled with institutional changes, account for this development.[165] The idea of rule of law, evidenced in notions of individual rights, constitutional authority and political accountability, began to have greater legal status in South Korea. Additionally, the Justices became more activist. This may be due to an institutional factor, the creation of the European-style centralized judicial review system, which altered their role.[166]

Nevertheless, as a case involving the National Security Act shows, there are limits to these developments. The National Security Act derives from the cold war era and was used extensively as a repressive instrument during the period of authoritarian rule. Although several other pieces of legislation from this era have been repealed, the National Security Act remains in force and is still invoked.[167] The question of the National Security Act's constitutionality was brought before the constitutional court by the Lawyers for a Democratic Society.[168] The main thrust of the court's ruling was that the Act was constitutional. Although, in the decision, the court's official designation of the Act highlighted its 'limited' constitutionality.[169] This differentiated the ruling from a decision of simple constitutionality without any reservation.[170]

The constitutional framework in Taiwan was drafted by the Kuomintang on the mainland. The constitution is an example of Sun Yat-sen's attempt to combine several strands of liberal democratic and socialist traditions with government institutions from China's past.[171] The constitution delineates the responsibilities of five major government bodies on the principle of the separation of powers. Notwithstanding these provisions, the democratic principles of the constitutional structure were frequently overridden by authoritarian government practice.[172] The full operation of the constitution in Taiwan was circumscribed by a series of emergency laws, administrative decrees, and interpretations by the Council of Grand Justices.

Extra-constitutional autocratic power, evident in martial law and the 'Temporary Provisions', had a profound impact on rule of law in Taiwan for almost four decades. Martial law specified ten categories of criminal offences by civilians that were to be handled by military tribunals.[173] The constitutional rights of the citizens were curtailed since they could no longer access normal judicial procedures. The effect of this is expanded upon in the next chapter which discusses the trial of the editors of the journal *Formosa*.

The standing of the judiciary was greatly undermined by its decision, detailed earlier, to suspend national elections in Taiwan until such time as the mainland was recovered. During martial law, the Council of Grand Justices operated essentially to legitimize, rather than constrain, the excesses of Kuomintang rule.[174] Since the process of democratization commenced, however, the Council has radically changed. The Grand Justices delivered the landmark decision in 1990 which resulted in national elections for entire National Assembly, and by implication, for the legislature.[175] During the past decade, they have struck down both legislation and administrative regulations on the basis of unconstitutionality.

In South Korea and Taiwan it appears that, since democratization, the attitudinal, institutional and political supports underpinning rule of law have developed. Rule of law appears to have moved beyond the process of adaptation, towards a process of learning. By contrast, in China a process of adaptation is in evidence.

Originally, the communist leadership established a legal system based on communist ideology and the Soviet model. These legal models were put to use as a means of class struggle.[176] The decision to vary the practice of rule of law in China related to the decision to pursue market-oriented economic development. Deng Xiaoping referred to it as the 'Two Hands Policy'. On the one hand, the economy must be developed; and on the other hand, the legal system must be strengthened.[177] Foreign legal terminology, structures and methodology found their way into Chinese laws made during the 1980s, while the rhetoric continued to emphasize the 'socialist' nature and Chinese characteristics of the new laws.[178]

The political elite's attitude towards the law is primarily utilitarian; the law is an instrument of the state. Judicial procedures reflect the dominance of a statist legal system, where the predominant concern is with an effort to achieve accurate outcomes, rather than fair procedures.[179] Judicial independence is an essential element of the separation of powers in the liberal model of democracy, but in China the state often interferes in judicial affairs, and judicial corruption is rife.[180] Recently, President Jiang Zemin articulated a doctrine of 'rule by virtue'.[181] He argues that 'rule by virtue' should operate in parallel with rule of law, and suggests that the Chinese Communist Party should govern the country by combining rule of law with 'rule by virtue'.[182]

Delineating a hybrid model

Political leaders in Taiwan and South Korea have developed their own political models, which combine some of the institutions of democracy with local norms and practices. These models are indicative of complex processes of cross-cultural interaction. East Asian political systems fuse local ideas about authority, power, and community with the political structures of democracy.

During his presidency Kim Young Sam articulated a South Korean model of democracy that was more communitarian than libertarian in nature; a model infused by a moral framework.[183] Kim's model emphasized Korean culture, the importance of purifying the authoritarian past and purging authoritarian elements from the democratic process.[184] Taiwan's President, Chen Shui-bian, has developed a political vision for Taiwan. Chen argues that Taiwan needs a complete transformation. Inspired by Tony Blair's 'Third Way' and Francis Fukuyama's concept of 'trust', Chen proposes a 'New Middle Road for Taiwan'.[185] According to Chen, the 'New Middle Road' will open the door to 'the alternation of political parties, while thoroughly resolving such structural problems as mafia money alliances'.[186] These efforts may be interpreted as attempts to respond to global and local imperatives. The statements by Chen and Kim represent a creative approach to developing a form of democracy that combines democracy and domestic norms.

China's leadership is continuing its practice of modifying ideas, ideologies and institutions from other cultures and societies. China has developed 'socialism with Chinese characteristics', and its own form of a 'socialist market economy'. Nonetheless, the persistence of tradition in China and the effect of the changing 'standard of civilization', in which democracy has become the new moral order, seems to be exacerbating aspects of China's tradition versus modernity dilemma, rather than ameliorating it.[187] This suggests that the effect of the emerging consensus, internationally, on the merit of electoral democracy may not necessarily be pro-democratic in its effects. Therefore, as Bhikhu Parekh contends, a polity is not a chance and fluctuating collection of individuals but has a history and a character, and needs to work out its political destiny in its own distinct way.[188]

Conclusion

Minimal, electoral democracy has achieved a normative status in global culture, and this development has played a role in the development of East Asia's political systems. Cross-cultural borrowing, adaptation and fusion have been central to this process. However, during the process of hybridization, the political institutions that have been developing in East Asia vary, both from each other and from the minimalist model of democracy.

In considering elections, political parties, free press, the rule of law in East Asian states, the effects of the contagion and diffusion of democratic ideas upon the region's political institutions are evident. This process has not resulted in a convergence between East Asian political institutions and practices and those of liberal democracies, nor does it imply East Asian civilizations are in conflict with other civilizations. Some aspects of democracy are congruent with East Asian political practice; others are not. The development of democratic forms in East Asia represents a process in which East Asian states are each adapting and learning their own distinctive style of democracy and substantive forms of politics. Although a minimal conception of electoral democracy is spreading across East Asia, the operative model of democracy is best understood as a hybrid. During its evolution the hybrid has synthesized elements of autocracy with electoral democracy, instituted democratic institutions associated with liberal democracies while retaining and reformulating local, non-liberal norms. Thus, although the impact of global norms upon democratic development in East Asian states is evident in their political institutions, the choice of political actions is a more complex and varied matter.

5 Protest and globalization

Introduction

The 1980s witnessed a global growth in democracy that included the previously recalcitrant Asian region. During the decade, democratic protest movements such as the Solidarity movement in Poland, the call to 'People Power' in the Philippines, South Korean worker and student protests, and the image of a man halting a line of tanks in Beijing's Tiananmen Square, became symbols of democratic struggle globally. Due to the globalization of television news, these events engaged international audiences in the form of a drama.

This chapter considers an interesting, but under-analysed, feature of the international dimension of democratization, namely, interactions between the international media, international audiences and democratic protest movements.[1] It highlights that the effects of interactions between international and domestic actors are not uni-directional. Rather, an interactive process influences actors across both the international and domestic domains. The account examines three democratic protest movements: the protest on international human rights day at Kaohsiung on 10 December 1979, the Kwangju democracy movement in South Korea during May 1980, and the democracy movement that developed in Beijing between April–June 1989.

Due to the values inherent in particular terms, the terminology used in the case studies can be problematic. Terms such as 'incidents', 'uprisings', 'insurrections' and 'massacre' colour a distinctive interpretation of the events. In the aftermath of such events government reports describe them as 'turmoil' or 'counter-revolutionary'. The choice of words carries political significance. Significantly, following South Korea's transition to democracy, the events at Kwangju were officially re-titled the 'May 18th Kwangju Democratization Movement'. Meanwhile, in Taiwan, as political liberalization increased, the prison sentences of those involved at Kaohsiung were commuted. By contrast, and perhaps unsurprisingly, no similar official revision has occurred in China.

This study treats each event as a democratic protest movement. Defining the nature of each event as such will trouble some people. For example, Geremie Barmié prefers to use the term 'Chinese Protest Movement of 1989', out of a concern that the term 'democracy' may not be able to contain the 'deep structure' of the events of April–June 1989.[2] The events are defined as democratic protest movements because the protestors desired the acceleration of the process of political liberalization, and hoped that popular protest would lead to political change. Most commonly, place names – Kaohsiung, Kwangju and Beijing – are used in this chapter to refer to the democratic protest movements. Nonetheless, it is recognized that the Chinese sphere of action was not confined to Beijing.[3]

The drama of democratization

Political scientists often employ literary devices to understand complex processes such as democratic transition. In particular, Laurence Whitehead points out how metaphors, analogies and models of 'elite pacts, crafting institutions and even the flow of ocean waves', assist understanding the transition phase of democratization.[4] Whitehead develops the metaphor of a dramatic public performance, because it advances 'comparative analysis of such processes' that may 'usefully complement' alternative perspectives on democratic transition.[5] The metaphor of a dramatic public performance provides a good framework with which to analyse the effect of interactions between democratic protest movements and the international dimension of democratization.

During the process of democratization those who remain on the sidelines of public affairs have to be persuaded that, on this occasion, the principles at stake are so important that they, too, must become involved.[6] At times, the international media and international audience become involved in the process. Whitehead cautions that the metaphor of the single stage risks neglecting what he terms extra-national and sub-national processes that are often equivalent in importance to national processes in understanding democratic transitions.[7] Extending the concept of audience to include both extra-national and sub-national processes alleviates this problem.

This chapter distinguishes between what it terms the elite international audience and the mass international audience, neither of which are regarded as homogenous. The concept of the elite international audience refers to the state elite of some Western countries and focuses on bilateral and multilateral action. The concept of the mass international audience is amorphous; however, it deserves study. In this context, the concept refers to people, including the diaspora, who witness the protest movement externally.

The metaphor of the drama of democratization is novel because it provides a device to explore and analyse aspects of the democratization process that are not often considered in political science. It invites the researcher to consider issues of motivation, symbolism, and psychology. As

Whitehead argues, democratic transitions are complex dynamic processes that cannot be wholly apprehended through formal modelling.[8] To understand political realities explanations must be developed that are not solely causal, but that are also more broadly interpretive.[9]

The democratic protest movements

The Kaohsiung protest was different from those at Kwangju and Beijing, which have some similarities. Kwangju and Beijing were both triggered by the sudden death of a key political figure; this was followed by a call for further political liberalization; the movements were student-led; and they ended with the imposition of martial law and violent repression.

In South Korea, the head of the Korean Civil Intelligence Association assassinated the President, Park Chung Hee, during dinner at the Blue House compound in 1979. In China, Chinese Communist Party reformer Hu Yaobang, who had previously been removed from his post as Party Secretary, died unexpectedly on 15 April 1989. Students reacted to these events by protesting peacefully for the acceleration of political reform. Students in China and South Korea have often been at the forefront of movements for political change. In South Korea on 19 April 1960, it was a student uprising that ended President Syngman Rhee's period of autocratic and corrupt rule. Since then, students have consistently led challenges against the legitimacy of non-democratic elements in the South Korean state.[10] Student protestors in China were rarely as radical in their demands as their South Korean counterparts. Nevertheless, during periods of political liberalization and factional cleavages, intellectuals and students in China have played a key role in protest movements.

Street theatre at Kaohsiung

Three factors set the stage for the events of 10 December 1979 in the streets of Kaohsiung: the repression of Taiwanese opposition during the 28 February 1947 uprising; the Chungli incident in 1977 and the Kuomintang's decision to postpone the 23 December 1978 elections after the Carter administration announced the normalization of relations between Beijing and Washington.

Taiwanese students and intellectuals began a month-long uprising against the Chiang Kai-shek regime on 28 February 1947. The protestors sought freedom, democracy and self-government.[11] During the uprising about 20,000 of the Taiwanese economic, political, cultural and social elite were killed.[12] The incident provided a keen and bloody example of the price that could be exacted for opposing Kuomintang rule.

During a local election at Chungli in 1977, supporters of former Kuomintang candidate, Hsu Hsin-liang, protested against vote counting irregularities. During the protest the worst violence since 28 February 1947 broke out, and one person was killed.[13] The incident highlights the growing significance to non-Party politicians of local elections. The 19 November 1977 elections for county executive, provincial assembly, county assembly and township executive positions returned a surprisingly high number of non-Party candidates.[14] The election results and the incident at Chungli led several non-Party candidates to believe that they were developing widespread support. Non-Party candidates began organizing for the 23 December 1978 supplementary national representative elections.[15]

Following the 16 December 1978 announcement of the normalization of relations between Beijing and Washington, the Kuomintang decided to postpone the supplementary national representative election. Non-Party candidates attempted to maintain momentum for the postponed election and continually sought to expand the parameters of acceptable political behaviour. The non-Kuomintang election campaign included 896 scheduled political rallies.[16] The candidates were developing their organizational skills and capacities, and increasingly resembled an incipient opposition party.

Several non-Party candidates used the Chinese tradition of literary journals to criticize the Kuomintang and push for democratization.[17] *The Eighties* and *Formosa* were the two most important journals during this period. *Formosa* quite openly functioned as a campaign base. *Formosa* opened local offices in the major cities, which more closely resembled party organizations than the offices of editors and reporters.[18] Their political meetings around the island attracted as many as a thousand people per meeting.[19] The political objectives of *Formosa* included parliamentary reform, direct election of mayors and the provincial governor of Taiwan, an independent judiciary, the end of martial law, the removal of Kuomintang control from schools, the military and courts, freedom of speech, and an amnesty for political prisoners. By the publication of the fourth issue it was the second most popular magazine on the island, after the local edition of *TV Guide*.[20] As the non-Party movement began to coalesce several destructive attacks were launched against *Formosa* offices and the homes of the magazine's staff, but the police were not inclined to take any action.[21]

Unlike the spontaneous protests in Kwangju and Beijing, the *Formosa* magazine sponsored the rally in Kaohsiung. It was planned as a precursor to a rally in Taipei on the anniversary of the normalization of relations between Beijing and Washington. On 10 December 1979, World Human Rights Day, police dressed in riot gear surrounded 30,000 rally participants, occasionally the police released tear gas on the protestors or prevented the crowd from moving forward.[22] The street rally at Kaohsiung suddenly became violent when protestors and military police clashed. Accounts differ about the cause of the confrontation. Marc Cohen reports that people, possibly associated with Kaohsiung's extensive underworld, attacked the police.[23] The police launched tear gas into the crowd, some of whom threw bricks, bottles and other debris back at them.[24] Audio tapes recorded at the rally indicate that the organizers urged calm and referred to the police as 'fellow Taiwanese'.[25] The protest was eventually suppressed with the minimum use of force.[26] This is a major difference between the protest at Kaohsiung and those at Kwangju and Beijing.

The drama of Kaohsiung continued in the courtroom. In the days after the rally key non-Party political leaders were arrested. Eight opposition activists were charged with sedition and prosecuted in a military court, another 32 were tried in civilian courts. The eight charged with sedition included four of the five individuals managing the *Formosa* magazine and others associated with it. Editor Huang Hsin-chieh was also indicted for conspiring to obtain money from communist agents in Japan. All eight confessed to the charges, but later asserted their confessions were induced through torture. The eight activists were found guilty of the charges and sentenced to lengthy prison terms. The other 32 accused, plus ten members of the Presbyterian Church connected with the Kaohsiung protest, were sentenced to prison terms ranging from ten months to six years.[27] An undercover Investigation Bureau agent who gave evidence during the trial publicly recanted in 1985.[28]

The Korean performance

Ch'oe Kyu-ha was Acting President after President Park Chung Hee's assassination. During this period, there was a political opening in South Korea; Emergency Decree no. 9 outlawing dissent was lifted, opposition leader Kim Dae Jung was released from house arrest, and 68 other dissidents were granted amnesty. This period came to an end on 12 December 1979, when General Chun Doo Hwan led what became known as the '12.12 coup'. General Chun consolidated his power base amid growing labour unrest and demonstrations at university campuses. South Korean students set the deadline of 15 May 1980 for General Chun to resign and for constitutional order to be re-established. As the deadline approached thousands of students clashed with police at university campuses around South Korea. On 17 May 1980, Chun Doo Hwan declared nationwide martial law, banning all political activity and closing the universities. Hundreds of democratic activists were arrested, including Kim Dae Jung.

The following day at Kwangju, in South Cholla province, black beret paratroopers violently dispersed a small group of student demonstrators. Several dozen civilians were brutally killed and many others seriously injured. Unlike the protest in Beijing, the protest at Kwangju rapidly deteriorated into violence. In response to the paratroopers' actions hundreds of people in Kwangju seized arms and fought against the military. Increasing numbers of citizens joined in demonstrations, and at its height over 200,000 people participated.[29] The protestors took control of Kwangju city; students formed a Citizens' Army, General Citizen Settlement Committee and Students' Settlement Committee. These committees assumed responsibility for negotiations, arranging funerals, providing public information, and weapons collection.[30] On 22 May 1980, the United States agreed to release Korean troops from the Republic of Korea–United States Combined Forces in order to assist with the suppression of the Kwangju demonstrations. In the early hours of 27 May 1980 the Korean military reassumed control of Kwangju. The government gave the official death toll as 191. Although it is widely accepted that many more were killed, there is little agreement on the absolute figure. However, Bruce Cumings contends that the number of students and young people killed at Kwangju is on the same, or greater, scale as those killed in Beijing during June 1989.[31]

The Beijing theatre

In Beijing, mourning activities associated with reformer Hu Yaobang's death on 15 April 1989 provided an opportunity for the mass expression of discontent with the pace, extent and effect of Deng Xiaoping's 'Four Modernizations' reform program. By 22 April 1989, thousands had gathered in Tiananmen Square to mourn Hu Yaobang, and to press the Chinese government to continue liberalization and economic reform. The protest soon evolved into a mass demand for extensive change. The crowds in Tiananmen Square grew at a rate that alarmed the Chinese government. *The People's Daily* published an editorial designed to shame the students into returning to their campuses on 26 April 1989. The editorial had the countervailing effect of mobilizing a high degree of popular support for the protestors. Unlike the protest at Kwangju, the protest was not confined to one location, but spread to Shanghai and other cities.[32]

The protest movement had begun to lose momentum by 12 May 1989. In response, the students initiated a hunger strike that reinvigorated the protest and inspired thousands of workers to support the students. Wang Dan describes the protest at that moment as such that 'if one person went on a hunger strike, one hundred would join in, and if a hundred joined, a thousand more would join … There is an emotional dynamic in all such mass movements … there was an unstoppable force pushing the movement to a confrontation with authorities'.[33] Over a million citizens filled the square in support of the students' non-violent protest.

Martial law was declared, but its full implementation delayed. *The New York Times* reported that tens of thousands of Beijing students and workers turned back more than 2,000 Peoples' Liberation Army troops who were marching toward Tiananmen Square.[34] During the pre-dawn hours of 4 June 1989, following a two-week impasse, the Peoples' Liberation Army cleared Tiananmen Square and its approach roads. Accounts of what occurred vary. Robin Munro argues that the 'theatre of the popular uprising and massacre, lay mainly on the periphery, above all, along western Changan Boulevard and out to the western suburbs', rather than in Tiananmen Square itself.[35] In a number of other cities demonstrations were staged in response, but they quickly dissipated. In the aftermath, protestors were detained and a number were executed. Workers bore the brunt of the reprisals.

The role and influence of the international media

The representation of the protests in the international media varied. These differences influenced the international audience's perception of, and response to, the events.

Peter Golding and Philip Elliot argue that journalists construct news stories according to a narrative structure similar to elements in human drama.[36] Constructing complex news stories as a drama captures the audience's attention. However, it can also create inaccurate understandings of the events. Media coverage of the trial of the so-called 'Kaohsiung Eight' contributed to the image of their martyrdom. *The New York Times'* coverage of Kwangju stressed the role of individuals, such as opposition leaders Kim Dae Jung and Kim Young Sam, and coup leader Chun Doo Hwan. Indeed, *The New York Times* reported on 20 May 1980 that the conflict developing in Kwangju was due to the arrest of Kim Dae Jung. It was not until two days later that the paper made explicit the cause of the uprising, that is, paratrooper brutality in dealing with the student demonstration on 18 May 1980 and thereafter.

The international media's emphasis on student leaders conferred on the protest movement in Beijing far greater cohesiveness than existed, and elevated the role of a small number of activists, such as Wuer Kaixi, Chai Ling, and Wang Dan. For example, *The New York Times* featured a profile of Wang Dan, whom they described as both a 'national figure', and the 'most influential of the student leaders'.[37] The international media's focus on those they perceived as key protagonists in each protest was at the expense of media analysis of the nature of the mass demonstrations.

The availability of news stories about the democratic protest movements also influenced the international audience's knowledge of the unfolding dramas. During the years separating the events in Kaohsiung and Kwangju from those in Beijing, a revolution in media technology occurred. This radically altered the availability of television news stories from overseas locations. The presence of a large foreign press corps (due to Soviet President Mikhail Gorbachev's visit to China), and the advent of satellite technology, contributed to the high availability of news stories about the Beijing protest.

The brevity of the Kaohsiung protest may account for the limited foreign media reporting of the event. Foreign and domestic press witnessed the proceedings in the military court and, arguably, for this reason it is the trial rather than the protest that gained significance internationally. The events during and after 10 December 1979 shed light on the abusive practices of the Kuomintang government and illuminated them for the world.

At Kwangju, the international media presence was also limited. Foreign journalists from Associated Press, *Suddeutsche Zeitung,* ARD-NDR German TV, *Los Angeles Times, The Times, Baltimore Sun, Le Monde, The New York Times*, and the *Asian Wall Street Journal* were able to report from Kwangju.[38] Not only was there less of a foreign media presence, it was logistically harder for news stories to be filed in South Korea than in China. Road blocks made it difficult to get in or out of Kwangju, and the city's telephone lines had been cut.

At Kaohsiung and Kwangju the international audience primarily gained information from the print media. Television news reports were less prevalent. Reports for ARD-NDR German TV were broadcast only after the journalist smuggled film footage from South Korea to Japan.[39] Nine years later, as James Lull observes, 'television viewers all over the world watched the incredible drama of the 1989 student and worker uprising in Beijing'.[40] Marshall McLuhan argues the 'medium is the message'.[41] Satellite technology brought another element into play in the coverage. Craig Calhoun highlights that he and others assumed the stance of 'eyewitnesses' in Beijing, cabling reports to London newspapers and holding interviews with American television stations. Paradoxically, they depended on, and were influenced by, the information contained in those same media reports.[42]

It is evident that the international media relied on vastly different sources of information in their coverage of the democratic protest movements. News coverage of the protest in Kaohsiung was situated against the backdrop of rapidly changing Sino-American relations. Analysis of *The New York Times* coverage of Kwangju shows a heavy reliance on the United States government and other official sources. Only a small number of stories feature the views of the Korean students. The prevalence of official sources in *The New York Times* is troubling in the light of Donald Sohn's study of United States diplomatic and military correspondence at the time of the Kwangju protests. Sohn argues that, in the aftermath of the 12.12 coup, Chun successfully manipulated the Carter administration into viewing Korea from a perspective advantageous to his own political purposes.[43] Chun achieved this through his control of all intelligence, diplomatic, and military communication channels. United States human intelligence sources dried up virtually overnight after the coup. The information constraints and the process of manipulation that the United States government experienced are also evident in *The New York Times* coverage of Kwangju.

From the outset, the Western media depicted the protestors in Beijing sympathetically, whereas the media portrayed protestors at Kaohsiung and Kwangju critically. The adjectives journalists used to describe the events aligned the protest movements with either primarily positive or primarily negative characteristics. The international media's construction of the drama in Beijing encouraged Western audience identification with the student protagonists. This is because the news media provides the audience with particular 'maps of meaning'; defining for the majority of the population not only what significant events are taking place, but, also, offering powerful interpretations of how to understand these events.[44] At the same time, contained within these interpretations are media attitudes toward the events and the people involved in them.

Shujen Wang's analysis of *The New York Times* coverage of Kwangju and Beijing reveals that the gathering of demonstrators in Beijing was frequently referred to as a 'pro-democracy movement', 'demonstration' or 'march'.[45] By contrast, Kwangju demonstrators were referred to as 'rebels', and were variously called 'mob', 'rioters', and 'insurgents'.[46] Those at Kwangju were depicted in *The New York Times* as 'looters', 'militants', and 'under little control'.[47] The language used in *The New York Times* to report the military's action in Beijing was often highly emotive: 'massacre', 'brutality', 'butchery' and 'barbarism'. By contrast, Kwangju was described as a 'clash', 'military operation', and 'disturbance'.

The *Far Eastern Economic Review* reflects a similar coverage pattern. Protestors in Kaohsiung were described as 'youths brandishing lighted torches, clubs and iron bars', while the Kuomintang 'handled the evening with forbearance and finesse'.[48] The *Far Eastern Economic Review* reported that the South Korean students' 'shrill voices posed impossible demands'.[49] The Kwangju protest was dismissed as 'a gesture by the students, necessary for their self esteem', in which the students were held accountable for setting loose a 'snow ball of dissent and violence' resulting in 'a path of obstinacy, extremism and death across the nation'.[50] Conversely, the *Far Eastern Economic Review* praised the students in China for their 'spontaneous courage' in contrast to the regime's 'savagery'.[51] Unlike the protestors at Beijing, protestors at Kaohsiung and Kwangju were not bestowed with any positive qualities by virtue of their youth.

The protestors themselves understood the effect international media reports could have. The Kuomintang was forced by domestic and international pressures to hold the dissident trials in open court and to allow the domestic and foreign media to cover them.[52] Legal representatives for the 'Kaohsiung Eight', and the defendants themselves, used the open trial as an opportunity to speak to the international and domestic audience, through the media. The prosecutors argued that the incident at Kaohsiung was part of a plot to overthrow the Kuomintang government.[53] In response, the defence lawyers made 'passionate and impressive defence speeches, more like scholarly lectures on human rights, the rule of law and democracy than customary criminal defence statements'.[54] One defendant, Yao Chia-wen, asked the court, 'Judge, do you honestly think we would attempt to overthrow the government with sticks and bamboo torches?'[55]

English poet and foreign correspondent James Fenton, reporting on the Kwangju protest for *The Times*, tells how a woman he encountered was 'desperate that the world outside should be told the truth of what was happening'.[56] She said to him, 'you are our corridor to life'.[57] Anthropologist Linda Lewis, who was also present, says that 'throughout the uprising, the lack of some overt American action was taken as evidence that the American Embassy in Seoul did not understand what was happening down south, and this idea came from the conviction ... that the United States government would step in and stop the violence'.[58] The citizens in Kwangju appeared to believe that if the outside world knew what was happening in their city, the outcome would be different.

Since the 1980s, globalization has resulted in the enhancement of the roles and powers of the media, particularly television news, which (through using satellite technology to tell the story of an event as it happens) can have direct consequences for the direction that event might take.[59] The international television news media creates a global audience for the event, influences the behaviour of the actors involved, and constructs world public opinion.[60] The difference globalization and satellite television made to the protest in Beijing was significant. During President Gorbachev's visit to China, the extensive coverage of the protest by the international media began to affect the students' presentation of themselves on what they by then realized was an international stage.[61] Protestors carried banners written in English, French and Russian, as well as Chinese, and used symbols of Western democracy and freedom. One slogan read 'International Opinion, Please Support Us'.[62]

As Craig Calhoun argues 'speaking to (or performing for) the foreign press had several functions. First, it mobilized international public opinion on the side of protestors against the government. Secondly, it spread word of the protests throughout China, as people listened to reports beamed back by BBC and the Voice of America'.[63] Particularly after the announcement of martial law, the Voice of America and the BBC Foreign Service played an influential role. According to Voice of America Director, Richard Carlson, during the crisis in 1989 between 60 and 100 million Chinese people listened to Voice of America every day.[64] Foreign news stories were recorded by Chinese listeners, printed onto paper and placed on bulletin boards, or read over loudspeaker systems.[65] The Chinese authorities viewed the role of Voice of America as contributing to the situation and jammed several of the channels.

Denis McQuail argues that more attention should be given to the various kinds of contagion, or diffusion activities, that are a consequence of media reporting.[66] As people within China learned, via the media, of the protest in Beijing, many were persuaded to participate. It has been estimated that 80 per cent of those occupying Tiananmen Square came from outside Beijing.[67] This played an interesting role, as Baogang He notes, for when the opportunity for compromise came, and the protestors voted whether or not to withdraw from Tiananmen Square, those who had just arrived in the city were reluctant to leave without achieving something.[68] They were particularly insistent on continuing the occupation.

The democratic effect of international media interactions with protestors in China was ambiguous. The international media indirectly influenced the students' decision to continue the protest, and also influenced the Chinese leadership's perception of the cause of the problem. Beijing Mayor Chen Xitong's account of the protest to the National People's Congress highlights this. He states:

... reactionary political forces in Hong Kong, Taiwan, the United States and other Western countries were also involved in the turmoil through various channels and by different means. Western news agencies showed unusual zeal. The Voice of America, in particular, aired news in three programs every day for a total of more than ten hours beamed to the Chinese mainland, spreading rumours, stirring up trouble and adding fuel to the turmoil.[69]

The interactive function of symbols

Symbols have an important function in any drama, including in the drama of democratization. Distinctive local and global cultures affected the symbolism deployed by the demonstrators. These symbols served to motivate and unify global and local actors in response to the democratic protest movements, as well as highlighting the strong national allegiance of the protestors.

There is not a great deal of information available about what took place during the protest at Kaohsiung, or the symbols which may have been employed by the protestors. Linda Chao and Ramon H. Myers describe that the *Formosa* leaders 'through microphones, spoke to the crowd, shouted political slogans, or sang songs'.[70] What is clear, however, is that as a consequence of the trial and sentencing of the 'Kaohsiung Eight', they developed a martyr symbolism domestically.[71] Some Taiwanese have deep seated feelings of colonization, and they respond emotionally to the martyr symbolism around such jailed leaders as the 'Kaohsiung Eight'. For newly elected non-Party politicians 'Kaohsiung' became a catchword in domestic politics.[72]

Moreover, the addition of defence lawyers into the opposition ranks, as a consequence of the trial of the 'Kaohsiung Eight', proved to be a formidable legal-institutional opposition line-up against the Kuomintang.[73] In particular, President Chen Shui-bian took on a leading role, both as defence lawyer for Huang Hsin-chieh, and later as a non-Party politician. In his autobiography he describes how previously he 'had known little about the opposition movement' and that this period of contact with some of the players allowed him to become familiar with the Taiwanese democracy movement and he was 'deeply moved by the opposition's power'.[74]

Subsequent South Korean protests used the tactics and symbols of overseas democracy movements. On the anniversary of Kwangju, students created their own news media, emulating the Big Character Posters and 'democracy walls' that had been used in China.[75] In 1989, demonstrators in

Beijing used local and global symbols of protest and democracy. During the early phase of the demonstrations, the protestors consciously tried to imitate the Democracy Wall movement of 1978–1979 and the May Fourth Movement. As the movement developed, the protestors borrowed the language, symbols, and icons of democracy and freedom fighters. The Chinese students learned protest skills and strategies from other countries. In particular, the experience of the Philippines had revealed to the Chinese protestors that a peaceful strategy could change a society.[76] The protestors' 'V-for victory' sign, the appearance of the term 'People Power' on banners, the hunger strike, and the 'Goddess of Democracy', had a particular resonance for American spectators. None more so than the figure of the 'Goddess of Democracy', its significance for the majority of members of the international audience was as a potent symbol of liberal democracy – the Statue of Liberty. The 'Goddess of Democracy' featured strongly in international media coverage of the protest, and became a key motif during international audience activity in support of the Chinese protestors. The appearance of the 'Goddess of Democracy' in other protests around the globe shows another aspect of the contagion effect of international media reports.

Songs often function in dramas to arouse the audience and unify the cast. In the drama of democratization they served a similar purpose. The power of motifs and songs is in their capacity to elicit a response from the audience. Demonstrators sang songs during the Kwangju and Beijing democratic protest movements to symbolize patriotism, and to unify disparate groups. Protestors in Beijing sang *The Internationale*, an official Chinese anthem, as a counter to the government's depiction of them as anti-communist. Kim Chung Keun notes that, from the very beginning, the people of Kwangju sang *Aekukga*, the South Korean national anthem. Kim Chung Keun describes how

> ... [t]he crowds would dissolve away and then re-form, building up numbers, and they would sing the anthem to recharge their wills and pledge loyalty to one another ... people tried traditional songs and folk songs. Of these *Airirang* and *Our Wishes* went best. That was because no matter who was doing the singing – men wearing neckties, hucksters from the stalls in the street markets, labourers, farmers, students, women – they all knew those two songs ... I would say the symbols of the Kwangju uprising – if traditional tunes can be symbols – were those two songs that people sang all day ... They brought together all types of beings, of whatever background – welded them as one to fight against unimaginable acts of violence by the army. And so those ordinary citizens rose as one.[77]

At both Kwangju and Beijing, although originally beginning with students, a cross-section of the population joined the protest, without reference to any pre-existing ties. As spectators joined the stage, singing songs together enabled the protestors to transcend their differences and assert their patriotism.

International audience responses to the drama

Whitehead argues that, as the drama of democratization unfolds, as in any theatre, the political audience is never unconditionally controlled from the stage.[78] Metaphorically, as well as literally, actors may be planted in the third row, spectators may be swept into the footlights for a quick turn, and rival performers may compete with each other for the allegiance of the audience.[79] The international audience responded to, and interacted with, the protests in Kaohsiung, Kwangju and Beijing differently. The dichotomous depiction of the protests in the international media, coupled with the development and effect of new media technology, contributed to these differences. In the case of Beijing, interactions between the democratic protest movement and the international dimension resulted in the contagion of the protests internationally, and, in the process, set the agenda for the international elite.

Kaohsiung

Of all the cases, the international audience's response was the most muted in the case of Kaohsiung. The international audience was primarily composed of overseas Taiwanese, Chinese, and the political elite in the United States. J. Bruce Jacobs identifies two groups of overseas opposition movements which he regards as important during this period: the Chinese communists and the Taiwanese independence movement.[80] The goal of the overseas Taiwanese independence movement was to create a democratic political system on Taiwan that would declare independence from China.

The independence movement was based primarily in Japan, the United States and Europe. It hoped that the United States might renounce its support of the Kuomintang and support the Taiwanese independence movement's democratic platform. During the trials, the Kuomintang unsuccessfully attempted to link the 'Kaohsiung Eight' with the overseas Taiwanese independence movement. The Kuomintang contention that the Kaohsiung protest was part of a Beijing-led plot to overthrow the regime was also unconvincing to many independent observers.

The trial revealed that torture had been used by interrogators to gain confessions from the accused. Hung-mao Tien argues that the incident is best understood as a political event in which the non-Party movement challenged the Kuomintang monopoly of power by holding the demonstration and by revealing the autocratic nature of Kuomintang rule in the trial itself.[81] Moreover, Taiwan's loss of diplomatic status within the international community affected reactions to the Kaoshiung protestors. Two years earlier, after the violence at Chungli, the Kuomintang had not responded with such widespread repression. The reasons for this vary, and include the Kuomintang's recognition that the *Formosa* group was amassing organizational power. However, the Kuomintang response was also influenced by the regime's heightened desire for stability at a time of perceived crisis. As a result, the 'Kaoshiung Eight' received less sympathy domestically than they might have obtained in more secure times. Public opinion surveys in Taiwan showed that a large majority of the population supported the government's actions.[82]

Kwangju

The mass international audience response to events in Kwangju was largely confined to the Korean diaspora located in the United States. The Korean diaspora initiated and participated in a number of commemorative activities. The Korean community throughout the United States commemorated the anniversary of the Kwangju protest through a series of lectures or cultural performances, involving plays, songs and movies. A number of activities were specifically targeted at non-Korean audiences, such as the touring play titled 'The Sound Of Liberation', which was performed in seven European countries and in Australia. Activities to support the Kwangju movement included the establishment of a Kwangju Victim Support Committee in Los Angeles, which raised funds and gathered information. Members of Young Koreans United from the United States, Canada and Australia petitioned the South Korean government to bring those involved in the coup and Kwangju repression to trial. Such overseas activities were not without risk, sometimes upon their return to South Korea activists were arrested under the National Security Act. Notwithstanding the Korean diaspora's efforts to focus international attention on Kwangju, the international mass audience did not support the Korean protestors to the same degree as they did the Chinese protestors in Beijing.

Beijing

Prior to 4 June 1989, the Chinese diaspora in Britain, Moscow, Hong Kong, Macao, Australia and the United States held peaceful demonstrations in support of the Beijing protest. These rallies borrowed the motifs of the Chinese protestors, symbolically unifying the protest movement internationally. The 'Goddess of Democracy' statue was replicated at rallies in Taipei, Hong Kong and Paris; and in New York and London a small number of overseas Chinese students began a hunger strike. In a park near the United Nations' building in New York, Chinese students fasted and called on the United Nations Security Council to initiate sanctions against China for human rights abuses.[83] A postcard campaign began in Manhattan's Chinatown to urge United States President Bush to bring sanctions against

China. The Chinese Language Journalists Association printed 40,000 post-cards urging the United States government to issue tough economic sanctions and to freeze diplomatic relations.

The international media's coverage fed into concerns about Great Britain's future hand-over of Hong Kong to China in 1997. Editorial comment in the *Far Eastern Economic Review* urged Hong Kong to bring its 'precarious future to the attention of the world and seek internationally the backing that a weak mean-spirited British government appears unwilling to provide'.[84] In Hong Kong, tens of thousands demonstrated in solidarity with the people in Beijing after the implementation of martial law, and in the following weeks that figure was dwarfed when more than a million people – one fifth of the population – took part in marches and rallies.[85] The Hong Kong Alliance in Support of the Patriotic Democratic Movement in China was formed; the group enjoyed mass support and raised millions of dollars to support the Chinese students.[86]

Notwithstanding the Hong Kong-based *Democracy Tide* paper's call for 'Chinese of the World to Unite', the Chinese diaspora in Southeast Asia did not join in the drama, preferring to stay in the audience.[87] Outside the Chinese embassy in Manila, protestors were not overseas Chinese, but were students from China studying in the Philippines. The Chinese in Singapore did not rally, and in Malaysia demonstrations by the Chinese community and the Malaysian Chinese Association disintegrated in the face of Malay disapproval.

Chinese diaspora living in liberal democracies were often the driving force behind campaigns to highlight the students' cause, although not exclusively so. Established ethnic and community groups, other non-government organizations and trade unions also participated. In Australia, the New South Wales Labour Council and the Australian Capital Territory Trades and Labour Council placed work bans on the Chinese embassy and consulate.[88] Non-government and philanthropic organizations also provided overseas Chinese students with support. In a number of liberal democracies citizens signed petitions, wrote letters to the editor and the government, lobbied political parties, and participated in consumer boycott campaigns and demonstrations. Protestors in the United States, Australia and Great Britain pushed for the relaxation of immigration regulations, the imposition of tougher sanctions against China, and clemency for arrested Chinese protestors. The concrete activities of the diaspora, non-government organizations, trade unions and citizens constrained the policy choices available to the international political elite.

Public opinion and political action

The international media coverage of Beijing motivated sections of the mass international audience to become involved in the drama. Due to a combination of the news media's portrayal of the protestors, new media technology and globalization, the mass international audience mobilized public opinion into political action. Several liberal democracies were invigorated through increased participation and activism, and, in the process, set the agenda of the international elite audience. In the cases of Kaohsiung and Kwangju, however, the mass international audience did not play a similarly significant role.

Not only was the international elite audience's response to the protests mediated by the agenda-setting role of the media and the mass international audience, power relationships also played a role. As such, it could be anticipated that political leaders in Taiwan and South Korea would have been more vulnerable than the Chinese leadership to the consequences of international opprobrium.

Although the Carter administration clearly enunciated a concern for human rights, in the case of East Asia, geo-political interests were paramount. Subsequent administrations continued this emphasis. After the events in Beijing, despite the fact that geo-politics in the region had altered by 1989, American foreign policy-makers continued to be concerned primarily with balancing the geo-political interests of the United States, China, Japan and the Soviet Union.[89]

As mentioned, international media coverage of events at Kaoshiung was limited. However, Taiwan's major ally, the United States, could not completely overlook the event. America's response to Kaohsiung was affected by the changing context of international relations. The normalization of relations between China and the United States (which became effective on 1 January 1979) and the termination by the United States of the Mutual Security Treaty, exposed the Kuomintang regime to greater international scrutiny and criticism on issues such as human rights.

Following the trial of the 'Kaohsiung Eight', American pressure on Taipei to improve human rights intensified.[90] In July 1979, the American Institute in Taiwan replaced the embassy on the island. David Dean, former director of the American Institute in Taiwan, has commented that, during this period, human rights abuse in Taiwan was a very crucial question.[91] There were many very critical Congressional hearings about Taiwan, and prominent senators and members of Congress wrote many letters to the leaders in Taiwan's government over cases such as Kaohsiung.[92] A number of high profile visitors to Taiwan also expressed concern for those detained. Lester Wolff, who was then the Chairperson of the House of Representatives Subcommittee on Asian and Pacific Affairs, and was the co-author of the Taiwan Relations Act, met with non-Kuomintang political leaders while visiting Taiwan in 1980. Upon his return to the United States he issued a lengthy statement to the effect that it was in Taiwan's long-term interests to see that human rights were protected.[93]

As domestic unrest in South Korea grew during the early 1980s, the United States was concerned to maintain regional stability. The United States issued clear statements to North Korea not to take advantage of the situation, and sent an aircraft carrier to the Korean coast. On 18 May and 19 May 1980, the State Department issued the following statement:

> We are deeply disturbed by the extension of martial law throughout the Republic of Korea, the closing of universities and the arrest of a number of political and student leaders ... We have made clear the seriousness of our concern to Korean leaders ... We urge all elements in Korean society to act with restraint at this difficult time. As we affirmed on October 26, 1979, the US Government will react strongly in accordance with its treaty obligations to any external attempt to exploit the situation in the Republic of Korea.[94]

The United States' actions during the Kwangju protest contributed to the emergence of strong feelings of anti-Americanism in South Korea. Combined Forces Commander General John Wickham's decision to release Korean troops to deal with the protest at Kwangju was regarded by many South Koreans as evidence of American complicity in the repression of the democracy movement. The United States military elite was free to do this without fear of domestic backlash because the American media did not publicize the brutality visited upon the students, or their democratic aspirations, to the domestic audience in the United States. This made it easier for the United States political elite to act without arousing negative public opinion. Dissident Moon Ik-kwan's view of the international dimension of South Korea's situation changed following his arrest for alleged activity plotting the events at Kwangju. He states:

> ... for the first time I was able to see the Korean problem in an international context. Syngman Rhee, Park Chung Hee, Chun Doo Hwan – to me, they had been the enemies. But all of a sudden I realized that America and Japan are pulling the strings behind them ... America knew what was happening [in Kwangju] and ... condoned it. That was shattering.[95]

The United States government focussed on high diplomacy, stressing their concern for individuals such as Kim Dae Jung, who had also been mentioned in international media reports. According to Ambassador Gleysteen, the United States embassy did not heed the developments at Kwangju because they were 'distracted at the time in Seoul with a very strong protest against Kim Dae Jung's arrest'.[96] The United States and Japan had diplomatic observers in court throughout Kim Dae Jung's trial on the charge of sedition. Japan and the United States were the first governments to protest publicly against the guilty verdict and death sentence Kim Dae Jung received soon afterwards Spain, Greece and Australia joined in.[97] The response of the international elite audience succeeded in having Kim Dae Jung's sentence commuted.

In 1988, the South Korean National Assembly convened a Special Committee on the Investigation of the May 18 Kwangju Democratization Movement, chaired by Kim Dae Jung. The committee asked the United States government 48 questions concerning their actions in South Korea during 1979–1980. The State Department issued its first comprehensive account of its activities and response to Kwangju, titled 'United States Government Statement on the Events in Kwangju, Republic of Korea, in May 1980'. The statement indirectly addressed the questions raised by the committee and revealed that the United States embassy in Seoul and the State Department had inadequately grasped the magnitude of Chun's coup. Although General Wickham presented verbal protests to the South Korean regime, the United States developed little policy leverage over the Chun regime. During May 1980, senior policy-makers in Washington 'reluctantly accepted' the release of Combined Forces troops to re-take Kwangju. General Wickham's autobiography concludes a chapter on Kwangju with the following summation 'we probably had little if any real influence over ROK [South Korean] internal developments, and we were little more than helpless bystanders as Chun shrewdly manoeuvred toward total power'.[98] Wickham is correct in his assessment that, in this case, they exerted 'little if any real influence'. However, the question of whether the United States could have been more than 'bystanders' remains contentious.

The elite international audience's response to events in Beijing reflected cold war allegiances. Initially, the Soviet Congress of People's Deputies condemned outside efforts to bring pressure on China, because the events in Beijing were purely an internal matter.[99] Britain, France, West Germany, Australia, Spain, Italy, the Netherlands and Sweden all immediately issued statements deploring Chinese government action. A few years later the Russian parliament also denounced the government's actions. In the aftermath of the event France, the Netherlands and Sweden froze political relations. Japan announced the suspension of economic development and cultural missions to Beijing, and a case-by-case review of aid projects already underway.[100] On 15 July 1989, at an economic summit in Paris, the leaders of seven major industrial capitalist nations issued a joint political declaration condemning China for its repression of the pro-democracy protest.[101]

In the immediate aftermath, President George Bush stated that he 'deeply deplore[s] the decision to use force against peaceful demonstrators ... We have been urging and continue to urge continued non-violence, restraint and dialogue'.[102] Editorial comment, human rights groups and Congress criticized President Bush for the weakness of his statements. Congress responded to public opinion and the lobbying activities of human rights groups and the Chinese diaspora. The Senate joined the House of Representatives in demanding tougher sanctions against China for its continued persecution of Chinese students and workers who supported the democracy movement.[103] President Bush stated that he wanted to make a 'reasoned, careful' response that 'takes into account both our long-term interests in recognition of a complex internal situation in China'.[104]

The extent of the public's demand for action was such that the Bush administration did introduce sanctions against China. The sanctions related to direct military sales and high technology transfers, the suspension of all high level government exchanges, prohibitions on Export–Import Bank programs, withholding development funds, and opposition to multilateral development bank loans to China.[105] However, within the executive branch, the Bush administration pursued a strategy of private diplomacy, built on personal relationships with China.[106] The Bush administration resisted attempts by Congress to broaden the scope of sanctions, based on its view that United States–China relations were more than bilateral and had broader geo-strategic significance.[107] Less than one month after Tiananmen Square had been cleared of protestors the administration sent Brent Scowcroft, President Bush's national security adviser, to Beijing to reassure China's leaders. The mission was kept secret because public opinion opposing contact with China was so strong. Before long, the sanctions that were announced in the aftermath of the crackdown in Beijing were either waived or modified.

Unlike Kaohsiung or Kwangju, the international audience's concern about events in Beijing found expression in multilateral institutions. Acting under United States pressure, the World Bank and Asian Development Bank temporarily suspended loans to China.

International audience concern about events in Beijing spilled into the international human rights regime. The United Nations Sub-Commission on Prevention of Discrimination and Protection of Minorities and the Human Rights Commission became the vehicle through which a number of countries in the United Nations reacted to events in Beijing. The issue dominated the 41st session of the Sub-Commission in August 1989. China unsuccessfully lobbied to avoid a resolution critical of its actions during the democratic protest movement, based on the principle of non-intervention and state sovereignty.[108] Before the 46th session of the Human Rights Commission in 1995, China lifted martial law, released 573 political prisoners, and sent a large delegation of more than forty diplomats to lobby against the reception of the Sub-Commission's resolution.[109] China succeeded in garnering enough support for a procedural no action vote to be passed. The response of the international elite audience has not generated widespread or deep democratic changes in China. In fact American pressure on China has caused a domestic backlash in China against the United States.[110] In particular, the State Department's annual Human Rights Report has been criticized by China as a blatant case of hegemonism.[111]

Conclusion

A comparison of the foreign media's coverage of events at Kaohsiung, Kwangju and Beijing has revealed the growing role the international media plays in depicting the drama of democratization for both local and global

actors. The role played by the media has altered significantly as a consequence of globalization and the advent of new media technologies. These
changes are facilitating an interactive process of exchange between local and
global actors.

During the protests at Kaohsiung and Kwangju the international media's
role was limited. By contrast, at Beijing the international media – particularly through the medium of instantaneous broadcasting – set the agenda,
created mass public opinion on a global stage, and, importantly, interacted
with and influenced the actors in the drama. In the case of Beijing, the mass
international audience responded to the symbols used by the protestors and
the international media's depiction of the events in a manner that invigorated their own democracies. Protests, petitions and lobbying activities
influenced the political elite, constraining the range of policy options available to them.

Ultimately, this effect was both contingent and transitory. When the
drama dies down and media interest in a story dissipates, it has proven difficult for would-be democratic activists in China to obtain or sustain the
attention of the international audience. Nonetheless, the growing role of the
media highlights the broader issue of the character of political globalization, which is considered further in the next chapter.

6 International non-government organizations

Introduction

A growing body of literature assesses the roles that international NGOs play in democratization.[1] The literature suggests that international NGOs serve a number of functions within the democratization process, including representing a global manifestation of civil society. Schmitter observes that there are an extraordinary variety of international parties, associations, foundations, movements, networks and firms that are ready to intervene, either to promote or protect democracy.[2] He argues that the extent of recent democratization and the fact that so few regressions have occurred is, in part, attributable to the concrete activities of these organizations. These activities are indicative of the role NGOs play in developing consent for democratic transitions.

This chapter considers the evolution and impact of international NGO democracy promotion activities in East Asia. The analysis is limited to the study of four NGOs and the cases are treated selectively. American-based organizations are selected for study because of the pre-eminent role the United States has played in the region.

The chapter argues that international NGO democracy promotion activity needs to be understood as a manifestation of political globalization. Political globalization, as conceptualized by Philip Cerny, refers to the shaping of the playing field of politics being increasingly determined not within insulated units (such as a particular state) but, rather, deriving from complex multi-level games played on multi-layered playing fields, above and across, as well as within, state bounds.[3]

Globalization and NGOs

Increasingly, the international architecture of collective institutions and formal agreements enshrines the principles of democracy and human rights and the legitimacy of international action to promote them.[4] International activities promoting democracy have grown significantly in the past twenty years and, in a post-cold war context, are a fertile area for NGO involvement.

Of the four NGOs that are the focus of this chapter one of them, the International Republican Institute, has promoting democracy abroad as its sole purpose. The other three – The Asia Foundation, the Ford Foundation and the Carter Center – have broader purposes but have been active in promoting democracy as well.

The Asia Foundation

The Asia Foundation states that it is a private, non-profit, non-governmental organization 'dedicated to advancing the mutual interests of the United States and the Asia Pacific region'.[5] The Asia Foundation receives funding from corporations, foundations, individuals, and government organizations from within the United States and Asian nations. Despite its claims to be a non-governmental organization, The Asia Foundation is better characterized as a quasi-governmental, but privately run, organization. All NGOs have to answer to their constituencies and fiscal authorities. In the case of The Asia Foundation, its heavy reliance upon government funding brings into question the autonomous status which is usually associated with organizations claiming to be non-governmental.[6] The bulk of The Asia Foundation's financial support stems from grants made by United States government agencies and from the State Department, while some support is also provided by other governments, multilateral organizations and private foundations.[7]

The United States government's relationship with The Asia Foundation has not been without controversy. In the context of the cold war, the 1967 exposé by a former agent that the Central Intelligence Agency (CIA) was a major funding source for The Asia Foundation sent 'shockwaves throughout the countries of Asia, particularly those where the Foundation maintained its field offices.'[8] The revelation led to the closure of several field offices in Southeast Asia.

Sino-American rapprochement altered The Asia Foundation's role in the region. It ceased a policy of assisting only anti-communist states. At present, The Asia Foundation collaborates with Asian and other partners from the public and private sectors to 'support leadership and institutional development, exchanges and dialogue, technical assistance, research, and policy engagement related to: governance and law; economic reform and development; women's political participation and international relations.'[9] The Asia Foundation has fourteen project offices within the United States and Asia. It has offices in Beijing, Hong Kong, South Korea and, until recently, Taiwan. These offices function with quite a high degree of autonomy from The Asia Foundation's San Francisco headquarters. As such, funding for local projects has tended to reflect the particular interests of the American representatives posted in each country.

The Asia Foundation's status in Taiwan changed in 1997. The Foundation was contemplating closing the Taiwan office in order to focus more of its resources on China. A number of previous grantees in Taiwan decided to negotiate with the Foundation to establish a joint venture. Former grantees established a locally incorporated non-profit organization known as the Asia Foundation in Taiwan (AFIT). As partners, the AFIT and The Asia Foundation have developed a program that 'stresses non-profit sector development; entrepreneurship and small and medium enterprise development; and enhancing cross-Strait and regional relations through co-operative projects'.[10] A primary focus of the office is to help cross-Strait exchanges. It is thought that AFIT can assist in this goal because it is 'easier culturally to work with China through Taiwan'.[11] The AFIT office receives roughly 70 per cent of its operational funding from sources in Taiwan and 30 per cent from the United States.

The South Korean office of The Asia Foundation was established at the end of the Korean War. The level of funding for the Foundation's South Korean office has been quite low in the past five years, and closing the office was contemplated. However, the importance of continuing an in-country presence and maintaining the Seoul office has increased since The Asia Foundation began its activities in North Korea.

In 1995, the President of The Asia Foundation offered assistance to North Korea. The North Korean government suggested commencing international skills training programs and educational efforts in the field of agriculture. The scope of activities has subsequently extended to include health, international law, and international economic and business practice 'in an effort to expose North Koreans to other countries in the region and the West'.[12] The Asia Foundation agreed to the North Koreans' original request for program assistance principally to develop a relationship.[13]

Unlike countries in Southeast Asia such as Thailand, where The Asia Foundation projects also receive funding from the United States Agency for International Development, the Korea program is driven by different factors. As both South Korea and Taiwan have developed economically and politically, the justification for retaining an in-country presence has altered. During the cold war The Asia Foundation's interest in Taiwan and South Korea was influenced by Taiwan and South Korea's function, in American foreign policy, as bastions against communism. Now, the organization's presence in these nations serves as a conduit to assist in the development of closer ties with North Korea and China.

International Republican Institute (IRI)

In 1983, during the Reagan administration, the Congress established the National Endowment for Democracy (NED). The IRI has become a core grant recipient of NED funding. The IRI is also funded by the United

States Agency for International Development, as well as by contributions from individuals, corporations and foundations. The financial connection of the IRI with the NED moors it to a specific ideological conception of democracy promotion. The NED was born from a conception of democracy promotion as a form of public diplomacy in the '"war of ideas" between communism and democracy'.[14] Some CIA political programs were transferred to the NED, reflecting an increased openness within the administration about its transnational promotion of certain kinds of political influence.[15] The discretionary programming of the NED continues to reflect an anti-communist focus, particularly in Asia through efforts in Burma, China, North Korea and Vietnam.[16]

IRI activity cannot, therefore, avoid reflecting American foreign policy interests. The IRI began work in Central and South America, and subsequently expanded its efforts to other regions. The IRI asserts that its programs are 'non-partisan and clearly adhere to fundamental American principles such as individual freedom, equal opportunity, and the entrepreneurial spirit that fosters economic development'.[17] IRI programs have, however, been criticized for being partisan. For instance, IRI pre-election political party training seminars held in Moscow during 1991 were criticized for displaying a distinct Republican Party slant through their emphasis on the virtues of free enterprise.[18]

The character of the IRI is revealed not only by its relationship with the NED but also by the Republican Party politicians who sit on its governing board of directors. Senator John McCain, who was a serious contender during 2000 for the Republican Party's nomination for President, chairs the IRI's board of directors. The board of directors includes Republicans from the Senate and the House of Representatives and as well as key American conservative figures. The IRI is thus ideologically, politically and financially intertwined with particular conservative interests within the United States.

The Carter Center

The connection between the Carter Center and the Democratic Party is not quite as overt as the relationship between the IRI and the Republican Party. Founded in 1982 by former Democrat President Jimmy Carter and his wife Rosalynn, the Carter Center is associated with Emory University. According to its own publicity, the Carter Center is not officially affiliated with any political, religious, or governmental organization. In contrast to the IRI, criticisms of political bias do not seem to be levelled against Carter Center programs. However, the Carter Center, through Jimmy Carter, has connections with the Democratic Party and could be considered to function as a quasi-think tank for that political party.

The Carter Center benefits from the high-level access to political and media channels that is a consequence of Jimmy Carter's involvement. The academic base of Emory University and Jimmy Carter's stature as a former

President of the United States of America combine to enable the Carter Center to embark on some distinctive and influential international activities. The Carter Center has assumed a role in international diplomacy. It created the International Human Rights Council to 'help prevent rights violations worldwide' and the International Negotiation Network to address civil conflicts in places such as Sudan, Bosnia, Ethiopia and the Korean Peninsula.[19] Jimmy Carter has at times taken on the role of a roving diplomat for the United States and his imprimatur is clearly stamped on the Carter Center's activities.[20] This is particularly so in relation to the Carter Center's work in China; Mr Carter himself regarding 'sound Sino-American relations, along with the importance of maintaining human rights as a foundation of American foreign policy, to be legacies of my [Presidential] administration'.[21]

A board of trustees, chaired by Jimmy Carter, governs the Carter Center. The board of trustees includes a former Democrat Senator and the United States' former Ambassador to South Korea. The Carter Center's 2004 annual operating budget of US$36 million is significantly smaller than the Ford Foundation's. The funding is derived from private donations from individuals, foundations, corporations and multilateral development assistance programs.

NGO connections with corporations are relevant considerations in an assessment of their role as international actors. The influence of corporate funding upon the nature of NGO activity is difficult to determine, but it would be unwise to assume that the NGO activities are independent of the funding source. Corporate support for, and interest in, Chinese political reform is likely to be connected to a perception of the importance of China as a potential market. The Carter Center acknowledges the support of the Coca-Cola Company, the Starr Foundation (which receives most of its funding from GIO Insurance), the Southern Company, and the Archer-Daniels-Midland Company in enabling it to begin its efforts in China and to undertake its first two election observation missions. Interestingly, it can be difficult to get corporations to fund the Carter Center's China program because some corporations fear the project is too political. In order to secure funding, the Carter Center emphasizes what it sees as the long-term benefits of the program, such as fostering the rule of law, and political stability. Some of the corporations that are willing to fund the China project do not want the Centre to publish their support because of its sensitive nature.[22]

The Carter Center invited a representative from Shell Developments China Limited to participate in its election observation mission in Fujian Province during August 2000. The Carter Center hoped to attract Shell funding. At the end of the trip, the Shell representative expressed scepticism about Shell assisting the Carter Center to promote village democracy.[23] Significantly, his major question regarding the Carter Center China program was 'will it contribute to stability?'

The Ford Foundation

The Ford Foundation was founded in 1936 and, since its creation, has been an independent, non-profit, non-government, philanthropic organization. The Ford Foundation does not have financial links with government or with political interest groups in the United States. Indeed, the Ford Foundation is not only avowedly non-governmental, it is not connected to any specific national government. The Ford Foundation's board of trustees, in contrast to The Asia Foundation, the Carter Center or the IRI, reflects an international focus and includes individuals from nations other than the United States, including Great Britain, India and South Africa.[24] An Australian currently leads the Ford Foundation's operations in China.

The Ford Foundation has provided over US$8 billion in grants and loans, funded from an investment portfolio that began with gifts and bequests of Ford Motor Company stock. Throughout the 1950s and 1960s, the Ford Foundation's budget for overseas activities exceeded that of all other private organizations and indeed of many United Nations and bilateral development organizations.[25] The Ford Foundation's investment portfolio was valued at US$14.5 billion at the end of the 2000 financial year.[26] The financial independence of the Ford Foundation gives it considerable latitude in determining the types of programs it funds, and its financial resources give it potential influence on the ground within host countries.

The Ford Foundation encourages activities and initiatives among people living and working where the 'problems' are located. Like The Asia Foundation it has offices in Asia, including an office in Beijing. It also has offices in New York, Africa, Latin America and Russia. Ford Foundation program officers in international offices 'explore opportunities to pursue the Foundation's goals, formulate strategies, and recommend proposals for funding'.[27] As a consequence of having offices and program staff in various countries, the Ford Foundation has the advantage of local knowledge and networks. Although the Foundation is financially independent, the desire to maintain an office in a particular country may influence its decision to fund politically sensitive or unpopular projects.

NGO approaches

A significant amount of democracy promotion activity stems from the United States and, in particular, from American-based NGOs. The development of democracy promotion activities rose in the mid-1960s, diminished in the 1970s, and increased dramatically from the late-1980s onwards.[28] Early NGO programs were not so self-consciously devoted to promoting democracy. Park Tae-jin, a long-term employee in The Asia Foundation's Seoul office, observes 'the vocabulary was different'.[29] Early NGO activities emphasized development. At present, however, the lexicon is of democracy and governance. One of the compelling reasons behind NGO and government support of democracy promotion is the belief that democracies do not go to war against each other.[30] As Miyume Tanji and Stephanie Lawson point out, this begs the question – what kind of democracies do not war with each other? They argue that the 'implicit mission of the democratic peace thesis seems to be the universalization of a particular concept of liberal democracy'.[31]

The model of democracy encouraged by American-based NGOs certainly reflects Western liberal democratic understandings. It seems to be underpinned by the assumption that democratic transitions all over the world share basic characteristics and that, if each major socio-political institution can become like counterpart institutions located within Western democracies, the particular society as a whole will become more democratic.[32]

Such democracy promotion activities have been criticized as a Western conceit. Some political analysts have proposed alternative models of political development, based on specifically 'Asian' understandings of concepts such as virtue, law and democracy, and they deny the universal applicability of Western ideas of democracy.[33] As outlined in Chapter 4, some argue that there are institutional, organizational and ideological constraints that not only preclude democracy, but also make democracy an inappropriate political form for Asian states.[34]

Consideration of such arguments about bias is not evident in the publications of the NGOs under study. There appears to be little explicit consideration of conceptions of democracy that consider the specific cultural, historical or political milieu, even though this might facilitate an outcome where democracy might develop and endure with deeper roots.

Early NGO activities in the region

The Asia Foundation and the Ford Foundation were among the first non-government organizations to be active in the region. The Asia Foundation was founded in 1954, and established permanent offices in the region soon after. It replaced the Committee for Free Asia, which was active between 1951 and 1953. It was anticipated that The Asia Foundation programs in South Korea and Taiwan would underpin American security and economic arrangements, which were designed to stop the spread of communist influence.

The Ford Foundation characterizes its provision, between 1952 and 1979, of more than US$40 million to support Chinese studies, national collections of Chinese-language library materials, and associations and committees studying China as part of its China program.[35] Interestingly, the beneficiaries of these grants were in the United States, United Kingdom, Australia, India and Japan. No American-based NGO was active in China until after 1979. The Ford Foundation did not open an office in China until 1988.

In the 1950s and 1960s, encouraging economic development was a primary focus of both policy-makers in the region and international non-government organizations. As discussed in Chapter 2, during the 1960s modernization theory dominated understandings of economic and political development. Translated into policy terms, this meant that the promotion of economic development was regarded as concomitantly promoting democracy. Thus, democratic development was regarded (if at all) as an indirect consequence of other programs. Early international NGO activities in the region reflected this logic. It was thought that every nation state could achieve modernization through the prudent management of domestic resources, and that the provision of foreign technical assistance and technologies could speed up this process.[36]

At first The Asia Foundation focussed its resources on the domestic elite. This is apparent in its programs during the 1950s in South Korea and Taiwan. However, both The Asia Foundation and the Ford Foundation programs in China from 1979 onwards exhibited a similar tendency. Scholars, senior bureaucrats, and other community leaders were the major beneficiaries of their programs. Funding for overseas study tours by local academics and the development of diplomatic skills among foreign affairs bureaucrats were aimed at assisting in the rapid development of diplomatic and trade ties. An interest in strengthening public administration and human resources was also evident. These types of programs, which focussed on budgeting, project development, and personnel management, had no specific democracy promotion focus.[37]

The suppression of the protest at Kaohsiung in Taiwan in 1979, the Park regime's repressive *Yushin* period in South Korea, and reforms within China led international NGOs to alter the emphasis of their programs. Nascent democratic trends in South Korea and Taiwan were encouraged through activities that supported governmental, electoral and legislative reforms, and media development programs. In China, although significant law and governance initiatives were added to the suite of international NGO programs, media programs remain a comparatively undeveloped area of international NGO activity.

Training, research and resources

An overview of some of The Asia Foundation and the Ford Foundation's programs reveals the evolution of their programs. Clearly, developing educational opportunities dominated early international NGO activities in East Asia. For example, in Taiwan The Asia Foundation programs focussed on strengthening the island's universities and in South Korea its programs enabled the provision of art supplies, paper (including rice paper), books, newsprint and offset paper. These programs aimed at filling the gap in supplies that was a consequence of the Korean War. Early international NGO programs in China involved the provision of books, direct support for academic and professional exchanges through conferences, short-term visits and workshops. Consistent with Chinese priorities, activities concentrated on scientific and technical knowledge, economics, and international relations.

The Asia Foundation's media and communications programs began in the 1960s when it provided assistance to enable South Korean participation in the Nieman Fellowship program at Harvard. A few years after his completion of the program, the first participant, Kim Yong-koo, was fired from his paper, *Hanguk Ilbo*, because of his alleged 'anti-government' reporting.[38] For ten years Korean candidates were accepted into the program. However, during the *Yushin* period, the Fellowship Committee ceased accepting nominees from South Korea. The decision was made in protest against the Park regime's blatantly repressive media policies. In Taiwan, The Asia Foundation helped to establish the first school of journalism, and continued to provide it with funding until 1980. The programs were designed to enhance professionalism through organizing local participation in national and international training seminars.

According to Rex Wang, at this time The Asia Foundation was the only organization supporting such activities.[39] Press freedom was highly constrained in Taiwan under martial law. The Asia Foundation sent four groups of journalists and a number of political cartoonists to the United States. The Asia Foundation programs in this field were aimed at encouraging the development of a free press. The Asia Foundation's media and communications programs in China have consistently been the smallest area of its programming, and – compared to its other areas of activity – the Ford Foundation is not very active in this area either.[40]

It is evident that domestic political developments impact upon in-country programming. After the events of June 4 1989, notwithstanding the domestic and international political sensitivities at the time, the Ford Foundation's Beijing office maneouvred to continue its programs. The Asia Foundation abandoned providing funding to the Congressional Fellowship Program during the *Yushin* period, and it was not reinstated until 1980. By contrast, from 1980 onwards, The Asia Foundation began a series of politically connected programs in Taiwan. The Congressional Fellowship Program was initiated after the Kaohsiung protest.[41] The Asia Foundation selected the participants, and the selection process tended to favour younger scholars and politicians, including non-Party politicians.[42] The program staff feared that if the political structure was not changed in Taiwan to 'give the opposition air, there might be a big revolution'.[43]

The Asia Foundation's rule of law programming began in South Korea in the early 1960s. Two revolutions occurred at the beginning of that decade, one a democratic revolution led by students and the other an authoritarian one led by the military. David Steinberg was appointed as a Representative to South Korea in 1963, and he began to cultivate the legal field. Initially, the emphasis was on the judiciary. Judges were sent to the United States, and an internship program initiated. Program participants then established their own training program. The Asia Foundation provided grants to Seoul National University Law School for research and the publication of legal textbooks. Professor Jay Murphy, from the University of Alabama, spent a year researching law in South Korea. Based on Professor Murphy's recommendations, further programs were initiated by The Asia Foundation.

In Taiwan, legal aid services were established in 1972 while Allen Choate was The Asia Foundation Representative. During the first two to three years, money was provided to support its growth, then in the fourth year, funding was based on project proposals for initiatives such as international exchanges, conferences and seminars. The program started in the face of Kuomintang disapproval. The police, who tried to establish that the society was a syndicate, investigated the legal aid society. According to Rex Wang, the program contributed to altering the concept of law and lawyer, the 'law was no longer simply about helping the establishment.'[44] The China Law Society (now the Taiwan Law Society) provided a centre where young lawyers could meet. Some of those imprisoned in 1980, after the Kaohsiung protest, were members of the society. In June 2000 President Chen Shui-bian met The Asia Foundation's Chairman, William Fuller. President Chen acknowledged that he was an indirect beneficiary of The Asia Foundation through his voluntary work for the legal aid society, participation at local conferences, and access to books.[45]

Acceptance of foreign financial and technical assistance for China's legal aid program is a sensitive matter for the Chinese government. The May 1997 Justice Ministry Notice on Legal Aid Work prohibited the acceptance of international aid.[46] Subsequently, the prohibition has been relaxed somewhat, but international NGOs offering to work in this area still undergo close scrutiny – especially when the offers are for assistance from US based organizations.[47] The Asia Foundation and the Ford Foundation are among the principal international NGOs supporting legal aid development in China. The Ford Foundation was a pioneer donor in the area of legal aid in China, supplying grants to a number of university-based and women's group-operated legal services.

During the 1980s, Ford Foundation collaboration in China extended to include other countries in Asia, the Middle East, Africa, and Latin America. After its Beijing office opened, the Ford Foundation continued its work in economics, law and international affairs, while developing new areas of work in rural poverty, resource management and reproductive health. Between its opening in 1988 and September 1995 the Ford Foundation made grants totalling about US$50 million in China.[48] The Ford Foundation's law, rights and governance program began with training law teachers and researchers, and this area of programming continues to be important to the Foundation.

According to Park Tae-jin, a program officer in South Korea, between the 1950s and the 1980s, The Asia Foundation was the 'only game in town' in the region. When The Asia Foundation first began its activities in the region there was little competition from other international non-governmental organizations. Its programs focussed on developing human capital in order to assist with economic development, and improving the media and rule of law according a liberal democratic model. Democratization was regarded as an implicit outcome of this process. The Asia Foundation's focus in East Asia shifted during the 1980s, to include a more specific interest in democracy promotion. Now, there are many organizations in the region who promote themselves as democratization focussed. The Asia Foundation and the Ford Foundation are just two of the large number of international NGOs working in the region.

Recent NGO activities in China

The chapter turns now to a detailed analysis of more recent democracy promotion efforts in the largest non-democracy in the region, China. The village self-governance projects, in which the NGOs under study here are involved, were not initiated at the grass-roots level in the villages. In 1993, China's Ministry of Civil Affairs, the ministry responsible for administering the Organic Law of Villagers' Committees, invited a number of international NGOs and multilateral bodies, such as the UNDP, to assist with and advise on China's village self-governance initiatives.[49] The Asia Foundation, the IRI, the Carter Center and the Ford Foundation focus on assisting and advising China's Ministry of Civil Affairs. Their democracy assistance programs in China cluster around three areas, training and research, conferences and election observation missions.

Training and research

Support from The Asia Foundation, the IRI, the Ford Foundation and the Carter Center has been used to conduct research and surveys, and to fund Chinese officials to observe elections in the United States.

The Carter Center has also provided funding and assistance for the establishment of an election data gathering operation, and the dissemination of election information, through the training of officials and the publication of election materials. A Memorandum of Understanding was signed on 14 March 1998 between the Carter Center and the Ministry of Civil Affairs. The Memorandum of Understanding relates to three areas: exchanges and visits; promoting standardized village election procedures; and establishing a data information network and training related to the information network.[50] Over the following three months, the Ministry of Civil Affairs and the Carter Center developed data collection forms and software, raised money for computers and training, and transmitted the forms to the villages.[51] Then, in late June 1998, the Carter Center conducted a mission to China to pilot the data collection system in three provinces. In June 1999, the Carter Center signed a new Memorandum of Understanding with the Ministry of Civil Affairs, designed to extend their activities into 2000. It is intended that the data collection system will generate information in relation to village elections throughout China, and that this information will be available on the internet. The Ministry of Civil Affairs will utilize the data to target training and resources in areas experiencing problems implementing village self-governance. By June 1999, more than 3,200 villages had contributed data, and a data verification project commenced in September 1999.

According to Zhang Mingliang, Director-General, Department of Basic-Level Governance at the Ministry of Civil Affairs, this project will 'eventually revolutionize election data gathering and analysis for officials at both the provincial and national levels', and will assist in determining where to concentrate resources on training or procedural standardization.[52] It is too early to evaluate whether the project will achieve this objective. There is a tension between funding direct training versus spending sums of money on hardware such as computers. It may be that the greatest interest in, and use for, the data collection project will be found within the international academic community rather than within China itself.

Conferences

The Asia Foundation funded the first conference on village self-governance in China. Soon after, in 1992, the Ford Foundation's activities began with the sponsorship of a conference in Beijing to discuss village self-governance. A range of international China scholars attended the 1992 Ford Foundation conference. Prominent among them were Kevin O'Brien, who had recently done field work in Fujian Province, and Tyrene White, who had conducted field studies in Liaoning Province. During the conference, both O'Brien and White stressed the importance of introducing 'one vote one value' to replace the existing system of proxy voting in which the patriarch cast the household's votes.[53]

The Ministry of Civil Affairs credits this Ford Foundation conference with the introduction in Fujian Province of a system of 'one vote one value'. Local leaders had resisted the system, arguing that women and elders were difficult to mobilize. Ministry officials drew upon the scholars' argument and warned the local officials that they were jeopardizing China's international image in resisting the reform.[54] In 1993 legislation was passed in Fujian Province enshrining universal suffrage. According to the IRI, the role of the Ford Foundation in this instance serves as an example of the 'vast potential impact of international assistance in reforming local governance ... where the suggestion of a single delegation effectively enfranchised over ten million people, particularly women'.[55]

This example is interesting, because it provides an insight into the way that the NGO presence assisted the Ministry of Civil Affairs to create local consent for the reform. The Ministry of Civil Affairs stressed to the provincial leaders that China's international image was at stake if they ignored the advice of the international scholars. Thus, it was not only the merit of the recommendation, or the fact that it was suggested by international observers that determined its fate. Rather, the Ministry of Civil Affairs succeeded in motivating provincial leaders by framing an image of local failure against China's global image.

On 7–8 August 2000 the Carter Center and the Ministry of Civil Affairs sponsored a conference to revise and update the National Procedures on Village Committee Elections. Fifty-five participants represented the provincial and central offices of the Ministry of Civil Affairs; also present were officials from the Committee on Internal and Judicial Affairs of the National People's Conference, the Central Organization Department of the Party, and scholars from universities in Hong Kong, China and the United States. The IRI had assisted in the preparatory work for the conference, which resulted in seven suggestions being debated at the conference. The Carter Center stressed the introduction of a more detailed national election law to assist in the standardization of village committee election procedures, the establishment of a national electoral commission, and the creation of stronger legal sanctions against electoral violations.[56]

The issues raised by the Carter Center at the conference reflect its current focus on national issues. IRI programs have tended to target Fujian Province. The Carter Center has struggled with the question of where to direct its China program – at the provincial or the national level. If NGOs engage in programs at the national level, the Ministry of Civil Affairs is more intrusive than if the organization focuses on provincial level reform. On the one hand, if NGOs focus their programs in a particular province, they have a degree of autonomy from the Chinese central government. The disadvantage of this strategy is that it limits the number of potential beneficiaries of their activities. On the other hand, if NGOs adopt a national focus, they experience greater central government interference.

Election observation

In 1994, the IRI conducted the first international NGO election observation mission in China in Fujian Province. Drawing upon its observations, the IRI recommended that the most urgent reform required was the provision to voters of practical opportunities to exercise their right to a secret ballot.[57] The recommendation was adopted, with the Ministry of Civil Affairs directly attributing the introduction of the secret ballot to the recommendation of the international observers.[58] Whereas no elections in Fujian Province had been conducted using secret ballots in 1989, by 1997 95 per cent of elections were conducted by secret ballot.[59] In 1998, the National People's Council promulgated a revised Organic Law of Villagers' Committees. Among the revisions was the inclusion, under article 14, of the provision to voters of the right to a secret ballot.

The Carter Center and the IRI have both noted improvements in electoral processes between their missions in areas that had been the subject of recommendations. Among these improvements were efforts to improve the secrecy of the ballot, to synchronize election days to improve civic education opportunities, to ban the use of proxy voting during elections, and to enable candidates to appoint monitors to oversee voting at polling stations. In its 1997 report, the IRI noted 15 changes to procedures that had been implemented since its 1994 mission.[60]

While it is difficult to ascertain the degree to which NGO recommendations and the provisions under the revised Organic Law will spread throughout China, it appears that the NGOs have contributed to the development of village self-governance, a process that is providing villagers in China with behavioural training and experience of democratic processes.

NGO approaches to observing elections

Unlike The Asia Foundation and the Ford Foundation, which have tended to adopt a facilitative approach in which they provide funding and assistance to improve the capacity of locals, the IRI and the Carter Center adopt a more participatory approach in which they directly observe the elections and make recommendations. In this section, a critique of the election-observation approach adopted by the IRI and the Carter Center is conducted. It is based upon an assessment of the 'mission statements' issued by the two organizations, and the author's observation of a Carter Center mission. The analysis reveals that the NGOs style of election observation gives little consideration to power relations and value differences. The analysis covers two IRI reports (relating to its election observation missions in Fujian Province during May 1994 and May 1997) and two Carter Center reports (relating to its missions in Fujian and Hebei Provinces during March 1997 and in Jilin and Liaoning Provinces during March 1998). Provincial level officials from the Ministry of Civil Affairs select which villages the NGOs will observe, and as a consequence, the best villages are showcased.

Each of the reports provides recommendations to the Ministry of Civil Affairs. The avowed purpose of the first IRI report included evaluation of the electoral process, identification of the strengths and weaknesses of the system, and the provision of recommendations to the Ministry for future elections.[61] The aim of the second IRI report was to observe and assess the 'development' of village committee elections in Fujian Province.[62] The purpose of the Carter Center's March 1997 report was to 'observe and assess village elections and to offer ideas to the Ministry of Civil Affairs on ways the process could be improved'.[63] In March 1998, the Carter Center mission broadened its purpose, reflecting the quasi-diplomacy in which the Carter Center engages. Its March 1998 report outlined the Carter Center's aim of developing long-term co-operation with the Ministry of Civil Affairs.[64]

The skills of the election observers selected by the two organizations to participate were quite different, yet they produced similar recommendations in their reports. Observers on IRI missions to China were a mix of United States-based IRI staff and American election officials and experts.[65] By contrast, the Carter Center missions included a significant number of academics. Its 1997 mission included a mix of independent scholars, a management consultant and the director of Program Development for The Asia Foundation, while the 1998 mission also included three photographer-cinematographers.[66]

Divergence between IRI and Carter Center reports might have been expected given the broad scope of the missions and the differences in the composition of their delegations. However, the structure, content and recommendations of the IRI and Carter Center reports are similar and relate primarily to technical improvements. The technical issues raised in the reports relate to training, candidate nomination processes, election monitoring, campaigning, fraud, various forms of balloting (for example, roving, proxy, absentee), secrecy and tools for illiterate voters. The utilization by the IRI and the Carter Center of a strategy of institutional modelling is reflected in the report recommendations. For example, the IRI and the Carter Center have both recommended establishing a national independent election commission.

The similarity between the IRI and the Carter Center reports reflects their shared assumptions about democracy promotion. Both NGOs employ an established US-derived frame of analysis in election observation missions. While this approach to election monitoring, advising and report writing has the virtue of being methodologically transparent, it is in danger of excluding from consideration other aspects that may be relevant to a particular local issue. For example, the Carter Center encourages officials to pay more attention to the electoral process and less to whether the villagers are electing competent individuals.[67] This highlights what seem to be value differences between the NGO and the local society. The NGO focuses on procedures, whereas the local actors, perhaps reflecting their own Confucian traditions, may prefer to be ruled by people who 'instrumentalize the virtue of the good ruler'.[68]

Strikingly, the NGOs under study do not define the type of democracy they are promoting and, at times, seem even to avoid using the term democracy. While taking care in the terminology used in their reports regarding village self-governance, the IRI and the Carter Center reports quote the views of Chinese officials and leaders on democracy without attempting to identify what meaning is intended. For example, the Carter Center cites then President Jiang Zemin's praise of village elections at the 15th Party Congress.[69] Yet at that Congress, Jiang Zemin had emphasized that the Party would not adopt Western models of democracy and, as Tianjin Shi highlights, the Ministry of Civil Affairs is careful to always refer to 'socialist democracy'.[70] However, an institutional modelling approach, notwithstanding its limitations, has the advantage of avoiding sensitive political issues when applied in China.

The IRI and Carter Center reports do not discuss or provide recommendations on matters relating to power relations among domestic actors. The question of why proxy voting is practised is not considered by the NGOs. By failing to consider the historical or cultural environment in which they operate, the NGOs miss an opportunity to discuss and debate strategies that might assist further in the development of village self-governance. Paradoxically, this neglect or oversight encourages a hybrid form of democracy to develop, in which electoral practices evolve with Chinese characteristics. The NGOs do not delve deeply into the nature of campaigning in China, the role of *guanxi*, clan influence in villages, or other issues with historical or cultural roots. As Thomas Carothers argues, there is a need to move beyond formalistic attempts at 'institutional modelling'; the real challenge for NGOs is to coax along processes of change that take account of the underlying interests and power relations in which institutions are embedded.[71] This suggests that greater consideration needs to be given to the local political environment than is at present the case.

The institutional modelling approach adopted by the IRI and the Carter Center may reflect a strategic choice by the NGOs, given the political environment in China. If the NGOs engage in activities that are perceived as challenging Chinese Communist Party authority and local power structures, the NGOs' longer-term ambitions might be thwarted. Alternatively, it may simply be a consequence of the limited time the NGOs actually spend in each village.

The village elections observed by the Carter Center in August 2000 in Dehua and Xianyou counties in Fujian Province did not enable time for an analysis of the issues raised above. Prior to the Carter Center's arrival in the village, township and provincial officials from Ministry of Civil Affairs briefed the Carter Center on preparatory activities associated with the election. The nomination and campaign processes were not witnessed by the NGO. However, in one instance an edited videotape of campaign speeches was shown to the Carter Center delegation the evening before the election was observed.

Immediately after observing the mechanics of the actual ballot the Carter Center and its entourage of members of the Ministry of Civil Affairs, the Ministry of Foreign Affairs, and foreign media representatives departs. Overall, only a small amount of time is spent in the villages. In Quibian village, the Carter Center delegation observed one of Fujian Province's first 'sea' elections, *haixian*, in which nomination for candidature is open to all village residents. The Carter Center arrived at 8.30 am. Polling had commenced at 8.00 am. The Carter Center delegation stayed until the completion of the ballot count at 12.30 pm, then left immediately to travel to Xianyou County. The next day, two different village elections were observed. Although there is the opportunity to observe the ballot, there is little opportunity to analyse or assess the nomination process, campaigning techniques, the transfer of power, or interactions between the village's Party Secretary, Chair of the Villager Committee, and local villagers. As a consequence, recommendations tend to relate to the limited features that are actually observed. For example, at times more than one voter was in the ballot booth, or the secrecy of the ballot was not assured. Thus, the delegation's recommendations tended to focus upon these types of procedural matters.

Nonetheless, the Ministry of Civil Affairs attributes to the NGOs significant improvements to village democracy, such as the introduction of a secret ballot and of 'one vote one value'. The importance of a growing number of Chinese villagers being able to choose a village committee, to replace the committee at regular intervals, through a transparent process based upon the equal input of each citizen should not be overlooked. Critics of electoralism undervalue procedural improvements. They also inadequately conceive the multiple effects of NGO involvement. NGO engagement in democracy promotion in China has set in motion a process of political game-playing that needs to be assessed. It is this game, in which local and international actors utilize the elections to pursue their interests, that is best understood as a process of political globalization.

Global and local interactions

Philip Cerny's concept of political globalization provides an insight into the interplay of interests between international and local actors in East Asia. Cerny argues that, as a consequence of political globalization, the playing field of politics is shaped by multi-level games played on multi-layered international playing fields.[72] Political globalization intertwines domestic politics and international relations, with political actors facing increasingly complex situations when evaluating their options.[73]

The involvement of The Asia Foundation, the IRI, the Carter Center and the Ford Foundation in the region can be usefully interpreted in this context in terms of various political games played by East Asian and American political actors. For example, the Ministry of Civil Affairs is a small and not particularly powerful department within the Chinese central government apparatus. However, the involvement of international NGOs in villagers' committee elections assists the Ministry to develop support in other areas of the Chinese bureaucracy for its work. Ministry officials have tried to balance the competing demands of both conservatives and reformers. Through wisely using the resources and influence of the NGOs, by refusing to accept any preconditions to NGO involvement and by retaining control over the type of training provided, Ministry officials have attempted to appease opponents of their village self-governance program. The Ministry of Civil Affairs uses the publicity and profile that international involvement generates to make it difficult for domestic opponents of villagers' committee elections to undermine the Ministry and its reform program.[74]

In 1995 the *Washington Post* featured a favourable article about China's village self-governance program.[75] The Ministry of Foreign Affairs noted the positive reporting of the initiative in the international media. The

Ministry of Foreign Affairs and the Ministry of Civil Affairs then began to collaborate to promote villagers' committee elections internationally.

The involvement of international observers and the complimentary statements in NGO reports assist the Chinese government to present a positive image internationally on the sensitive issue of political rights.[76] Comments by one senior Chinese bureaucrat illustrate how NGO involvement assists in sending a positive message about Chinese political reform to the United States. Zeng Jianhui, the Chair of the Foreign Affairs Committee of the National People's Congress, thanked the Carter Center for its involvement stating that 'beyond helping Americans understand village elections you have done much to help the Chinese improve our elections by the recommendations in your reports'.[77]

Top leaders in China have begun praising village self-governance and associating themselves locally and internationally with the success stories. Former President Jiang Zemin characterized village self-governance as one of the 'great inventions' of Chinese farmers, and the usually conservative Li Peng visited Jilin Province to observe election nomination procedures.[78] Zhu Rongji, Premier of China, when asked in a news conference about the likelihood of elections spreading to the positions of Premier and President, responded by referring to an affirmative report written by an American foundation on the village elections.[79]

There is some debate about the degree to which village elections are being used as a public-relations stunt. Nathan is one observer who has suggested that the Ministry of Foreign Affairs is using the elections as a propaganda tool to a large degree.[80] On the other hand, Kelliher argues that, notwithstanding the utilization of village elections as a propaganda tool, the intent and purpose of the democratic reforms remain primarily instrumental.[81]

Even if the impetus for the introduction of villagers' committee elections was not to project a positive image internationally, the elections provide a public relations opportunity that is increasingly being exploited. In contrast to previous NGO missions, including the Carter Center's March 1997 mission, the Chinese government permitted the Carter Center mission in March 1998 to be accompanied by journalists from the *New York Times*, *Time*, CBS News and members of the Chinese press.

The degree to which the elections are being used to project a positive image internationally can be assessed by considering a number of articles written in the English-language Chinese newspaper the *China Daily* about Carter Center missions. The *China Daily* has been selected for analysis here because English-language papers are specifically aimed at an international audience.

A pattern emerges of increasing utilization of the media by the Chinese government to publicize its village election reforms abroad. The first Carter Center election observation mission in 1997 received no coverage in the *China Daily*. The second election observation mission of March 1998 generated two *China Daily* articles.[82] These articles profile the reforms, the Carter

Center's involvement, and quote Robert Pastor's praise of the process. Pastor, who was then Director of the Carter Center's China Program, said:

> China is doing it right. They are starting at the village level, trying to make sure that the technical elements of an election are working properly before they start moving that process up the ladder to the national level.[83]

Coverage in the *China Daily* of the Carter Center's July 1998 mission increased to four articles, including one by a member of the Carter Center mission.[84] The articles positively report the rural reforms, their impact on rural Chinese, and again, refer to the Carter Center's contribution and comments.

The growth of media coverage seems indicative of the desire of the Chinese government to promote internationally its reforms in village self-governance. By framing the coverage against a backdrop of the Carter Center's involvement, the articles convey an air of objectivity.

The degree to which NGOs are themselves engaging in a political game is rarely analysed. The Carter Center's interaction with the media is sophisticated. The Carter Center conducts media conferences in China and in the United States about its missions. While working for the Carter Center, Robert Pastor contributed articles regarding the Chinese elections to a range of print media publications.[85] During its March 1998 mission, the Carter Center delegation included two Emmy Award-winning documentary filmmakers and a photographer. The Carter Center wants to help 'publicize village elections both for training purposes within China and also to make them better known to a wider outside audience'.[86]

NGO reports have an audience in the United States. The high profile of IRI and Carter Center board members and mission participants, and the political networks in which they are engaged, give a correspondingly high profile to their reports, both within the United States and internationally. Corporations and governments often take an interest in such NGO reports because they frequently represent the first available information on political developments in developing countries.

Governments increasingly regard contributing international observers as a way of improving relations with other nations.[87] The involvement of US-based NGOs highlighted the issue of village elections for both the Republican and Democrat politicians. The IRI submitted a study paper to the Joint Economic Committee of the United States Congress in August 1998, titled 'China's Economic Future: Challenges to United States Policy', which included an analysis of village self-governance. Jimmy Carter briefed former Vice President Al Gore on Carter Center involvement in village self-governance in advance of the Vice President's trip to China, and Robert Pastor briefed officials from the National Security Council and the State Department.[88] During a Beijing press conference, Vice President Gore deflected a question on the sensitive topic of human rights by referring to discussions he had on the topic of villagers' committee elections with the President and the Premier of China.[89]

To some extent, governments wanting to improve their relationship with China have pointed to the apparent progress made on village elections to justify increasing their own engagement with China. Interest in the village elections is part of the bigger picture that governments are trying to paint of China, because it makes it easier for them to become more engaged with China. It is against this backdrop of complex and challenging relations between the United States and China that US-based NGO activities in China should be situated. This broader perspective does not devalue the achievements of the international NGOs, but rather, broadens our understanding of the functions and effects of some of their activities.

Conclusion

This chapter has analysed the characterization of The Asia Foundation, the IRI, the Carter Center and the Ford Foundation as non-governmental organizations, and considered NGO connections with clusters of power within the United States. It highlighted that, with the exception of the Ford Foundation, the NGOs studied are imbricated with particular ideological and political power groupings in the United States. While the IRI and the Carter Center participate directly in programs, such as their election observation missions, the Ford Foundation and The Asia Foundation tend to focus more exclusively on facilitating local capacity building through the provision of grants.

A review and assessment of some of the NGOs' programs acknowledged the contribution of the work of the NGOs, in particular in their role as agents of consent. However, it also revealed some limitations to the IRI and the Carter Center's method of democracy promotion. Moreover, human resource development and technical improvements attributable to the NGO programs represent only one aspect of the impact of NGO engagement in democracy promotion. The Asia Foundation's initial interest in South Korea and Taiwan reflected their geo-strategic importance to the United States. There is a paradox, however: where once The Asia Foundation's activities in South Korea and Taiwan were aimed at blocking the influence of their communist neighbours, The Asia Foundation now uses its presence in South Korea and Taiwan as a springboard for its programs in China and North Korea.

NGO involvement in promoting villagers' committee elections in China can be understood more broadly as illustrating the process of political globalization. Interpreted in this broader perspective, it becomes apparent that national and international actors are promoting and exploiting political reforms in China's villages in pursuit of their interests and political agendas. Though the impact is usually modest, democracy promotion activities are one of the most important means at policy-makers' disposal for advancing democratic transitions in other countries.[90] The increased salience of NGO activity since 1990, and the extent to which their activities might be manipulated by regimes, indicates that the interactive process between the domestic and international dimensions of democratization is complex and multifaceted.

Conclusion

Introduction

This book has shown that regime change in South Korea, Taiwan and China has been dialectically related to the international dimension of democratization and that (especially in the context of globalization) interactions between the international and domestic dimensions are complex and multi-directional. From the end of World War II until the present both incremental and sudden changes in international relations have occurred. These changes included shifts in the balance of power, ideological imperatives, and normative interests. A comparison of South Korea's and Taiwan's experience of international integration with that of China has revealed the effect of globalization upon the political development of the region.

Comparisons and patterns

The book has analysed the extent to which changes in the external context placed constraints or opportunities upon democratization, and shown under what circumstances the international context affected the choice of political institutions and actions. It has revealed a number of general tendencies rather than any one efficient cause. The research has also identified a number of differences between each of the cases, which affected their interactions with the international dimension of democratization.

If, as this book has contended, the international dimension evolved during the 1980s and 1990s in ways that facilitated democratic transition in South Korea and Taiwan, why did it not have a similar effect upon China, which remains a one-party state? The analysis has shown that, by the middle of the 1980s, the balance had shifted from international constraints against regime change in the region toward increased opportunities. In both South Korea and Taiwan this transformation coincided with changes in the balance of power among domestic social forces. The domestic and international dimensions of democratization interacted in ways that created a political opening, and moulded the opportunity for a transition from authoritarian rule toward democracy in South Korea and Taiwan. China experienced a brief period of political opening during this period, but it was quickly closed off by the authoritarian regime. Although the scope for influence by external actors and processes widened, China lacked domestic forces that were sufficiently powerful, motivated and aligned to produce democratic change.[1] Clearly, an international context conducive to democratization is an insufficient condition on its own; its impact and effect are dependent upon domestic political actors.

Another mediating factor, which explains why the impact of the international dimension within the region differed, is the degree of impermeability among the states concerned. From the end of World War II onwards, Taiwan and South Korea were permeated by external (particularly American) political, economic and cultural influences. By contrast, during the first 30 years of Chinese Communist Party rule, China was quite impermeable and its external relations with major powers were contentious. In the late 1970s Deng Xiaoping implemented policies designed to increase rapidly China's international economic integration. However, at the same time (and somewhat contradictorily), the political leadership in China initiated strategies aimed at insulating Chinese society from the 'polluting' effects of international integration.

The force of globalization has affected the Chinese Communist Party's ongoing efforts to protect the regime from external democratizing influences. The diffuse effects of participation in the global economy, engagement with and by multilateral institutions, cultural interactions, advances in communications technology, and the programs of international NGOs are increasing the permeability of the Chinese state. Autocratic regimes in South Korea and Taiwan were not exposed to the cross-cutting spectrum of international structures and processes interested in encouraging transparent government, accountability, and democratic development that the regime in China currently faces.

This research has identified that China's interactions with the international system also set it apart from South Korea and Taiwan. Both South Korea's and Taiwan's political, economic and security systems were vulnerable to shifts in American foreign policy. China's political system is less susceptible to external sanctions (both positive and negative). This is because of China's power internationally and regionally, and its practice of 'linkage *realpolitik*'. Clearly, China has not been a passive participant in the international system.

Since China became enmeshed in the international system, and especially since the political crisis in June 1989, China has used its material strength and a range of complex political and diplomatic manoeuvres to ensure that those aspects of the international order that it regards as undermining its sovereignty or threatening its stability are not invoked against it. China's interactions with the international system demonstrate the need to conceive of the multi-directional nature of influence when considering the international dimension of democratization.

The book has also identified a number of distinguishing features in the international dimension of democratization in South Korea and Taiwan. One of these concerns the way in which the 1988 Olympics affected South Korean democratization. Its role as the host country functioned to constrain the South Korean government from using force against the democracy movement, because the 'eyes of the world' were upon them. An important feature of South Korean political development was its bilateral relationship with the United States. The nature of the relationship has its roots in the Korean War and continues into the present. The book demonstrated that this relationship was a crucial external factor affecting the South Korean political elite's choice of institutions and actions. Its relationship with the United States affected the political, economic and security institutions of South Korea, and its policies.

By contrast, Taiwan's political, economic and cultural development has been greatly affected by two states, the United States and China. Over time, their relative degree of influence has altered, with China's role increasing in importance. Relations between the United States and China directly impacted upon Taiwan's status in the international community. Initially, this resulted in Taiwan's inclusion and China's exclusion from the United Nations. Subsequently, Sino-American rapprochement contributed to a reversal of that situation and, during the 1970s, China assumed a position in major international bodies, while Taiwan was excluded. Unlike North Korea and South Korea (where with the dual entry into the United Nations the sovereignty of the two halves has become part of the international status quo), Taiwan's lack of international diplomatic status remains a divisive issue, both internationally and domestically.

There are several important differences between China and Taiwan's response to, and experience of, international isolation. Between 1950 and 1972 China was shut out of the Western international order economically and diplomatically. The combination of these two factors reinforced totalitarian tendencies within the Chinese regime. By contrast, after the loss of its seat at the United Nations in 1972 Taiwan was politically but not economically isolated. Moreover, the loss of diplomatic recognition was the catalyst for a political crisis within the Kuomintang, and contributed to democratic development in Taiwan. For China the assumption of a position among the international community of states exposed Chinese government political practice to a higher degree of scrutiny and criticism. In response, the Chinese political leadership has engaged in human rights dialogue, while also attempting to control some of the terms of the debate. Thus, although integration and interdependence has not led to democratization in China, it has entangled China in human rights discourse.

Time contexts

Changes in the external context created both constraints and opportunities for democratization in the region. This is because changes in international relations impinged upon the range of plausible options available to domestic political actors. This suggests the importance of differentiating between time periods when assessing the international context.

Three distinct periods may be identified. The first began in 1945 and lasted until the early 1970s. In this period, the United States constituted the dominant source of external influence over the region. The United States exerted its power through both multilateral and bilateral channels. Bilaterally, the United States influenced the economic, political and security agenda of both South Korea and Taiwan. It negotiated security agreements and fostered preferential trade and aid arrangements. Multilaterally, the United States led the United Nations' decision to engage in the Korean War and to continue to recognize the Kuomintang regime in Taiwan as the legitimate leaders of China. Although the United Nations Charter established a right to democratic governance, in the context of the cold war this right was pragmatically interpreted by the major powers. Because the United States was keen to create a regional environment inhospitable to communism, autocratic rule in the East Asia region was tolerated provided it was not communist. American foreign policy succeeded in excluding China from the Western political and economic structures. This not only affected China's development prospects, but it also insulated the Chinese population from the diffusion of democratic ideas. During this phase, the international context actually functioned to inhibit democratic change in East Asia.

The second phase began during the 1970s with Sino-American rapprochement, and lasted until 1989. China's integration into the international order occurred at a time when the global balance of power shifted and the premonitory effects of globalization began to exert their influence. Regional economic relations increased in importance and, within the international community, the pursuit of economic interests superseded cold war ideological concerns. In addition, an international interest in human rights and democracy promotion grew. This normative shift increased the costs to authoritarian regimes of repressive and autocratic tactics. South Korea and Taiwan underwent a democratic transition during this period, and China embarked on a strategy of economic reform. In the course of these changes, hybrid political systems developed in the region.

The collapse of the Berlin Wall marked the beginning of a third phase. Interestingly, the effects of changes in the international context during this period were not uniform across different regional contexts. For example, the former Soviet Union's political and economic reform strategy, which precipitated its eventual collapse, had a democratizing effect in Europe. In East Asia, however, the demonstration effect of this event was decidedly antidemocratic. The Chinese Communist Party regarded the Soviet Union's experiences as a compelling example of the dangers of extensive political liberalization. In order to avoid national fragmentation China has accelerated economic reform while limiting political reform. In addition, in its efforts to maintain national unity, the Chinese state has employed repressive tactics in regional areas seeking greater autonomy, such as Tibet and

Xinjiang. The Chinese government has had some success in this strategy notwithstanding an expansion of normative concerns internationally.

International structures

The book suggests then that the significance, for democratization, of international structures may differ over time and place. Further, it contends that international economic and political structures significantly affected the choice of institutions and actions in East Asia.

Directly and indirectly, international economic and market factors conditioned aspects of political development in the region. The political context of the cold war crucially affected South Korea, Taiwan and China's development strategies and experience of international integration. The external context was used by the region's regimes to justify certain authoritarian political forms. As a consequence, the relative strength and autonomy of civil society was limited. International economic integration indirectly influenced the development of democracy movements in South Korea, Taiwan and China. America's trade and foreign policy began to focus on economic competition, and the labour and human rights standards in East Asia. These changes in the international context coincided with domestic changes. In South Korea and Taiwan they were the consequence of the cumulative effects of economic growth. In China, the Chinese Communist Party's market-oriented economic reforms contributed to a mounting crisis of domestic legitimacy.

International political interactions, exemplified by United Nations activities, directly and indirectly impacted upon the region's political regimes. The play of power politics within the United Nations had a notably ambiguous effect upon democratization in the region. United Nations intervention in Korea contributed to its stance on the question of the legitimacy of the Kuomintang versus the Chinese Communist Party government. On the one hand this was because the United Nations regarded China as a belligerent in the war, but on the other hand, it was also because the United States had come to regard Taiwan as a key component of a strategy to consolidate American security interests in the Pacific. Indirectly and unintentionally, the reversal of the United Nations position on the question of Taiwan's international status assisted Taiwan's nascent opposition movement to push for political reform. Since the Chinese government replaced the Kuomintang as a Permanent Member of the United Nations Security Council it has been on the receiving end of the United Nations expanded normative agenda. China's interactions with United Nations regimes represent a complex dialectic.

It is evident that international political structures, such as the United Nations, have had both a positive and an adverse impact upon democratization in the region. Interestingly, these effects have rarely been the result of explicit United Nations objectives. Rather, they have been unintentional consequences, occasioned when its most powerful members have used the international regime to pursue their particular interests in the region.

Diffuse international cultural exchanges are of less significance to regime change than political and economic interactions. The global culture of democracy has affected domestic actors' choice of political institutions. However, global culture has had a minimal impact upon domestic political behaviour. As such, whether or not political institutions function to create procedural or substantive democracy is largely determined by local political actors.

International actors

The case studies make evident the contingent nature of international actors' influence upon regime change in the region. This is because international actors are especially susceptible to shifts in the broader international context, and within their own interest groupings.

The multi-directional influence of the international dimension of democratization is particularly relevant to consideration of international actors, and the complexities associated with globalization. The democratizing effects of the democracy movement in Beijing during June 1989 extended beyond China's borders. Within several established democracies the international audience's response to the event stimulated active citizenship and constrained the range of policy choices available to the Western political elite. However, as the Tiananmen Square example demonstrates, even with poignant images and ingenious means of transmission, power is still an irreducible component of the international context, and coercion is still a resource available to national autocrats.[2]

American-based NGO programs in the region often reflect American foreign policy interests. As such, The Asia Foundation's activities in South Korea and Taiwan initially lacked a specific democracy promotion focus and served to underpin American security interests. A connection between American foreign policy and The Asia Foundation's programs in East Asia can still be identified. Their offices in Taiwan and South Korea are used as a springboard for their programs in China and North Korea.

United States-based NGO village self-government programs have contributed to a number of technical improvements to China's village democracy. However, the impact of the NGOs is broader than this. The examples discussed demonstrated the way in which the political elite in China and America spotlight certain NGO programs in order to foster closer relations, and deflect criticism of China's human rights record. It is apparent that the purpose and independence of such NGO programming should be considered. In some instances drawing a distinction between state and non-state actors is a difficult business.

Comments on previous research and theorizing

What, finally, is the significance of this research in terms of its contribution to theorizing on the international dimension of democratization?

The book demonstrated that studies of the international dimension of democratization ought to conceive this interactive process in multi-directional terms. This is done in order to avoid a dichotomous analysis in which *either* the domestic *or* the international dimension is exclusively assessed as an interdependent variable. Further, this research suggests that such an approach is particularly relevant to studies considering the role of international actors.

This research has made some progress toward filling a gap in empirical studies of the international dimension of democratization, which has curiously overlooked the Asian region. The empirical analysis has revealed that the international context has played a much greater role in the process of regime change in East Asia than is often acknowledged.

The book demonstrates that an approach which considers the international dimension of democratization is applicable beyond the Latin American and European contexts where it was initially formulated. This is important because, as Peter Evans observes, for research to be useful it needs to be conceptualized in ways that are potentially separable from the settings in which they were originally devised, that is, they have to speak to other cases as well.[3] Moreover, East Asia's experience suggests that combinations of three international factors – control, contagion and consent – have affected regime change in the region. For example, the influence of control is evident in the political outcome in South Korea. The influence of the American military command, the United Nations, and the threatening presence of North Korea indirectly and directly influenced South Korean political institutions and politics. Nonetheless, the South Korean case demonstrates that, in the absence of domestic consent for democratic norms, control is insufficiently capable of fostering democracy.

The effects of contagion were particularly evident in the region after the Philippines' democratic transition in 1986. The democracy movement in the Philippines influenced the strategies of democratic protestors throughout East Asia. The globalization of television news amplified the effects of such contagion. The 1989 democracy movement in Beijing highlighted the ambiguous democratizing function of contagion. Contagion affected the Chinese government's interpretation of the event and the student protestors' decision to continue to occupy Tiananmen Square.

Consent is the more complex of the factors, and involves four sub-categories: territorial limits, international and regional structures, national actors and their relationship with transnational groupings, as well as demonstration effects. Consent has been a vital factor affecting democratization in East Asia. International consent for territorial boundaries has been a key variable influencing politics in the region. South Korean policies designed to reunify the Korean peninsula, and the relationship between Taiwan and China, remain crucially affected by broader issues arising from international relations.

The creation of regional and international structures, in which membership is conditional upon a state's democratic status, is less relevant to East Asia than Europe. In no Asian regional organization is democracy a condition of membership. The region's experiences of conditionality have been limited to IMF and other financial institutions' measures. These were especially apparent after the Asian financial crisis, where some good governance conditions were imposed upon South Korea.

National actors from the region have a complex relationship with transnational groupings. The diaspora of each of the countries considered has contributed to the region's development both in economic and political terms. In addition, some social movements and political exiles from East Asia have benefited from international protection and a high profile. The importance of these relationships is evident in the role the international community played, intervening to protect the life of Kim Dae Jung twice during South Korea's authoritarian years.

Although international factors associated with democratic transition have been apparent across Latin America, Europe and East Asia, it is necessary, in concluding, to highlight a few of the regional differences. In the other cases (Europe in particular) regional organizations acted to encourage democracy; East Asia lacks such a regional impulse. Indeed, unlike the other regions there is not a regional human rights regime in East Asia. European and Latin American countries are close to the seat of the world's modern democracies, and many have had prior experience of democracy. The East Asian examples considered are not only geographically distant from the world's most powerful democracies, but also have had limited or no prior democratic experience. These features make the international dimension of democratization in East Asia particularly worthy of study.

Clearly, the impact of international structures of power upon East Asian political development has more in common with Latin America than with Europe. The geo-political interests of the United States generated direct interventions and support for the repressive apparatus of the state in several Latin American countries, and thus created an unfavourable balance of power between the state and civil society for democratization.[4] There are some obvious parallels between this and the experiences of South Korea and Taiwan during the cold war. By contrast, pressures from the northern European democracies (and in part also the United States) supported very different democratizing developments in Spain, Portugal and Greece.[5] The United States remains the single most influential external actor in the East Asian region, and the way in which it perceives its geo-political interests into the future will continue to have important consequences for the region's political systems.

Notes

Introduction

1 Adrian Karatnycky, 'The 1998 Freedom House Survey: The Decline of Illiberal Democracy', *Journal of Democracy*, 10, 1, 1999, p. 119.
2 Laurence Whitehead (ed.), *The International Dimensions of Democratization: Europe and the Americas*, New York: Oxford University Press, 1998; Geoffrey Pridham, Eric Herring and George Sanford (eds), *Building Democracy? The International Dimension of Democratization in Eastern Europe*, London: Leicester University Press, 1997; Geoffrey Pridham and Tatu Vanhanen (eds), *Democratization in Eastern Europe: Domestic and International Perspectives*, London, New York: Routledge, 1994; Bruce Parrot and Karen Dawisha (eds), *The International Dimension of Post-Communist Transitions in Russia and the New States of Eurasia*, Armonk, New York: M. E. Sharpe, 1997.
3 Although the role of the international context is implied in many studies of regime change in East Asia, it has rarely been the express focus. Examples in which the international context is the central focus include Ahn Byung-Joon, 'Korea's International Environment', in Thomas W. Robinson (ed.), *Democracy and Development in East Asia: Taiwan, South Korea and the Philippines*, Washington DC: The AEI Press, 1991, pp. 155–168 and Martin L. Lasater, 'Taiwan's International Environment', in Thomas W. Robinson (ed.), *Democracy and Development in East Asia: Taiwan, South Korea and the Philippines*, Washington DC: The AEI Press, 1991, pp. 91–104, and Robert Compton, *East Asian Democratization: Impact of Globalization, Culture and Economy*, Westport: Praeger, 2000. Compton analyses several of the opportunities and constraints presented to the region's leaders by globalization and changes in the international context.
4 The book focuses upon only a few of countries in the region: South Korea, Taiwan and China. Japan is not included as a case study although references to Japan are made throughout the text.
5 These research questions were drawn from a number proposed by Philippe C. Schmitter. See Philippe C. Schmitter, 'The Influence of the International Context upon the Choice of National Institutions and Policies in Neo-Democracies', in Laurence Whitehead (ed.), *The International Dimensions of Democratization: Europe and the Americas*, New York: Oxford University Press, 1998, p. 28.
6 For a discussion of the development of democracy in Japan see Robert E. Ward, 'Reflections on the Allied Occupation and Planned Political Change in Japan', in Robert E. Ward (ed.), *Political Development in Modern Japan*, Princeton:

Princeton University Press, 1969, pp. 477–537; Rikki Kersten, *Democracy in Postwar Japan: Maruyama Masao and the Search for Autonomy*, London: Routledge, 1996; and, Tetsuya Kataoka, *The Price of a Constitution: The Origin of Japan's Post-war Politics*, New York: Crane Russak, 1991.

7 Although it would provide for an undeniably interesting study, the research does not focus on Hong Kong. This is because of the unstable and fluid nature of political developments in Hong Kong, especially since its return to China. Nonetheless, it warrants careful observation from the perspective of the international dimension of democratization.

8 Minxen Pei, 'Creeping Democratization in China', *Journal of Democracy*, 6, 4, 1995, pp. 65–79.

9 Arend Lijphart, 'Comparative Politics and the Comparative Method', *The American Political Science Review*, 65, 1971, p. 683.

10 Ibid.

11 Thomas Carothers, 'The Resurgence of United States Political Development Assistance to Latin America in the 1980s', in Laurence Whitehead (ed.), *The International Dimensions of Democratization: Europe and the Americas*, New York: Oxford University Press, 1998, pp. 125–145; Kathryn Sikkink, 'The Effectiveness of US Human Rights Policy 1973–1980', in Laurence Whitehead (ed.), *The International Dimensions of Democratization: Europe and the Americas*, New York: Oxford University Press, 1998, pp. 93–124.

12 Alan Angell, 'International Support for the Chilean Opposition', in Laurence Whitehead (ed.), *The International Dimensions of Democratization: Europe and the Americas*, New York: Oxford University Press, 1998, pp. 175–200.

13 Francis Fukuyama, *The End of History and the Last Man*, London: Penguin, 1992.

14 Scott Mainwaring, 'Transitions to Democracy and Democratic Consolidation: Theoretical and Comparative Issues', in Scott Mainwaring, Guillermo O'Donnell and J. Samuel Valenzuela (eds), *Issues in Democratic Consolidation: The New South American Democracies in Comparative Perspective*, Notre Dame, Indiana: University of Notre Dame Press, 1992, p. 298.

15 Guillermo O'Donnell and Philippe C. Schmitter, *Transitions from Authoritarian Rule: Tentative Conclusions about Uncertain Democracies*, fourth impression, Baltimore, London: The Johns Hopkins University Press, 1993, pp. 7–11.

16 Ibid.

17 There are of course many different definitions of democracy. David Held outlines eight distinct models in David Held, *Models of Democracy*, 2nd edition, Cambridge: Polity Press, 1996, pp. 278–283.

18 One of the most popular conceptions of minimal democracy is that articulated by Joseph A. Schumpeter in *Capitalism, Socialism and Democracy*, 3rd edition, New York: Harper and Row, 1976. Here the definition has been modified to include universal suffrage, a criterion overlooked by Schumpeter.

19 Larry Diamond, *Developing Democracy: Toward Consolidation*, Baltimore: The Johns Hopkins University Press, 1999, pp. 10–11. Diamond characterizes four types of democracy: pseudo-democracies and non-democracies, electoral, liberal, and mid-range.

20 Ibid., p. 54.

21 Laurence Whitehead, 'Three International Dimensions of Democratization', in Laurence Whitehead (ed.), *The International Dimensions of Democratization: Europe and the Americas*, New York: Oxford University Press, 1998, pp. 3–25.

22 Philip G. Cerny, 'Paradoxes of the Competition State: The Dynamics of Political Globalization', *Government and Opposition*, 32, 2, 1997, pp. 251–274.

1 Considering the international dimension of democratization

1 Geoffrey Pridham, Eric Herring and George Sanford, 'Introduction', in Geoffrey Pridham, Eric Herring and George Sanford (eds), *Building Democracy? The International Dimensions of Democratization in Eastern Europe*, London: Leicester University Press, 1997, p. 1.
2 Ibid.
3 Geoffrey Pridham, 'Democratic Transition and the International Environment: A Research Agenda', *Centre for Mediterranean Studies-Occasional Paper*, 1, February, 1991, p. 1.
4 Laurence Whitehead, 'Three International Dimensions of Democratization', in Laurence Whitehead (ed.), *The International Dimensions of Democratization: Europe and the Americas*, New York: Oxford University Press, 1998, p. 3.
5 Guillermo O'Donnell and Philippe C. Schmitter, *Transitions from Authoritarian Rule: Tentative Conclusions about Uncertain Democracies*, 4th impression, Baltimore, London: The Johns Hopkins University Press, 1993.
6 Ruth Berins Collier argues that most contributions to transitions literature have either implicitly or explicitly followed O'Donnell and Schmitter's framework. See Ruth Berins Collier, *Paths Toward Democracy: The Working Class and Elites in Western Europe and South America*, Cambridge: Cambridge University Press, 1999, p. 5.
7 This observation does not negate the importance of the concepts developed by O'Donnell and Schmitter, a number of which are employed in this research. Rather, it highlights differences between the pattern of transition in Latin America and East Asia.
8 Indeed Thomas Carothers argues that, although useful for explaining several trends between the 1970s and 1990s, the transition paradigm has outgrown its utility. This is because many of the countries commonly regarded as 'transitional' are not in transition to democracy, and of those democratic transitions that are underway several are not following the model articulated by O'Donnell and Schmitter. See Thomas Carothers, 'The End of the Transition Paradigm', *Journal of Democracy*, 13, 1, 2002, pp. 5–21.
9 Jeff Haynes, *Democracy in the Developing World: Africa, Asia, Latin America and the Middle East*, Cambridge: Polity Press, 2001, p. 33.
10 Whitehead, 'Three International Dimensions', p. 5.
11 Philippe C. Schmitter, 'The Influence of the International Context upon the Choice of National Institutions and Policies in Neo-Democracies', in Laurence Whitehead (ed.), *The International Dimensions of Democratization: Europe and the Americas*, New York: Oxford University Press, 1998, p. 40.
12 Whitehead, 'Three International Dimensions', p. 10.
13 Ibid., p. 15.
14 Ibid., p. 14.
15 Ibid., p. 19.
16 Schmitter, 'The Influence of the International Context', p. 29.
17 Ibid., p. 30.
18 Whitehead, 'Three International Dimensions', p. 20.
19 Ibid.
20 Ibid.
21 Ibid., pp. 21–22.
22 Geoffrey Pridham, 'The International Dimension of Democratization: Theory, Practice and Inter-regional Comparisons', in Geoffrey Pridham, Eric Herring and George Sanford (eds), *Building Democracy? The International Dimensions of Democratization in Eastern Europe*, London: Leicester University Press, 1997, p. 11.

23 Ibid., p. 12.
24 Schmitter, 'The Influence of the International Context', p. 39.
25 Karen Dawisha and Michael Turner, 'The Interaction Between Internal and External Agency in Post-Communist Transitions', in Bruce Parrot and Karen Dawisha (eds), *The International Dimension of Post-Communist Transitions in Russia and the New States of Eurasia*, Armonk, New York: M. E. Sharpe, 1997, pp. 404–405.
26 Ibid., p. 404.
27 Leonardo Morlino, 'Democratic Establishments: A Dimensional Analysis', in Enrique Baloyra (ed.), *Comparing New Democracies: Transition and Consolidation in Mediterranean Europe and the Southern Cone*, Boulder: Westview Press, 1987, p. 72.
28 Dawisha and Turner, 'The Interaction', pp. 400–403.
29 Ibid., p. 401.
30 Ibid., p. 402.
31 Ibid., p. 401.
32 Ibid.

2 Development, democracy and the international economy

1 Dietrich Rueschemeyer, Evelyne Huber Stephens and John D. Stephens, *Capitalist Development and Democracy*, Oxford: Polity Press, 1992, p. 9, p. 69 and p. 74.
2 Geoffrey R. D. Underhill, 'State, Market and Global Political Economy: A Genealogy of an (inter-?) Discipline', *International Affairs*, 76, 4, 2000, p. 806.
3 David Collier and James E. Mahon Jr., 'Conceptual "Stretching" Revisited: Adapting Categories in Comparative Analysis', *American Political Science Review*, 87, 4, December, 1993, p. 845.
4 See generally Wolfgang Sachs (ed.), *The Development Dictionary: A Guide to Knowledge as Power*, London, New Jersey: Zed, 1992; Myron Weiner and Samuel P. Huntington (eds), *Understanding Political Development*, Boston: Little and Brown, 1987; and Mark Hobart (ed.), *An Anthropological Critique of Development: The Growth of Ignorance*, London, New York: Routledge, 1993.
5 Walt Rostow, *The Stages of Economic Growth: A Non-Communist Manifesto*, 3rd edition, Cambridge: Cambridge University Press, 1990.
6 Amartya K. Sen, *Development as Freedom*, New York: Knopf, 1999.
7 Interestingly, Jack Donnelly rejects the concept of sustainable human development on analytical grounds. He argues that it defines democracy, human rights, peace and justice as subsets of development. As a consequence, Donnelly argues, the concept of sustainable human development does not address the question of the relationship between economic development and the different subsets. See Jack Donnelly, 'Human Rights, Democracy and Development', *Human Rights Quarterly*, 21, 1999, pp. 608–632.
8 Seymour Martin Lipset, 'Some Social Requisites of Democracy: Economic Development and Political Legitimacy', *American Political Science Review*, 53, March, 1959, pp. 69–105; Barrington Moore Jr., *Social Origins of Dictatorship and Democracy: Lord and Peasant in the Making of the Modern World*, Harmondsworth: Penguin, 1973; Theda Skocpol, *States and Social Revolutions: A Comparative Analysis of France, Russia and China*, Cambridge: Cambridge University Press, 1979.
9 Rueschemeyer, Stephens and Stephens, *Capitalist Development and Democracy*, p. 1.
10 Peter Bernholz, 'Democracy and Capitalism: Are they compatible in the long-run?', *Journal of Evolutionary Economics*, 10, 2000, p. 7.

11 See for example Tun-jen Cheng, 'Is the Dog Barking? The Middleclass and Democratic Movements in the East Asian NICs', *International Studies Notes: Research Paper*, 89–05, Spring, 1990; Sung-Joo Han, 'South Korean Politics in Transition', in Larry Diamond, Juan Linz and Seymour Martin Lipset (eds), *Democracy in Developing Countries*, vol. 3, Boulder: Lynne Rienner, 1989, pp. 267–299; Lucian W. Pye, *Asian Power and Politics: The Cultural Dimensions of Authority*, Cambridge, Massachusetts: The Belknap Press of Harvard University Press, 1985, p. 233.

12 Gabriel Almond and G. Bingham Powell Jr., *Comparative Politics: A Developmental Approach*, Boston: Little Brown and Co., 1966, p. 3.

13 Bruce Cumings, 'The Origins and Development of the Northeast Asian Political Economy: Industrial Sectors, Product Cycles, and Political Consequences', *International Organization*, 38, 1984, pp. 3–4.

14 Guillermo O'Donnell and Philippe C. Schmitter, *Transitions from Authoritarian Rule: Tentative Conclusions about Uncertain Democracies*, 4th impression, Baltimore, London: The Johns Hopkins University Press, 1993, p. 6.

15 James Cotton, 'Korea in Comparative Perspective', in James Cotton (ed.), *Politics and Policy in the New Korean State: From Roh Tae-woo to Kim Young-sam*, Melbourne: Longman, 1995, p. 228. A good example of this approach can be found in the work of Bruce Cumings. See in particular Bruce Cumings, 'World System and Authoritarian Regimes in Korea, 1948–1984', in E. A. Winckler and S. Greenhalgh (eds), *Contending Approaches to the Political Economy of Taiwan*, Armonk, New York: M. E. Sharpe, 1989, pp. 249–269.

16 For a critique of Bruce Cumings' approach see James Cotton, 'Understanding the State in South Korea: Bureaucratic-Authoritarian or State Autonomy Theory', *Comparative Political Studies*, 24, 4, January, 1992, pp. 512–531. For an empirical study and rejection of the relevance of dependency theory to East Asia see Richard E. Barrett and Soomi Chin, 'Export-oriented States in the Capitalist World System: Similarities and Differences', in Frederic C. Deyo (ed.), *The Political Economy of New Asian Industrialism*, Ithaca, New York: Cornell University Press, 1987, pp. 12–23.

17 Peter J. Katzenstein, Robert O. Keohane and Stephen D. Krasner, 'International Organization and the Study of World Politics', *International Organization*, 52, 4, Autumn, 1999, p. 648.

18 Chalmers Johnson, *MITI and the Japanese Miracle: The Growth of Industrial Policy 1925–1975*, Stanford: Stanford University Press, 1982; Chalmers Johnson, 'South Korean Democratization: the Role of Economic Development', in James Cotton (ed.), *Korea Under Roh Tae Woo: Democratization, Northern Policy and Inter-Korean Relations*, Sydney: Allen and Unwin, 1993, pp. 82–107; Chalmers Johnson, 'Political Institutions and Economic Performance: The Government–Business Relationship in Japan, South Korea and Taiwan', in Frederic C. Deyo (ed.), *The Political Economy of New Asian Industrialism*, Ithaca, New York: Cornell University Press, 1987, pp. 136–165; Robert Wade, *Governing the Market: Economic Theory and the Role of Government in East Asian Industrialization*, Princeton: Princeton University Press, 1990; and Alice H. Amsden, *Asia's New Giant: South Korea and Late Industrialization*, New York: Oxford University Press, 1989.

19 Chalmers, 'Political Institutions', p. 147.

20 Wade, *Governing the Market*, p. 26.

21 Ibid., p. 27.

22 Ibid., p. 7.

23 Riordan Roett and Russell Crandell, 'The Global Economic Crisis, Contagion and Institutions: New Realities in Latin America and Asia', *International Political Science Review*, 20, 3, 1999, p. 278.

24 Steve Chan, 'Cores and Peripheries: Interaction Patterns in Asia', *Comparative Political Studies*, 15, 3, October, 1982, p. 317.

25 Stephan Haggard and Chung-in Moon, *Pacific Dynamics: The International Politics of Industrial Change*, Boulder: Westview Press, 1989, p. 6.

26 Cumings, 'The Origins of Development', p. 11.

27 Tun-jen Cheng, 'Democratizing the Quasi-Leninist Regime', *World Politics*, 41, 4, 1989, pp. 471–499.

28 Cited in Colin Mackerras (ed.), *Asia Since 1945: History Through Documents*, Melbourne: Longman Cheshire, 1992, p. 239.

29 Robert Gilpin, *The Political Economy of International Relations*, Princeton: Princeton University Press, 1987, p. 133.

30 Hsin-Huang Michael Hsiao and Chen Hsiao-shi, 'Taiwan', in Ian Marsh, Jean Blondel and Takashi Inoguchi (eds), *Democracy, Governance and Economic Performance: East and Southeast Asia*, Tokyo: United Nations University Press, 1999, p. 109.

31 John Lie, *Han Unbound: The Political Economy of South Korea*, Stanford: Stanford University Press, 1998, p. 20.

32 Kwang Suk-kim and Michael Foemer, *Growth and Structural Transformation*, Cambridge, Massachusetts: Council on East Asian Studies, Harvard, 1981, p. 43.

33 Norman Jacobs, *The Korean Road to Modernization and Development*, Urbana: University of Illinois Press, 1985, pp. 157–158.

34 Ibid.

35 For a cogent argument about how the region has turned external disadvantage and international circumstances to its advantage see Stephan Haggard, *Pathways from the Periphery*, Ithaca, New York: Cornell University Press, 1990.

36 Wade, *Governing the Market*, p. 96.

37 Lie, *Han Unbound*, p. 62.

38 Ibid.

39 Ibid., p. 63.

40 Kevin G. Cai, 'The Political Economy of Economic Regionalism in Northeast Asia: A Unique and Dynamic Pattern', *East Asia: An International Quarterly*, 17, 2, 1999, p. 8.

41 Cumings, 'The Origins of Development', p. 13.

42 Jian Chen, *China's Road to the Korean War: The Making of the Sino-American Confrontation*, New York: Columbia University Press, 1994, pp. 64–65.

43 Yongjin Zhang, *China in International Society Since 1949: Alienation and Beyond*, Hampshire, London: Macmillan; New York: St. Martin's Press, 1998, p. 26.

44 Ibid., p. 23.

45 For further details see Rosemary Foot, *The Practice of Power: US Relations with China since 1949*, Oxford: Oxford University Press, 1995, pp. 52–65.

46 David Zweig, *Internationalizing China: Domestic Interests and Global Linkages*, Ithaca and London: Cornell University Press, 2002, p. 1.

47 John K. Fairbank and Edwin O. Reischauer, *China: Tradition and Transformation*, revised edition, Sydney: Allen and Unwin, 1990, p. 499.

48 Yongjin Zhang, *China in International Society*, p. 29.

49 Rueschemeyer, Stephens and Stephens, *Capitalist Development and Democracy*, p. 66.

50 Carter J. Eckert, Ki-baik Lee, Ick Lew Young, Michael Robinson and Edward W. Wagner, *Korea Old and New: A History*, Seoul: Published for the Korea Institute, Harvard University by Ilchokak, 1990, p. 349.

51 C. L. Chiou, *Democratizing Oriental Despotism: China from 4 May 1919 to 4 June 1989 and Taiwan from 28 February 1947 to 28 June 1990*, New York: St. Martin's Press, 1995, pp. 1–2.

52 Cotton, 'Korea in Comparative Perspective', p. 232.
53 Mark Gayn, 'What Price Rhee? Profile of a Despot', *The Nation*, 13 March, 1954, p. 214.
54 Eckert et al., *Korea Old and New*, p. 355.
55 Sung-Joo Han, 'South Korean Politics', pp. 270–272.
56 Eckert et al., *Korea Old and New*, p. 361.
57 Donald Stone MacDonald, *The Koreans: Contemporary Politics and Society*, 2nd edition, Boulder: Westview Press, 1990, pp. 219–222.
58 Stephan Haggard, 'The Newly Industrializing Countries in the International System', *World Politics*, 38, 2, January, 1986, p. 348.
59 Stephan Haggard and Robert Kaufman, *The Political Economy of Democratic Transitions*, Princeton: Princeton University Press, 1995, p. 30.
60 Hagan Koo, 'From Farm to Factory: Proletarianization in Korea', *American Sociological Review*, 55, October, 1990, p. 673.
61 Frederic C. Deyo, 'State and Labour: Modes of Political Exclusion in East Asian Development', in Frederic C. Deyo (ed.), *The Political Economy of New Asian Industrialism*, Ithaca, New York: Cornell University Press, 1987, p. 185.
62 James M. West, 'South Korea's Entry Into the International Labor Organization: Perspectives on Corporatist Labor Law During a Late Industrial Revolution', *Stanford Journal of International Law*, 23, 2, Summer, 1987, p. 489.
63 Ibid., pp. 490–491.
64 Deyo, 'State and Labour', p. 184.
65 Sean Cooney, 'A Community Changes: Taiwan's Council of Grand Justices and Liberal Democratic Reform', in Kanishka Jayasuriya (ed.), *Law, Capitalism and Power in Asia: The Rule of Law and Legal Institutions*, London, New York: Routledge, 1999, p. 264.
66 For more on the Japanese employment system and its adoption by other countries see Anthony Woodiwiss, *Globalization, Human Rights, and Labour Law in Pacific Asia*, Cambridge: Cambridge University Press, 1998, pp. 69–80.
67 Edwin A. Winckler, 'Taiwan Transition?', in Tun-jen Cheng and Stephan Haggard (eds), *Political Change in Taiwan*, Boulder: Lynne Rienner, 1992, p. 242.
68 Haggard, 'Newly Industrializing', p. 355.
69 West, 'South Korea's Entry', p. 493.
70 Hsin-Huang Michael Hsiao and Cheng Hsiao-shi, 'Taiwan', p. 110.
71 Ibid., p. 118.
72 Tun-jen Chen, 'Democratizing', p. 481.
73 Deyo, 'State and Labour', p. 194.
74 Stephan Haggard, 'Business, Politics and Policy in Northeast and Southeast Asia', in Andrew MacIntyre (ed.), *Business and Government in Industrializing Asia*, Sydney: Allen and Unwin, 1994, p. 274.
75 Chen, *China's Road to the Korean War*, pp. 222–223.
76 Ibid.
77 Andrew J. Nathan, *China's Crisis: Dilemmas of Reform and Prospects for Democracy*, New York: Columbia University Press, 1990, p. 4.
78 Zweig, *Internationalizing China*, p. 1.
79 Xuewu Gu, 'China's Policy Towards Russia', *Aussenpolitik*, 111, 1993, p. 290 and p. 294.
80 Alastair Iain Johnston observes that, more recently, references to globalization in Chinese academic journals have outstripped references to multipolarization. See Alastair Iain Johnston, 'Is China a Status Quo Power?', *International Security*, 27, 4, Spring, 2003, pp. 34–35.
81 Chae-Jin Lee, 'The United States and Korea: Dynamics of Changing Relations', in Young Whan Kihl (ed.), *Korea and the World: Beyond the Cold War*, Boulder: Westview Press, 1994, p. 70.

82 Geoff Simons, *Korea: The Search for Sovereignty*, London: Macmillan, 1995, p. 17.

83 David Lampton, 'America's China Policy in the Age of the Finance Minister: Clinton Ends Linkage', *The China Quarterly*, 139, September, 1994, p. 599.

84 Andrew J. Nathan, 'What's Wrong with American Taiwan Policy?', *Washington Quarterly*, 23, 2 Spring, 2000, pp. 93–106.

85 David Martin Jones, 'Myths of the Meltdown: The Curious Case of the Developmental State in the Asia Pacific', *London Defence Studies*, 48, 1999, p. 5.

86 Christopher M. Dent, 'ASEM and the "Cinderella Complex" of EU–East Asia Economic Relations', *Pacific Affairs*, Spring, 2001, p. 30.

87 Amy Kaslow, 'Pacific Rim Beckons European Business', *Christian Science Monitor*, December–January, 1994–1995, p. 21.

88 See for example, Stephen Oxman, Otto Triffterer, Francisco Cruz, *South Korea: Human Rights in Emerging Politics*, Switzerland: International Commission of Jurists, 1987.

89 Rosemary Foot, *Rights Beyond Borders: The Global Community and the Struggle Over Human Rights in China*, Oxford: Oxford University Press, 2000, p. 84.

90 Andrew J. Nathan, 'Human Rights in Chinese Foreign Policy', *The China Quarterly*, 139, September, 1994, p. 631.

91 Amnesty International, *Political Imprisonment in the People's Republic of China*, London: Amnesty International, 1978. The report focussed on arbitrary arrest, the use of torture to obtain confessions, and detention without trial.

92 James D. Seymour, 'Human Rights and the World Response to the Crackdown in China', *China Information*, 4, 4, Spring, 1990, p. 5.

93 Takashi Inoguchi, 'Three Frameworks in Search of a Policy: US Democracy Promotion in Asia Pacific', in Michael Cox, John G. Ikenberry, Takashi Inoguchi (eds), *American Democracy Promotion: Impulses, Strategies and Impacts*, Oxford: Oxford University Press, 2000, p. 276.

94 Zha Daojiong, 'Chinese Perspectives on International Political Economy', *Political Science*, 49, 1, July, 1997, p. 74.

95 Wade, *Governing the Market*, p. 96.

96 Kanishka Jayasuriya, 'Political Economy of Democratization in East Asia', *Asian Perspective*, 18, 2, Fall–Winter, 1994, p. 160.

97 Richard Rosecrance, *The Rise of the Trading State*, New York: Basic Books, 1986, pp. 136–154.

98 Cai, 'The Political Economy', p. 8.

99 Chyungly Lee, 'Impact of the East Asian Financial Crisis on the Asia–Pacific Regional Order: A Geo-Economic Perspective', *Issues and Studies*, 35, 4, July–August, 1999, p. 119.

100 Kenichi Ohmae, 'The Rise of the Region State', *Foreign Affairs*, 72, Spring, 1993, p. 88.

101 Cai, 'The Political Economy', pp. 27–28.

102 Gary Gereffi, 'More than the Market, More than the State: Global Commodity Chains and Industrial Upgrading in East Asia', in Steve Chan, Cal Clark and Danny Lam (eds), *Beyond the Developmental State: East Asia's Political Economies Reconsidered*, Hampshire: Macmillan Press, 1998, p. 39.

103 Steve Chan, 'Peace by Pieces? Mainland–Taiwan Transaction Flows', in Steve Chan, Cal Clark and Danny Lam (eds), *Beyond the Developmental State: East Asia's Political Economies Reconsidered*, Hampshire: Macmillan Press, 1998, p. 70.

104 See David Zweig, *Internationalizing China*, for a cogent argument about the role external forces, bureaucratic agents, domestic structure and a feedback loop

based on the distributional consequences of internationalization have played in the internationalization of China's economy.

105 Yongjin Zhang, *China in International Society*, p. 84.
106 Nathan, *China's Crisis*, p. 99. China has also been influenced by Southeast Asian experiences. In particular, Chinese policy-makers have been impressed by Singapore's marriage of economic growth with political stability and control.
107 Barry Naughton, 'China's Emergence and Prospects as a Trading Nation', *Brookings Papers on Economic Activity*, 2, 1996, p. 302.
108 Yasheng Huang, *Selling China: Foreign Direct Investment During the Reform Era*, Cambridge: Cambridge University Press, 2003.
109 Ibid., p. 335.
110 Edward Xin Gu, 'Foreign Direct Investment and the Restructuring of Chinese State-Owned Enterprises (1992–1995): A New Institutionalist Perspective', *China Information*, 12, 3, Winter, 1997–1998, p. 46.
111 Naughton, 'China's Emergence', pp. 326–327.
112 Gu, 'Foreign Direct Investment', p. 51.
113 Cheng-tian Kuo, 'Privatization', p. 76.
114 Gu, 'Foreign Direct Investment', pp. 68–69.
115 Huang, Yasheng, *Selling China*, p. 350.
116 Ibid.
117 Improving economic development in the western regions of Tibet and Xinjiang is regarded by the Chinese state as one way to help to settle ethnic unrest in these areas.
118 Michael Mandelbaum, 'Westernizing Russia and China', *Foreign Affairs*, 76, 3, May–June, 1997, p. 83.
119 Jean C. Oi, 'Fiscal Reform and the Economic Foundations of Local State Corporatism in China', *World Politics*, 45, October, 1992, p. 100.
120 Ibid., p. 100.
121 Ibid., p. 102.
122 Nicholas R. Lardy, 'Comments', *Brookings Papers on Economic Activity*, 2, 1996, p. 338.
123 Oi, 'Fiscal Reform', p. 99.
124 Cheng-tian Kuo, 'Privatization within the Chinese State', in Steve Chan, Cal Clark and Danny Lam (eds), *Beyond the Developmental State: East Asia's Political Economies Reconsidered*, Hampshire: Macmillan Press, 1998, p. 72.
125 *Time*, 24 June, 1974, p. 46.
126 John Lewis, 'In Search of a Moderate Image', *Far Eastern Economic Review*, 103, 5 January, 1979, p. 13.
127 David Martin Jones, 'Democratization, Civil Society, and Illiberal Middle Class Culture in Pacific Asia', *Comparative Politics*, 30, 2, 1998, pp. 147–169.
128 Ibid., p. 147.
129 Ibid., p. 149.
130 Ibid., p. 152.
131 Ibid., p. 153 and p. 159.
132 Wenli Zhu, 'International Political Economy from a Chinese Angle', *Journal of Contemporary China*, 10, 26, 2001, p. 49.
133 For a detailed analysis of the inflation, and economic policy making conflicts see You Ji, 'Zhao Ziyang and the Politics of Inflation', *The Australian Journal of Chinese Affairs*, 25, January, 1991, pp. 69–91.
134 For a detailed analysis of the extent to which the 1989 protest movement spread to other provinces and cities see Andrew J. Nathan and Perry Link (eds), *The Tiananmen Papers*, London: Little, Brown and Company, 2001.
135 Naughton, 'China's Emergence', p. 281.
136 Ibid., pp. 281–282 and p. 287.

137 Philip G. Cerny, 'Globalization and the Changing Logic of Collective Action', *International Organization*, 49, 4, Autumn, 1995, p. 603.
138 Ibid., p. 607.
139 Susan Strange, *The Retreat of the State: The Diffusion of Power in the World Economy*, Cambridge: Cambridge University Press, 1996 and Linda Weiss, *The Myth of the Powerless State*, Ithaca, New York: Cornell University Press, 1998.
140 For an early and prescient critique of the prospects of continued Asian economic success see Paul Krugman, 'The Myth of Asia's Miracle', *Foreign Affairs*, 73, 6, November–December, 1994, pp. 62–78.
141 Nathan, 'Human Rights', p. 622.
142 Charles Bickers, G. Pierre Goad, Chester Dawson, Charles S. Lee, 'China's Challenge', *Far Eastern Economic Review*, 162, 23 September, 1999, pp. 43–44.
143 Dani Rodrik, *The New Global Economy and Developing Countries: Making Openness Work*, Baltimore: The Johns Hopkins University Press, 1999, p. 9.
144 David Martin Jones and Mike Smith, 'Tigers Ready to Roar', *The World Today*, 55, 10, October, 1999, p. 17.
145 Devesh Kapur, 'The IMF: A Cure of a Curse', *Foreign Policy*, 111, Summer, 1998, p. 124.
146 John D. Steinbruner, *Principles of Global Security*, Washington DC: Brookings Institution, 2000, p. 213.
147 Naughton, 'China's Emergence', p. 277.
148 Rodrik, *The New Global Economy*, pp. 144–145.
149 Dent, 'ASEM', p. 41.
150 Ibid.
151 World Bank, *World Development Report*, Washington: World Bank, 1996.
152 Roett and Crandall, 'The Global Economic Crisis', p. 278.
153 Ibid., p. 274.
154 Rodrik, *The New Global Economy*, p. 139.
155 Ibid., p. 17.
156 Cited in Amitav Acharya, 'Southeast Asia's Democratic Moment', *Asian Survey*, 39, 3, May–June, 1999, p. 421. See also Adrian Karatnycky, 'The 1998 Freedom House Survey: The Decline of Illiberal Democracy', *Journal of Democracy*, 10, 1, 1999, p. 122.
157 Claudia Rosett, 'Mapping the New World Markets', in Brian T. Johnson, Kim R. Holmes, Melanie Kirkpatrick (eds), *1999 Index of Economic Freedom*, New York: The Heritage Foundation and Dow Jones and Co. Inc, 1999, p. 37.
158 Michel Chossodovsky, from the University of Ottawa, argues that the details of the IMF reform program had been decided in consultation with the US Treasury, Wall Street's commercial and merchant banks as well as major banking interests in Japan and the European Union. Michael Chossodovsky, Korea Web Weekly, http://www.kimsoft.com//1997/sk/imfc.htm, accessed 24 March, 1999.
159 David Hale, 'The IMF, Now More Than Ever: The Case for Financial Peacekeeping', *Foreign Affairs*, 77, 6, November–December, 1998, p. 11.
160 Bruce Cumings, 'The Korean Crisis and the End of "Late Development"', *New Left Review*, 231, September–October, 1998, p. 45.
161 Nicola Bullard, Walden Bello and Kamal Malhotra, *Taming the Tigers: The IMF and the Asian Crisis*, Bangkok: Focus on the Global South, Chulalongkorn University, 1998, p. 3.
162 G. John Ikenberry, 'America's Liberal Grand Strategy: Democracy and National Security in the Post-War Era', in Michael Cox, John G. Ikenberry, Takashi Inoguchi (eds), *American Democracy Promotion: Impulses, Strategies and Impacts*, Oxford: Oxford University Press, 2000, p. 117.
163 Ibid.

164 Ibid., p. 118.
165 Ibid.
166 Johnston, 'Status Quo Power?', p. 53.
167 Ibid.
168 Jin Canrong, 'The US Global Strategy in the Post-Cold War Era and Its Implications for China–United States Relations: A Chinese Perspective', *Journal of Contemporary China*, 10, 27, 2001, p. 313.
169 Yong Deng and Sherry Gray, 'Introduction: Growing Pains – China Debates its International Future', *Journal of Contemporary China*, 10, 26, 2001, p. 9.
170 Song Qiang, Zhang Zangang and Qiao Bian, *China Can Say No [Zhongguo keyi shuo bu]*, Beijing: *Zhonghua gongshang lianhe chubanshe*, 1996.
171 For a description of China's commitments see Qingjiang Kong, 'China's WTO Accession: Commitments and Implications', *Journal of International Economic Law*, 3, 4, 2000, pp. 655–690.
172 Zweig, *Internationalizing China*, p. 277.
173 Ibid.

3 International regimes: the role of the United Nations

1 For further detail on the Westphalia model see David Held, *Democracy and the Global Order: From the Modern State to Cosmopolitan Governance*, London: Polity Press, 1996, p. 78.
2 Clive Archer, *International Organizations*, 2nd edition, London, New York: Routledge, 1995, p. 4.
3 Held, *Democracy and the Global Order*, p. 81.
4 David Held and Andrew McGrew, 'Globalization and the Liberal Democratic State', *Government and Opposition*, 28, 2, 1993, p. 262.
5 Susan Strange, *The Retreat of the State: The Diffusion of Power in the World Economy*, Cambridge: Cambridge University Press, 1996, p. ix.
6 Richard Falk, 'The World Order between Inter-State Law and the Law of Humanity: The Role of Civil Society Institutions', in Daniele Archibugi and David Held (eds), *Cosmopolitan Democracy: An Agenda for a New World Order*, Cambridge: Polity Press, 1995, pp. 166–167.
7 Asia–Europe Foundation Monograph, *The Third Informal ASEM Seminar on Human Rights*, Paris, France, 19–20 June, 2000, p. 46.
8 Ibid., p. 47.
9 Robert Cooper, *The Post-Modern State and the World Order*, London: Demos, 1996.
10 Ibid., p. 19.
11 Ibid., p. 23.
12 Robert O. Keohane and Joseph S. Nye, *Power and Interdependence*, 3rd edition, New York: Longman, 2001, p. 17.
13 Robert Gilpin, *The Political Economy of International Relations*, Princeton: Princeton University Press, 1987, p. 132.
14 Oran R. Young, 'Regime Dynamics: The Rise and Fall of International Regimes', *International Organization*, 36, 2, Spring, 1982, pp. 290–291.
15 United Nations, http://www.un.org.Depts/dpa/ead/website5.htm, accessed 8 February, 2002.
16 Ibid.
17 The division carries out activities across six theme areas: governing institutions, decentralized governance, public sector management and accountability, urban development, governance in crisis countries, and capacity development.

18 Laurence Whitehead, 'Preface', in Laurence Whitehead (ed.), *The International Dimensions of Democratization: Europe and the Americas*, New York: Oxford University Press, 1998, p. vi.

19 For an analysis that credits the European Community with a key role promoting democracy in Southern Europe see Basilios Tsingos, 'Underwriting Democracy: The European Community and Greece', in Laurence Whitehead (ed.), *The International Dimensions of Democratization: Europe and the Americas*, New York: Oxford University Press, 1998, pp. 285–314. For a critical analysis of the disappointing role of the European Community in relation to Eastern Europe see John Pinder, 'The European Community and Democracy in Central and Eastern Europe', in Geoffrey Pridham, Eric Herring, and George Sanford (eds), *Building Democracy? The International Dimension of Democratization in Eastern Europe*, London: Leicester University Press, 1997, pp. 110–132.

20 Laurence Whitehead, 'Three International Dimensions of Democratization', in Laurence Whitehead (ed.), *The International Dimensions of Democratization: Europe and the Americas*, New York: Oxford University Press, 1998, p. 19.

21 Although the Organization of American States declared during a 1991 convention that member states were required to maintain democratic forms of governance consistent with its charter, in practice the Organization of American States commitment to democracy has not been strong.

22 Vikram K. Chand, 'Democratization from the Outside in: NGOs and International Efforts to Promote Open Elections', in Thomas G. Weiss (ed.), *Beyond UN Subcontracting: Task-Sharing with Regional Security Arrangements and Service Providing NGOs*, London: Macmillan; New York: St. Martin's Press, 1998, pp. 161–163.

23 The belief that democracies are inherently more peaceful than autocracies has its origins in Immanuel Kant's work. See Immanuel Kant, *Perpetual Peace, and Other Essays on Politics, History and Morals*, trans. Ted Murphy, Indianapolis: Hackett Publishing Co., 1983. Recently, a growing literature has developed the 'democratic peace' thesis. See for example, Michael W. Doyle, 'Liberalism and World Politics', *American Political Science Review*, 80, 4, 1986, pp. 1151–1169; Bruce Russett with W. Antholis, E. Ember, M. Ember and Z. Maos, *Grasping the Democratic Peace: Principles for a Post-Cold War World*, Princeton: Princeton University Press, 1993; Michael W. Doyle, *Ways of War and Peace*, New York: W. W. Norton and Company, 1997.

24 Whitehead, 'Three International Dimensions', p. 16.

25 Daniele Archibugi, Sveva Balduini and Marco Donati, 'The United Nations as an Agency of Global Democracy', in Barry Holden (ed.), *Global Democracy: Key Debates*, London, New York: Routledge, 2000, p. 126.

26 Archer, *International Organizations*, p. 136.

27 Hung-mao Tien, *The Great Transition: Political and Social Change in the Republic of China*, Stanford: Hoover Institution Press, Stanford University, 1989, p. 217.

28 Ralph Clough, *Island China*, Cambridge, Massachusetts: Harvard University Press, 1978, p. 529.

29 Hung-mao Tien, *The Great Transition*, p. 221.

30 Ibid., p. 219.

31 Ross. H. Munro, 'Giving Taipei a Place at the Table', *Foreign Affairs*, 73, 6, November–December, 1994, p. 109.

32 Cited in Pei-chi Chung, 'The Cultural Other and National Identity in the Taiwanese and South Korean Media', *Gazette*, 62, 2, 2000, p. 110.

33 Baogang He, 'Power, Responsibility and Sovereignty: China's Policy towards Taiwan's Bid for a UN Seat', in Yongjin Zhang and Greg Austin (eds), *Power and Responsibility in Chinese Foreign Policy*, Canberra: Asia Pacific Press, 2001, p. 208.

34   Strange, *Retreat of the State*, p. 13.
35   United Nations, http://www.un.org/Overview/growth/htm, accessed 8 February, 2002.
36   Byung Chul Koh, 'The Foreign and Unification Policies of the Republic of Korea', in Soong Hoom Kil and Chung-in Moon (eds), *Understanding Korean Politics: An Introduction*, New York: State University of New York Press, 2001, p. 235.
37   Ibid.
38   Ibid., p. 236.
39   Martin Hewson and Timothy J. Sinclair, 'The Emergence of Global Governance Theory', in Martin Hewson and Timothy J. Sinclair (eds), *Approaches to Global Governance Theory*, New York: State University of New York Press, 1999, p. 4.
40   The United Nations Development Programme argues that in an era of democratic transitions in developing and former socialist countries, 'people's participation is becoming the central issue of our time', *Human Development Report*, New York: United Nations Development Programme, 1993, p. 1.
41   Bruce Cumings, *The Origins of the Korean War: Liberation and the Emergence of Separate Regime 1945–1947*, vol. 1, 3rd edition, Princeton: Princeton University Press, 1989, p. 103.
42   Kim Chum-kon, *The Korean War 1950–1953*, Seoul: Kwangmyong, 1980, p. 15.
43   Ibid., p. 17.
44   For an extensive examination of the reasons behind this stance see Cumings, *The Origins of the Korean War*, vol. 1.
45   Soong Hoom Kil, 'Development of Korean Politics: A Historical Profile', in Soong Hoom Kil and Chung-in Moon (eds), *Understanding Korean Politics: An Introduction*, New York: State University of New York Press, 2001, p. 41.
46   Ibid., p. 35.
47   John P. Lovell, 'The Military and Politics in Postwar Korea', in Edward Reynolds Wright (ed.), *Korean Politics in Transition*, Seattle: University of Washington Press, 1975, p. 161.
48   Bruce Cumings, *The Origins of the Korean War: The Roaring of the Cataract 1947–1950*, vol. 2, Princeton: Princeton University Press, 1990, p. 66.
49   Cecilia Lynch, 'The Promise and Problems of Internationalism', *Global Governance*, 5, 1, January–March, 1999, p. 92.
50   Ibid.
51   Dean Acheson, *The Korean War*, New York: W. W. Norton Co., 1971, p. 34.
52   Ibid., p. 33.
53   Ibid., p. 58.
54   Cumings, *The Origins of the Korean War*, vol. 2, p. 737.
55   Chen, *China's Road to the Korean War*, p. 218.
56   Ibid.
57   Allen S. Whiting, *China Crosses the Yalu: The Decision to Enter the Korean War*, New York: Macmillan, 1960.
58   Carl Berger, *The Korea Knot: A Military Political History*, revised edition, Philadelphia: University of Pennsylvania Press, 1968, p. 161.
59   Donald Stone MacDonald, *The Koreans: Contemporary Politics and Society*, 2nd edition, Boulder: Westview Press, 1990, pp. 51–52.
60   Chen, *China's Road to the Korean War*, p. 223.
61   MacDonald, *The Koreans*, pp. 51–52.
62   Lovell, 'The Military and Politics', p. 164.
63   Ibid., p. 165.
64   Jung Bock Lee, 'The Political Process in Korea', in Soong Hoom Kil and Chung-in Moon (eds), *Understanding Korean Politics: An Introduction*, New York: State University of New York Press, 2001, p. 163.

65 Lovell, 'The Military and Politics', p. 178.
66 David Brown, 'Democratization and the Renegotiation of Ethnicity', in Daniel A. Bell, David Brown, Kanishka Jayasuriya and David Martin Jones, *Towards Illiberal Democracy in Pacific Asia*, New York: St. Martin's Press, 1995, pp. 135–137.
67 Ibid.
68 Ibid.
69 Ibid., pp. 150–152.
70 Young Whan Kihl, 'Democratization and Foreign Policy', in James Cotton (ed.), *Politics and Policy in the New Korean State: From Roh Tae-woo to Kim Young-sam*, Melbourne: Longman, 1995, p. 124.
71 Evgeny V. Afanasiev, 'Vladimir Putin's New Foreign Policy and Russian Views of the Situation on the Korean Peninsula', *The Korean Journal of Defense Analysis*, 12, 2, Winter, 2000, p. 11.
72 James Cotton, 'The Koreas in 1999: Between Confrontation and Engagement', *Parliamentary Library of Australia Research Paper*, 14, http://www.gov.au/library/pubs/rp/1998–99/99rp14.htm, accessed 5 February, 2002.
73 Ralph A. Cossa, 'US–ROK–Japan: Why a "Virtual Alliance" Makes Sense', *The Korean Journal of Defense Analysis*, 12, 1, Summer, 2000, p. 76.
74 Yong-Chool Ha, 'South Korea in 2000: A Summit and the Search for New Institutional Identity', *Asian Survey*, 41, 1, January–February, 2001, p. 31.
75 William O. Odom, 'The US Military in Unified Korea', *The Korean Journal of Defense Analysis*, 12, 1, Summer, 2000, p. 8. See also William J. Taylor, Jr., *Great Power Interests in Korean Unification*, Washington, DC: Center for Strategic and International Studies, 1998.
76 You Ji, 'China and North Korea: A Fragile Relationship of Strategic Convenience', *Journal of Contemporary China*, 10, 28, 2001, p. 387 and p. 392.
77 Yun-han Chu, *Crafting Democracy in Taiwan*, Taipei: Institute for National Policy Research, 1992, pp. 18–19.
78 Ibid.
79 François Mengin, 'State and Identity', in Steve Tsang and Hung-mao Tien (eds), *Democratization in Taiwan: Implications for China*, London: Macmillan Press, 1999, p. 117.
80 Pei-chi Chung, 'The Cultural Other', p. 105.
81 Yangsun Chou and Andrew J. Nathan, 'Democratizing Transition in Taiwan', *Asian Survey*, 27, 3, March, 1987, pp. 277–297.
82 Linda Chao and Ramon H. Myers, 'How Elections Promoted Democracy in Taiwan Under Martial Law', *The China Quarterly*, 162, June, 2000, p. 387.
83 Tun-jen Cheng, 'Democratizing The Quasi-Leninist Regime in Taiwan', *World Politics*, 41, 4, 1989, p. 475.
84 Suisheng Zhao, *Power by Design: Constitution-Making in Nationalist China*, Honolulu: University of Hawai'i Press, 1996, pp. 147–148.
85 Lijun Sheng, 'China Eyes Taiwan: Why a Breakthrough is so Difficult', *The Journal of Strategic Studies*, 21, 1, March, 1998, p. 65.
86 Evan Luard, *Britain and China*, London: Chatto and Windus, 1962, p. 78.
87 Ibid., pp. 76–77.
88 Yun-han Chu, *Crafting Democracy in Taiwan*, p. 24.
89 Ibid., p. 34.
90 Ngo Tak-wing, 'Civil Society and Political Liberalization in Taiwan', *Bulletin of Concerned Asian Scholars*, 25, 1, 1993, p. 9.
91 Ibid.
92 For further detail on the process see Yangsun Chou and Andrew J. Nathan, 'Democratizing Transition in Taiwan'.

93 Samuel S. Kim, 'Human Rights in China's International Relations', in Edward Friedman and Barrett L. McCormick (eds), *What if China Doesn't Democratize? Implications for War and Peace*, Armonk, New York: M. E. Sharpe, 2000, pp. 129–162.

94 Samuel S. Kim, *China, the United Nations and World Order*, Princeton: Princeton University Press, 1979.

95 Ibid., p. 104.

96 Ibid., p. 196.

97 Rosemary Foot, *Rights Beyond Borders: The Global Community and the Struggle over Human Rights in China*, Oxford: Oxford University Press, 2000, p. 96.

98 Ibid., p. 16.

99 Samuel S. Kim, 'China's International Organizational Behaviour', in Thomas W. Robinson and David Shambaugh (eds), *Chinese Foreign Policy in Theory and Practice*, Oxford: Clarendon Press, 1994, p. 409.

100 Robert O. Keohane, 'The Demand for International Regimes', *International Organization*, 36, 2, Spring, 1982, p. 329.

101 Thomas M. Franck, 'The Emerging Right to Democratic Governance', *American Journal of International Law*, 86, 1, January, 1992, p. 90.

102 Jack Donnelley, 'The Social Construction of International Human Rights', in Tim Dunne and Nicholas J. Wheeler (eds), *Human Rights in Global Politics*, Cambridge: Cambridge University Press, 1999, p. 84.

103 Thomas Carothers, 'Democracy and Human Rights: Policy Allies or Rivals', *The Washington Quarterly*, 17, 3, Summer, 1994, pp. 109–120.

104 Fred Halliday, *Rethinking International Relations*, Basingstoke: Macmillan, 1994, p. 95.

105 Ann Kent, *China, the United Nations and Human Rights: The Limits of Compliance*, Philadelphia: University of Pennsylvania Press, 1999, p. 46.

106 Andrew Hurrell, 'Power, Principles and Prudence: Protecting Human Rights in a Deeply Divided World', in Tim Dunne and Nicholas J. Wheeler (eds), *Human Rights in Global Politics*, Cambridge: Cambridge University Press, 1999, p. 277.

107 Kim, 'Human Rights in China's International Relations', p. 130. Kim contends that there is nothing distinctively Chinese about this approach, rather, it derives from Soviet theory.

108 Ann Kent, *Between Freedom and Subsistence: China and Human Rights*, New York: Oxford University Press, 1993, p. 222.

109 Quansheng Zhao and Barry Press, 'The US Promotion of Human Rights and China's Response', *Issues and Studies*, 34, 8, August, 1998, p. 45.

110 For further detail on the Bangkok Declaration see Christina M. Cerna, 'Universality of Human Rights and Cultural Diversity: Implementation of Human Rights in Different Socio-Cultural Contexts', *Human Rights Quarterly*, 16, 1994, pp. 740–752, and M. C. Davis (ed.), *Human Rights and Chinese Values: Legal, Philosophical and Political Perspectives*, New York: Oxford University Press, 1995.

111 Samuel S. Kim, 'Human Rights in China's International Relations', p. 149.

112 Foot, *Rights Beyond Borders*, p. 18.

113 Yong Deng and Sherry Gray, 'Introduction: Growing Pains – China Debates its International Future', *Journal of Contemporary China*, 10, 26, 2001, p. 6.

114 Wu Xinbo, 'Four Contradictions Constraining China's Foreign Policy Behaviour', *Journal of Contemporary China*, 10, 27, 2001, p. 293.

115 Ibid., p. 296.

116 UNDP CPR/96/503.

117 Baogang He and Jing Zhang, 'Evaluation Report of CPR/96/503 – Rural

Official Training', Evaluation Conducted for the United Nations Development Programme, 2–11 August, 2001, p. 3.

118 Foot, *Rights Beyond Borders*, p. 153.

119 Mary Kaldor, 'Transnational Civil Society', in Tim Dunne and Nicholas J. Wheeler (eds), *Human Rights in Global Politics*, Cambridge: Cambridge University Press, 1999, p. 195.

120 Alastair Iain Johnston, 'Is China a Status Quo Power?', *International Security*, 27, 4, Spring, 2003, p. 49.

4   Global and local cultural interactions: fusing democratic institutions with domestic ideas

1 John Dunn, *Western Political Theory in the Face of the Future*, Cambridge: Cambridge University Press, 1979, p. 1.

2 Joseph A. Schumpeter, *Capitalism, Socialism and Democracy*, 3rd edition, New York: Harper and Row, 1976, p. 269.

3 Larry Diamond, *Developing Democracy: Towards Consolidation*, Baltimore: The Johns Hopkins University Press, 1999, p. 10–11.

4 Daniel A. Bell and Kanishka Jayasuriya, 'Understanding Illiberal Democracy: A Framework', in Daniel A. Bell, David Brown, Kanishka Jayasuriya and David Martin Jones, *Towards Illiberal Democracy in Pacific Asia*, London: Macmillan, 1995, p. 2.

5 Francis Fukuyama, *The End of History and the Last Man*, London: Penguin, 1992, p. xi.

6 Dunn, *Western Political Theory in the Face of the Future*, p. 4.

7 Ibid., p. 10.

8 Ibid., p. 11.

9 David Beetham, *The Legitimation of Power*, London: Macmillan, 1991, p. 134.

10 Thomas M. Franck, 'The Emerging Right to Democratic Governance', *American Journal of International Law*, 86, 1, January, 1992, pp. 46–56.

11 Andrew Hurrell, 'Power, Principles and Prudence: Protecting Human Rights in a Deeply Divided World', in Tim Dunne and Nicholas J. Wheeler (eds), *Human Rights in Global Politics*, Cambridge: Cambridge University Press, 1999, p. 279.

12 Jack Donnelly, 'Human Rights: A New Standard of Civilization?', *International Affairs*, 74, 1, 1998, p. 19.

13 Harry Harding, 'Breaking the Impasse Over Human Rights', in Ezra Vogel (ed.), *Living with China: U.S./China Relations in the Twenty-first Century*, New York: Norton, 1998, p. 170.

14 Marina Svensson, *The Chinese Conception of Human Rights: The Debate on Human Rights in China 1898–1949*, Lund: Studentlitteratur, 1996, p. 49.

15 Thomas Carothers, 'Democracy and Human Rights: Policy Allies or Rivals', *The Washington Quarterly*, 17, 13, Summer, 1994, p. 110.

16 Ibid., p. 114.

17 Donnelly, 'Human Rights: A New Standard', p. 1.

18 Dunn, *Western Political Theory*, p. 2.

19 Bilahari Kausikan argues that differences among Western and East Asian countries have been exaggerated because of a common failure to make a critical distinction between democracy as a political theory of legitimation of government and democracy as a mechanism, or instrument of government. See Bilahari Kausikan, 'The "Asian Values" Debate: A View From Singapore', in Larry Diamond and Marc F. Plattner (eds), *Democracy in East Asia*, Baltimore, London: The Johns Hopkins University Press, 1998, pp. 17–27.

20 Jack Donnelly, 'Human Rights, Democracy, and Development', *Human Rights Quarterly*, 21, 1999, p. 618.
21 Adam Przeworski, 'Minimalist Conception of Democracy: A Defense', in Ian Shapiro and Casiano Hacker-Córdon (eds), *Democracy's Value*, Cambridge: Cambridge University Press, 1999, p. 43.
22 Ibid., p. 44.
23 Ibid., pp. 45–49.
24 Robert J. C. Young, *Colonial Desire: Hybridity in Theory, Culture and Race*, London: Routledge, 1995, p. 5.
25 Sidney Verba, 'Comparative Political Culture', in Lucian W. Pye and Sidney Verba (eds), *Political Culture and Political Development*, Princeton: Princeton University Press, 1965, p. 517.
26 Karen Dawisha and Michael Turner, 'The Interaction Between Internal and External Agency in Post-Communist Transitions', in Bruce Parrot and Karen Dawisha (eds), *The International Dimension of Post-Communist Transitions in Russia and the New States of Eurasia*, Armonk, New York: M. E. Sharpe, 1997, pp. 400–403.
27 James L. Watson, 'Introduction', in James L. Watson (ed.), *Golden Arches East: McDonald's in East Asia*, California: Stanford University Press, 1997, p. 8.
28 Ibid.
29 Lucian W. Pye, 'Introduction: Political Culture and Political Development', in Lucian W. Pye and Sidney Verba (eds), *Political Culture and Political Development*, Princeton: Princeton University Press, 1965, p. 19.
30 Samuel P. Huntington, *The Clash of Civilizations and the Remaking of World Order*, London: Simon and Schuster, 1997.
31 Samuel P. Huntington, 'The Clash of Civilizations?', *Foreign Affairs*, 72, 3, Summer, 1993, p. 22.
32 Huntington, *The Clash*, pp. 310–311.
33 Ibid., p. 321.
34 Alfred Stepan, 'Religion, Democracy and the "Twin Tolerations"', *Journal of Democracy*, 11, 4, 2000, p. 44.
35 Ibid.
36 Kim Dae Jung, 'A Response to Lee Kuan Yew: Is Culture Destiny? The Myth of Asia's Anti-Democratic Values', *Foreign Affairs*, 73, November–December, 1994, pp. 189–194.
37 Ian Neary, 'Political Culture and Human Rights in Japan, Korea and Taiwan', *Nissan Occasional Paper Series*, 28, Oxford: Nissan Institute of Japanese Studies, 1998, p. 1.
38 David Kelly, 'The Search for Freedom as a Universal Value', in David Kelly and Anthony Reid (eds), *Asian Freedoms: The Idea of Freedom in East and Southeast Asia*, Cambridge: Cambridge University Press, 1998, p. 94.
39 Baogang He, *The Democratization of China*, London: Routledge, 1996, p. 161.
40 Lee Teng-hui, 'Chinese Culture and Political Renewal', *Journal of Democracy*, 6, 4, 1995, p. 6.
41 Ibid.
42 Ibid., p. 7.
43 Kim Dae Jung, 'A Response', p. 191.
44 Ibid., p. 192.
45 Svensson, *The Chinese Conception*, p. 15.
46 Bilahari Kausikan, 'The "Asian Values" Debate', p. 33.
47 Lucian W. Pye, 'Introduction: Political Culture and Political Development', in Lucian W. Pye and Sidney Verba (eds), *Political Culture and Political Development*, Princeton: Princeton University Press, p. 19.
48 Charles Taylor, 'Conditions of an Unforced Consensus on Human Rights', in

Joanne R. Bauer and Daniel A. Bell (eds), *The East Asian Challenge for Human Rights*, Cambridge: Cambridge University Press, 1999, pp. 124–146.

49 Fukuyama, *The End of History*, p. 287.
50 Francis Fukuyama, 'Asian Values in the Wake of the Asian Crisis', *The Review of Korean Studies*, 2, September, 1999, p. 21.
51 Fukuyama, *The End of History*, p. 338.
52 David Held, 'Anything but a dog's life? Further comments on Fukuyama, Callinicos, and Giddens', *Theory and Society*, 22, 1993, p. 295.
53 Inoue Tatsuo, 'Liberal Democracy and Asian Orientalism', in Joanne R. Bauer and Daniel A. Bell (eds), *The East Asian Challenge for Human Rights*, Cambridge: Cambridge University Press, 1999, p. 27.
54 Fareed Zakaria, 'The Rise of Illiberal Democracy', *Foreign Affairs*, 76, 6, November–December, 1997, p. 24.
55 Inoue Tatsuo, 'Liberal Democracy', pp. 27–28.
56 Mark T. Berger, 'Mythologies: The East Asian Miracle and Post-Cold War Capitalism', *positions*, 4, 1, 1996, p. 121.
57 Tu Weiming, 'A Confucian Perspective on the Core Values of the Global Community', *The Review of Korean Studies*, 2, September, 1999, p. 55.
58 Bhikhu Parekh, 'The Cultural Particularity of Liberal Democracy', in David Held (ed.), *Prospects for Democracy: North, South, East, West*, Cambridge: Polity Press, 1993, p. 167.
59 Haechang Choung, 'The Philosophical Turn and Creative Progress in Korean Philosophy', *The Review of Korean Studies*, 2, September, 1999, p. 87.
60 Young-chan Ro, 'Korean World View and Values: Economic Implications', *The Review of Korean Studies*, 2, September, 1999, p. 51.
61 Laurence Whitehead, 'The Democratization of Taiwan: A Comparative Perspective', in Steve Tsang and Hung-mao Tien (eds), *The Democratization of Taiwan: Implications for China*, London: Macmillan, 1999, p. 171.
62 C. L. Chiou, *Democratizing Oriental Despotism: China from 4 May 1919 to 4 June 1989 and Taiwan from 28 February 1947 to 28 June 1990*, New York: St. Martin's Press, 1995, p. 74.
63 Lucian W. Pye, *Asian Power and Politics: The Cultural Dimensions of Authority*, Cambridge, Massachusetts: Belknap Press of Harvard University Press, 1985, p. 51.
64 Ibid.
65 Laurence Whitehead, 'Stirrings of Mutual Recognition', *Journal of Democracy*, 11, 4, 2000, p. 68.
66 Kishore Mahbubani, 'The Pacific Way', *Foreign Affairs*, 74, 1, January–February, 1995, p. 102.
67 Liu Binyan, 'Civilization Grafting: No Culture is an Island', *Foreign Affairs*, 72, 1, September–October, 1993, p. 19.
68 Eliza Lee, 'Human Rights and Non-Western Values', in Michael Davis (ed.), *Human Rights and Chinese Values: Legal, Philosophical and Political Perspectives*, New York: Oxford University Press, 1995, p. 87.
69 These differences of opinion point to the internal heterogeneity of the Asian region.
70 Christina M. Cerna, 'Universality of Human Rights and Cultural Diversity: Implementation of Human Rights in Difference Socio-Cultural Contexts', *Human Rights Quarterly*, 16, 1994, pp. 740–752.
71 Onuma Yasuaki, 'Toward an Intercivilizational Approach to Human Rights', in Joanne R. Bauer and Daniel A. Bell (eds), *The East Asian Challenge for Human Rights*, Cambridge: Cambridge University Press, 1999, pp. 103–123.
72 Pye, *Asian Power and Politics*, p. 342.

73 Jan Nederveen Pieterse, 'Globalization as Hybridization', *International Sociology*, 9, 2, June, 1994, p. 173.
74 Larry Diamond and Ramon H. Myers, 'Introduction: Elections and Democracy in Greater China', *The China Quarterly*, 162, June, 2000, p. 367.
75 Bell and Jayasuriya, 'Understanding Illiberal Democracy', p. 2.
76 Ibid., p. 9 and p. 15.
77 Pye, *Asian Power and Politics*, p. 331.
78 Donald Stone MacDonald, *The Koreans: Contemporary Politics and Society*, 2nd edition, Boulder: Westview Press, 1990, p. 16.
79 Chung-Si Ahn, 'Democratization and Political Reform in Korea: Development, Culture, Leadership and Institutional Change', in Doh Chull Shin, Myeong-Han Zoh and Myung Chey (eds), *Korea in the Global Wave of Democratization*, Seoul: Seoul National University Press, 1994, p. 169.
80 Jung Bock Lee, 'The Political Process in Korea', in Soon Hoom Kil and Chung-in Moon (eds), *Understanding Korean Politics: An Introduction*, New York: State University of New York Press, 2001, p. 148.
81 James Cotton, 'From Authoritarianism to Democracy in South Korea', in James Cotton (ed.), *Korea Under Roh Tae Woo: Northern Policy and Inter-Korean Relations*, Sydney: Allen and Unwin, 1993, p. 33.
82 Byung-Kook Kim, 'Korea's Crisis of Success', in Larry Diamond and Marc F. Plattner (eds), *Democracy in East Asia*, Baltimore, London: The Johns Hopkins University Press, 1998, p. 127.
83 Ibid.
84 Philippe Schmitter, 'Danger and Dilemmas of Democracy', *Journal of Democracy*, 5, 2, 1994, p. 59.
85 Linda Chao and Ramon H. Myers, *The First Chinese Democracy: Political Life in the Republic of China*, Baltimore: The Johns Hopkins University Press, 1998, pp. 3–4.
86 Ibid., p. 4.
87 Linda Chao and Ramon H. Myers, 'How Elections are Promoting Democracy in Taiwan Under Martial Law', *China Quarterly*, 162, June, 2000, p. 389.
88 Chao and Myers, *The First Chinese Democracy*, p. 60.
89 Chiou, *Democratizing Oriental Despotism*, p. 80.
90 Hung-mao Tien, 'Elections and Taiwan's Democratic Development', in Hung-mao Tien and Charles Chi-hsiang Chang (eds), *Taiwan's Electoral Politics and Democratic Transition: Riding the Third Wave*, Armonk, New York: M. E. Sharpe, 1996, p. 23.
91 John F. Copper, 'Taiwan's 2000 Presidential and Vice Presidential Election: Consolidating Democracy and Creating a New Era of Politics', *Maryland Series in Contemporary Asian Studies*, 157, 2, 2000, p. 45. James Soong split from the Kuomintang and ran as an independent after Lee Teng-hui supported Lien Chan's candidacy ahead of James Soong's.
92 Kevin J. O'Brien and Lianjiang Li, 'Accommodating "Democracy", in a One Party State: Introducing Village Elections in China', *The China Quarterly*, 162, June, 2000, p. 488.
93 Baogang He, 'Are Village Elections Competitive?: The Case Study of Zhejiang', in J. Chen (ed.), *China's Challenge in the Twenty-first Century*, Hong Kong: City University of Hong Kong Press, 2002.
94 Ibid.
95 Jean C. Oi and Scott Rozelle, 'Elections and Power: The Locus of Decision-Making in Chinese Villages', *The China Quarterly*, 162, June, 2000, p. 537.
96 Fareed Zakaria, 'The Rise of Illiberal Democracy', *Foreign Affairs*, 76, 6, November–December, 1997, p. 24.
97 MacDonald, *The Koreans*, p. 141.

98 Ibid.
99 The China Youth Party was the officially endorsed 'opposition' party.
100 Chiou, *Democratizing Oriental Despotism*, p. 75.
101 Byung-Kook Kim, 'Korea's Crisis of Success', p. 129.
102 Doh C. Shin, *Mass Politics and Culture in Democratizing Korea*, Cambridge: Cambridge University Press, 1999, p. 179.
103 Sunhyuk Kim, 'Patronage Politics as an Obstacle to Democracy in South Korea: Regional Networks and Democratic Consolidation', in Howard Handelman and Mark Tessler (eds), *Democracy and Its Limits: Lessons from Asia, Latin America and the Middle East*, Notre Dame: University of Notre Dame Press, 1999, p. 119.
104 Byung-Kook Kim, 'Korea's Crisis of Success', p. 130.
105 Sunhyuk Kim, 'Patronage Politics', p. 123.
106 Byung-Kook Kim, 'Politics of Democratic Consolidation in Korea', paper presented at the 16th World Congress of the International Political Science Association, Berlin, August 21–25, 1994, p. 33.
107 David Steinberg, 'Korea: Triumph and Turmoil', *Journal of Democracy*, 9, 2, 1998, p. 80.
108 Ibid., p. 82.
109 Byung-Kook Kim, 'Korea's Crisis of Success', pp. 117–118.
110 Consider the preeminent role of Kim Dae Jung, Kim Jong Pil and Kim Young Sam in South Korean politics.
111 Shim Jae Hoon and Andrew Sherry, 'Cutting the Knot', *Far Eastern Economic Review*, 158, 30 November, 1995, pp. 66–72.
112 David Martin Jones, *Political Development in Pacific Asia*, Cambridge: Polity Press, 1997, p. 157.
113 Jean Blondel and Ian Marsh, 'Conclusion', in Ian Marsh, Jean Blondel and Takashi Inoguchi (eds), *Democracy, Governance and Economic Performance: East and Southeast Asia*, Tokyo: United Nations University Press, 1999, p. 338.
114 Joseph Bosco, 'Factions versus Ideology: Mobilization Strategies in Taiwan's Elections', *The China Quarterly*, 137, March, 1994, p. 30.
115 Teh-fu Huang, 'Elections and the Evolution of the Kuomintang', in Hung-mao Tien and Charles Chi-hsiang Chang (eds), *Taiwan's Electoral Politics and Democratic Transition: Riding the Third Wave*, Armonk, New York: M. E. Sharpe, 1996, p. 127.
116 Ibid.
117 Yun-han Chu, *Crafting Democracy in Taiwan*, Taipei: Institute for National Policy Research, 1992, p. 152.
118 Ibid.
119 Ming-tong Chen, 'Local Factions and Elections in Taiwan's Democratization', in Hung-mao Tien and Charles Chi-hsiang Chang (eds), *Taiwan's Electoral Politics and Democratic Transition: Riding the Third Wave*, Armonk, New York: M. E. Sharpe, 1996, pp. 176–177.
120 Bosco, 'Factions', p. 39.
121 Ibid.
122 Mayfair Mei-Hui Yang, 'The Gift Economy and State Power in China', *Comparative Studies in Society and History*, 31, 1, 1989, p. 35.
123 Ibid., p. 40. See also Joseph Bosco, 'Taiwan Factions: Guanxi, Patronage and the State in Local Politics', in Murray A. Rubinstein (ed.), *The Other Taiwan: 1945 to the Present*, Armonk, New York: M. E. Sharpe, 1994, pp. 114–144.
124 Yun-han Chu, 'Challenges', p. 127.
125 Yun-han Chu and Larry Diamond, 'Taiwan's 1998 Elections: Implications for Democratic Consolidation', *Asian Survey*, 39, 5, September–October, 1999, p. 819.

126 Ibid., p. 815.
127 Baogang He, 'Are Elections Competitive?'.
128 Carter Center–Ministry of Civil Affairs Seminar on Standardizing Village Committee Election Procedures, Beijing, 6–7 August, 2000.
129 Børge Bakken, 'Principled and Unprincipled Democracy: The Chinese Approach to Evaluation and Election', in Hans Antlöv and Ngo Tak-Wing (eds), *The Cultural Construction of Politics in Asia*, Surrey: Curzon Press, 2000, p. 109.
130 Ibid., p. 110.
131 Ibid.
132 Speaking at the Carter Center–Ministry of Civil Affairs Seminar on Standardizing Village Committee Election Procedures, Beijing, 6–7 August, 2000.
133 Andrew J. Nathan, 'Historical Perspectives on Chinese Democracy: The Overseas Democracy Movement Today', in R. Jeans (ed.), *Roads Not Taken: The Struggle of Opposition Parties in Twentieth Century China*, Boulder: Westview Press, 1992, p. 313.
134 Ibid., p. 315.
135 Yuen Ying Chan and Peter Kwong, 'Trashing the Hopes of Tiananmen?', *The Nation*, April, 1990, p. 560.
136 Edmund S. K. Fung and Chen Jie, 'Changing Perceptions: The Attitudes of the PRC Chinese Towards Australia and China, 1989–1996', *Australia–Asia Paper*, 78, November, 1996, p. 19.
137 Ibid.
138 Verba, 'Comparative Political Culture', pp. 550–551.
139 Alastair Iain Johnston, 'Learning Versus Adaptation: Explaining Change in China's Arms Control Policy in the 1980s and 1990s', *The China Journal*, 35, January, 1996, pp. 27–62. Johnston distinguishes between learning and adapting. He argues that learning involves a fundamental change in assumptions and approach, whereas adapting implies adjusting to changing circumstances.
140 Doh Shin, *Mass Politics and Culture in Democratizing Korea*, Cambridge: Cambridge University Press, 1999, p. 180.
141 Yun-han Chu, *Crafting Democracy in Taiwan*, p. 25.
142 Steinberg, 'Korea', p. 82.
143 Wm. Theodore de Bary, 'Confucianism and Human Rights in China', in Larry Diamond and Marc F. Plattner (eds), *Democracy in East Asia*, Baltimore, London: The Johns Hopkins University Press, 1998, p. 43.
144 Ibid.
145 Quoted in Roger du Mars, 'South Korea: Fear is a Hard Habit to Break', in Louise Williams and Roland Rich (eds), *Losing Control: Freedom of the Press in Asia*, Canberra: Asia Pacific Press, 2000, p. 194.
146 Ibid.
147 Ibid.
148 David Steinberg, 'The Role of the US Press in Improving Inter-Korean Relations', *The Korea Times*, 3 November, 2001, p. 4 and p. 7.
149 du Mars, 'South Korea', p. 201.
150 Gary D. Rawnsley and Ming-Yeh T. Rawnsley, 'Regime Transition and the Media in Taiwan', *Democratization*, 5, 2, Summer, 1998, p. 111.
151 Chiou, *Democratizing Oriental Despotism*, p. 72.
152 Ma-li Yang and Dennis Engbarth, 'Taiwan: All Politics, No Privacy', in Louise Williams and Roland Rich (eds), *Losing Control: Freedom of the Press in Asia*, Canberra: Asia Pacific Press, 2000, p. 208.
153 Ibid., p. 212.

154 Ibid.
155 Ibid., p. 217.
156 Rawnsley and Rawnsley, 'Regime Transition', p. 108.
157 Yuezhi Zhao, *Media, Market, and Democracy in China: Between the Party and the Bottom Line*, Urbana and Chicago: University of Illinois Press, 1998, p. 1.
158 Ibid., p. 34.
159 Ibid., p. 2.
160 David Clark, 'The Many Meanings of Rule of Law', in Kanishka Jayasuriya (ed.), *Law, Capitalism and Power in Asia: The Rule of Law and Legal Institutions*, London, New York: Routledge, 1999, p. 37.
161 Ibid.
162 Jianfu Chen, 'Market Economy and the Internationalization of Civil and Commercial Law in the People's Republic of China', in Kanishka Jayasuriya (ed.), *Law, Capitalism and Power in Asia: The Rule of Law and Legal Institutions*, London, New York: Routledge, 1999, p. 69.
163 Kanishka Jayasuriya, 'Introduction: A framework for the analysis of legal institutions in East Asia', in Kanishka Jayasuriya (ed.), *Law, Capitalism and Power in Asia: The Rule of Law and Legal Institutions*, London, New York: Routledge, 1999, p. 3.
164 Kun Yang, 'Judicial Review and Social Change in the Korean Democratizing Process', *The American Journal of Comparative Law*, 41, 1993, p. 2.
165 Ibid.
166 Ibid., p. 6.
167 Ibid.
168 A group of human rights lawyers active during the 1970s formed the organization 'Lawyers for Democratic Society' after the constitutional reforms of 1987. The organization has become the centre for public interest activities, including constitutional litigation.
169 Ibid.
170 Ibid., p. 7.
171 Cooney, 'A Community Changes', p. 254.
172 Hung-mao Tien, *The Great Transition*, p. 108.
173 Ibid., p. 111.
174 Cooney, 'A Community', p. 257.
175 Ibid., p. 259.
176 Jianfu Chen, 'Market Economy', p. 77.
177 Ibid., p. 70.
178 Ibid., p. 78.
179 Kanishka Jayasuriya, 'Corporatism and Judicial Independence within Statist Legal Institutions in East Asia', in Kanishka Jayasuriya (ed.), *Law, Capitalism and Power in Asia: The Rule of Law and Legal Institutions*, London, New York: Routledge, 1999, p. 197.
180 Zou Keyuan, 'Reforming China's Judicial System: New Endeavours Toward Rule of Law', paper presented at East Asian Institute Conference on The Challenges to China's Fourth Generation Leadership, Singapore, 8–9 November, 2001, p. 5 and p. 10.
181 It is not only Jiang Zemin who has contemplated how such a system might work in contemporary China. Daniel A. Bell has proposed a bicameral model of democracy for China in which the upper house would be appointed on the basis of merit, while the lower house would be democratically elected. See Daniel A. Bell, *East Meets West: Human Rights and Democracy in East Asia*, Princeton: Princeton University Press, 2000, pp. 277–332.
182 Zheng Yongnian and Lai Hongyi, 'Rule by Virtue: Jiang Zemin's New Moral Order for the Party', *East Asian Institute Background Brief*, 83, March, 2001.

183 Steinberg, 'Korea', p. 82.
184 Doh Shin, *Mass Politics*, p. 218.
185 Chen Shui-bian, *The Son of Taiwan: The Life of Chen Shui-Bian and his Dreams for Taiwan*, trans. David J. Toman, Taipei: Taiwan Publishing Co. Ltd, 2000, pp. 119–126.
186 Ibid.
187 Chengxin Pan, 'Understanding Chinese Identity in International Relations: A Critique of Western Approaches', *Political Science*, 51, 2, December, 1999, p. 140.
188 Bhikhu Parekh, 'Cultural Particularity', p. 167.

5 Protest and globalization

1 An earlier version of this argument was first published in the journal *Democratization*. See Becky Shelley, 'Protest and Globalization: Media, Symbols and Audience in the Drama of Democratization', *Democratization*, 8, 4, Winter, 2001, pp. 155–174.
2 Geremie Barmié, 'A Day in the Death of China', *Far Eastern Economic Review*, 146, 9 November, 1989, p. 45.
3 For detail on protest activities throughout China between April and June 1989, see Andrew J. Nathan and Perry Link, *The Tiananmen Papers*, London: Little, Brown and Co., 2001.
4 Laurence Whitehead, 'The Drama of Democratization', *Journal of Democracy*, 10, 4, 1999, p. 84. Laurence Whithead's heuristic metaphor was first published as a journal article. Whitehead subsequently expanded and developed it further in his book *Democratization: Theory and Experience*, Oxford: Oxford University Press, 2002.
5 Whitehead, 'Drama', p. 96.
6 Ibid., p. 86.
7 Ibid., p. 96.
8 Whitehead, *Democratization*, p. 37.
9 Ibid., p. 38.
10 Su-Hoon Lee, 'Transitional Politics of Korea, 1987–1992: Activation of Civil Society', *Pacific Affairs*, 66, 1993–1994, pp. 354–355.
11 C. L. Chiou, *Democratizing Oriental Despotism: China from 4 May 1919 to 4 June 1989 and Taiwan from 28 February 1947 to 28 June 1990*, New York: St. Martin's Press, 1995, p. 1.
12 Ibid.
13 Linda Chao and Ramon H. Myers, *The First Chinese Democracy: Political Life in the Republic of China on Taiwan*, Baltimore: The Johns Hopkins University press, 1988, p. 63.
14 J. Bruce Jacobs, 'Political Opposition and Taiwan's Political Future', *The Australian Journal of Chinese Affairs*, 6, 1981, p. 27.
15 Ibid.
16 Chao and Myers, *The First Chinese Democracy*, p. 64.
17 The *Free China* journal was published during the 1950s. It advocated the ideas of freedom and democracy, and built upon the May Fourth culturalist tradition of intellectual criticism. The journal was shut down and its editor arrested following the publication of an editorial in support of Lei Chen's call for opposition politics.
18 I-chou Liu, 'The Development of the Opposition', in Steve Tsang and Hung-mao Tien (eds), *Democratization in Taiwan: Implications for China*, Hong Kong: Hong Kong University Press, 1999, p. 69.
19 Chao and Myers, *The First Chinese Democracy*, p. 57.

20 Marc J. Cohen, *Taiwan at the Crossroads: Human Rights, Political Development and Social Change on the Beautiful Island*, Washington DC: Asia Resource Centre, 1991, p. 38.

21 Ibid.

22 Ibid., p. 39.

23 Ibid.

24 Chao and Myers, *The First Chinese Democracy*, p. 58.

25 Cohen, *Taiwan at the Crossroads*, p. 39.

26 Steve Tsang and Hung-mao Tien, 'Introduction', in Steve Tsang and Hung-mao Tien (eds), *Democratization in Taiwan: Implications for China*, Hong Kong: Hong Kong University Press, 1999, p. 12.

27 Phil Kurata, 'The Sound of Silence', *Far Eastern Economic Review*, 108, 13 June, 1980, p. 16.

28 Cohen, *Taiwan at the Crossroads*, p. 39.

29 Donald N. Clark, 'Introduction', in Donald N. Clark (ed.), *The Kwangju Uprising: Shadows Over the Regime in South Korea*, Boulder: Westview Press, 1988, p. 13.

30 *The 5.18 History Compilation Committee of Kwangju City*, trans. Lee Kyung-soon and Ellen Bishop, City of Kwangju, 1998, pp. 147–149.

31 Bruce Cumings, *Korea's Place in the Sun: A Modern History*, New York: W. W. Norton and Co., 1997, p. 338.

32 See for example Nathan and Link (eds), *The Tiananmen Papers*, pp. 214–216 and p. 304.

33 Wang Chaohua, Wang Dan and Li Minqi, 'Dialogue on the Future of China', *New Left Review*, 235, 1999, p. 69.

34 Nicholas D. Kristof, 'Beijing Residents Block Army Move Near City Centre', *The New York Times*, 3 June, 1989, 1.

35 Robin Munro, 'Who Died in Beijing and Why', *The Nation*, June, 1990, p. 812.

36 Peter Golding and Philip Elliot, *Making the News*, London: Longman, 1979, p. 123.

37 Sheryl Wu Dunn, 'A Portrait of a Young Man as a Beijing Student Leader', *The New York Times*, 3 June, 1989, p. 4.

38 Henry Scott-Stokes and Lee Jai Eui (eds), *The Kwangju Uprising: Eyewitness Press Accounts of Korea's Tiananmen*, Armonk, New York: M. E. Sharpe, 2000, p. xix.

39 Jurgen Hinzpeter, 'I Bow My Head', in Henry Scott-Stokes and Lee Jai Eui (eds), *The Kwangju Uprising: Eyewitness Press Accounts of Korea's Tiananmen*, Armonk, New York: M. E. Sharpe, 2000, pp. 63–76.

40 James Lull, *China Turned On: Television, Reform and Resistance*, London: Routledge, 1991, p. 1.

41 Marshall McLuhan, *Understanding the Media: The Extensions of Man*, London: Routledge, Kegan and Paul, 1964, p. 15.

42 Craig Calhoun, 'Tiananmen, Television, and the Public Sphere: Internationalization of Culture and the Beijing Spring of 1989', *Public Culture*, 2, 1, Fall, 1989, p. 54.

43 Donald Sohn, 'Chun Doo Hwan's Manipulation of the Kwangju Popular Uprising', unpublished thesis, Cornell University, 1998, pp. 1–15.

44 Stuart Hall, Chas Critcher, Tony Jefferson, John Clarke and Brian Robert, *Policing the Crisis: Mugging, the State and Law and Order*, London: Macmillan, 1978, pp. 53–60.

45 Shujen Wang, 'Ideology and Foreign News Coverage: Propaganda Model Re-examined', *Asian Journal of Communications*, 5, 1, 1995, p. 117.

46 Ibid.

47 Henry Kamm, 'South Korea Troops Recapture Kwangju in Pre-dawn Strike', *The New York Times*, 27 May, 1980, pp. 1–6.
48 Phil Kurata, 'Violence in the Name of Reason', *Far Eastern Economic Review*, 106, 28 December, 1979, p. 27.
49 *Far Eastern Economic Review*, 'South Korea Focus '80', 108, 30 May, 1980, p. 40.
50 Ibid.
51 Robert Delfs, 'The People's Republic', *Far Eastern Economic Review*, 144, 1 June, 1989, p. 12; Emily Lau, 'Mourning the Dead', *Far Eastern Economic Review*, 144, 27 April, 1989, pp. 11–12.
52 Chiou, *Democratizing Oriental Despotism*, p. 94.
53 Hung-mao Tien, *The Great Transition: Political and Social Change in the Republic of China*, Stanford: Hoover Institution Press, 1989, p. 97.
54 Chiou, *Democratizing Oriental Despotism*, p. 94.
55 Phil Kurata, 'Democracy Goes on Trial with the Dissidents', *Far Eastern Economic Review*, 108, 4 April, 1980, p. 10.
56 James Fenton, *All the Wrong Places: Adrift in the Politics of Asia*, London: Viking, 1988, p. 241.
57 Ibid.
58 Linda Lewis, 'The "Kwangju Incident" Observed: An Anthropological Perspective on Civil Uprisings', in Donald Clark (ed.), *The Kwangju Uprising: Shadows Over the Regime in South Korea*, Boulder: Westview Press, 1988, p. 23.
59 James Curran and Michael Gurevitch, *Mass Media and Society*, London: Edward Arnold, 1991, pp. 178–193.
60 Ibid.
61 Suzanne Ogden, 'The Conflict Escalates as the Students Defend their Patriotism', in Suzanne Ogden, Kathleen Hartford, Lawrence Sullivan and David Zweig (eds), *China's Search for Democracy: The Student and Mass Movement of 1989*, Armonk, New York: M. E. Sharpe, 1992, p. 130.
62 Ibid., p. 212.
63 Calhoun, 'Tiananmen, Television', p. 58.
64 Lull, *China Turned On*, p. 191.
65 Ibid.
66 Denis McQuail, 'The Influence and Effects of Mass Media', in James Curran, Michael Gurevitch and Janet Woollacott (eds), *Mass Communication and Society*, London: Edward Arnold, 1977, p. 86.
67 Baogang He, *The Democratization of China*, p. 79.
68 Ibid.
69 Translated in Michel Oksenberg, Lawrence R. Sullivan and Marc Lambert (eds), *Beijing Spring, 1989: Confrontation and Conflict: The Basic Documents*, Armonk, New York: M. E. Sharpe, 1990, p. 86.
70 Chao and Myers, *The First Chinese Democracy*, p. 57.
71 Yangsun Chou and Andrew J. Nathan, 'Democratizing Transition in Taiwan', *Asian Survey*, 27, 3, March, 1987, p. 289.
72 *Far Eastern Economic Review*, 'Evolution or Revolution', editorial, 161, 5 February, 1998, p. 6.
73 Chiou, *Democratizing Oriental Despotism*, p. 85.
74 Chen Shui-bian, *The Son of Taiwan: The Life of Chen Shui-bian and his Dreams for Taiwan*, trans. David J. Toman, Taipei: Taiwan Publishing Co. Ltd., 2000, pp. 67–69.
75 James Palais, *Human Rights in Korea*, Washington DC: Asia Watch, 1986, p. 98.
76 Baogang He, *The Democratization of China*, London: Routledge, 1996, p. 82.
77 Kim Chung Keun, 'Days and Nights on the Street', in Henry Scott-Stokes and Lee Jai Eui (eds), *The Kwangju Uprising: Eyewitness Press Accounts of Korea's Tiananmen*, Armonk, New York: M. E. Sharpe, 2000, pp. 10–11.

78 Whitehead, 'Drama', p. 92.

79 Ibid.

80 Jacobs, 'Taiwan's Political Future', p. 22.

81 Hung-mao Tien, *The Great Transition*, p. 97.

82 John F. Copper, 'Taiwan's Recent Election: Progress Toward a Democratic System', in James C. Hsiung (ed.), *Contemporary Republic of China: The Taiwan Experience 1950–1980*, Westport: Praeger, 1981, p. 376.

83 Michael T. Kaufman, 'Moynihan Jeered at China Protest', *The New York Times*, 10 June, 1989, p. 6.

84 *Far Eastern Economic Review*, 'Britain's Obligation', editorial, 144, 22 June, 1989, p. 12.

85 Frank Ching, 'Toward Colonial Sunset: The Wilson Regime 1987–1992', in Ming K. Chan (ed.), *Precarious Balance: Hong Kong Between China and Britain 1842–1992*, Armonk, New York: M. E. Sharpe, 1994, p. 178.

86 Ibid., p. 179.

87 Lynn Pann, N. Balakrishnan and Paul Handley, 'Stirring the Blood', *Far Eastern Economic Review*, 145, 24 August, 1989, pp. 16–17.

88 Kim Richard Nossal, *The Beijing Massacre: Australian Responses*, Canberra: Australian Foreign Policy Papers, Australian National University, 1993, p. 33.

89 Warren John Tenney, 'U.S. Responses to the Tiananmen and Kwangju Incidents: American Relations with China and Korea', *Journal of North East Asian Studies*, 11, 4, 1992, p. 61.

90 Chao and Myers, *The First Chinese Democracy*, p. 120.

91 'From the Stage to the Page', *Free China Review*, 49, 7, July, 1999, p. 33.

92 Ibid.

93 Phil Kurata, 'Soft-line Prosecution', *Far Eastern Economic Review*, 107, 7 March, 1980, p. 22.

94 John Wickham, *Korea on the Brink: From the '12/12 Incident' to the Kwangju Uprising*, Washington DC: National Defense University Press, 1999, pp. 203–204.

95 Tenney, 'U.S. Responses', p. 66.

96 Mark Peterson, 'Americans and the Kwangju Incident', in Donald Clark (ed.), *The Kwangju Uprising: Shadows Over the Regime in South Korea*, Boulder: Westview Press, 1988, p. 60.

97 Shim Jae Hoon, 'Chun's Hand Can Stay the Noose', *Far Eastern Economic Review*, 109, 19 September, 1980, p. 13.

98 Wickham, *Korea on the Brink*, p. 149.

99 Bill Keller, 'Eager Not to Offend, Soviet Congress Criticizes Outside Pressure on China', *The New York Times*, 7 June, 1989, p. 10.

100 Steven R. Weisman, 'Japan, China's Main Foreign Benefactor Puts Billions in Aid in Doubt', *The New York Times*, 7 June, 1989, p. 10.

101 The nations included the United States, Japan, France, West Germany, Britain, Italy and Canada.

102 Robert Pear, 'President Assails Shootings in China', *The New York Times*, 4 June, 1989, p. 21.

103 M. C. Tai, 'Face Healing', *Far Eastern Economic Review*, 145, 27 July, 1989, pp. 11–12.

104 Weinraub, Bernard, 'President Spurns other Sanctions', *The New York Times*, 6 June, 1989, p. 14.

105 Jing-dong Yuan, 'Sanctions, Domestic Politics and US–China Policy', *Issues and Studies*, 33, 10 October, 1997, p. 95.

106 Tenney, 'U.S. Responses', p. 69.

107 Jing-dong Yuan, 'Sanctions', p. 96.

108 Hun Yi Jan, 'Interaction Between Mainland China and the UN Human Rights Regime', *Issues and Studies*, 24, 4, November–December, 1998, p. 76.
109 Ibid.
110 Ming Wan, 'Policies, Resource Commitments and Values: A Comparison of United States and Japanese Approaches to Human Rights in China', in John D. Montgomery (ed.), *Human Rights: Positive Policies in Asia and the Pacific Rim*, Hollis: Hollis Publishing Co, 1998, p. 44.
111 Quansheng Zhao and Barry Press, 'The US Promotion of Human Rights and China's Response', p. 49.

6 International non-government organizations

1 For example Philippe Schmitter, 'On Civil Society and the Consolidation of Democracy: Ten General Propositions and Nine Speculations about their Relation in Asian Democracies', paper presented at International Conference on Consolidating the Third Wave Democracies: Trends and Challenges, Taipei, Taiwan, 1995, and Gordon White, 'Civil Society, Democratization and Development (I): Clearing the Analytical Ground', *Democratization*, 1, 3, 1994, pp. 375–390.
2 Philippe C. Schmitter, 'The Influence of the International Context upon the Choice of National Institutions and Policies in Neo-Democracies', in Laurence Whitehead (ed.), *The International Dimensions of Democratization: Europe and the Americas*, New York: Oxford University Press, 1998, p. 38.
3 Philip G. Cerny, 'Paradoxes of the Competition State: The Dynamics of Political Globalization', *Government and Opposition*, 32, 2, 1997, p. 253.
4 Larry Diamond, *Developing Democracy: Towards Consolidation*, Baltimore: The Johns Hopkins University Press, 1999, p. 221.
5 Allen Choate, 'Legal Aid in China', *The Asia Foundation: Working Paper Series*, 12, San Francisco: The Asia Foundation, 2000.
6 Leon Gordenker and Thomas G. Weiss, 'Devolving Responsibilities: A Framework for Analyzing NGOs and Services', in Thomas G. Weiss (ed.), *Beyond UN Subcontracting: Task-Sharing with Regional Security Arrangements and Service-Providing NGOs*, Hampshire: Macmillan; New York: St. Martin's Press, 1998, p. 38.
7 In the 1999–2000 financial year US$23,746,000 came from the United States government, while US$5,420,000 was provided by other governments, multilateral organizations and private foundations. Another US$12,156,000 came from net assets from restrictions. The Asia Foundation, *The Asia Foundation Annual Report 2000*, San Francisco: Asia Foundation, 2000, p. 24.
8 Cho Tong-jae, 'The Asia Foundation: Korea Office History 1951–1970', unpublished paper, available from Seoul office of The Asia Foundation, p. 58.
9 Choate, 'Legal Aid'.
10 'Taiwan', Asia Foundation in Taiwan, undated publication.
11 Sunny Ho, Program Officer, Asia Foundation in Taiwan, 24 August, 2000.
12 The Asia Foundation, http://www.asiafoundation.org/programs/prog-asia-kore.html, accessed 7 March, 2002.
13 Scott Snyder, The Asia Foundation Representative in Seoul, 17 August, 2000.
14 Thomas Carothers, 'The NED at 10', *Foreign Policy*, 95, Summer, 1994, p. 134.
15 Lori Fisler Damrosch, 'Politics Across Borders: Non-intervention and Non-forcible Influence over Domestic Affairs', *American Journal of International Law*, 83, 1, 1989, p. 18.
16 National Endowment for Democracy, http://www.ned.org/page_3/asia.html, accessed 15 October, 1999.

17 International Republican Institute, http://www.iri.org.aboutiri/iri.html, accessed 21 April, 1998.

18 Karen Jason, 'The Role of International Non-governmental Organizations in International Election Observing', *New York University Journal of International Law and Politics*, 24, 4, 1991–1992, p. 1822.

19 Carter Center, http:sol;/www.emory.edu/CARTER_CENTER/homepage.htm, accessed 21 April, 1998.

20 Some of Jimmy Carter's efforts in this regard have provoked the ire of the present Republican administration. In particular, his visit to Cuba in 2002 drew criticism from President George W. Bush and others.

21 Jimmy Carter, 'It's Wrong to Demonize China', *Carter Center: Reports and Speeches*, 1998, http://www.emory.edu/CARTER_CENTER/OPEDS/chinaop. htm, accessed 3 May, 1998.

22 Charles Costello, Director, Carter Center China Program, 30 July, 2000.

23 Shell Developments Limited Representative, 4 August, 2000.

24 Ford Foundation, http://www.fordfound.org/about/mission.html, accessed 18 March, 2002.

25 Colette Chabbott, 'Development INGOs', in John Boli and George M. Thomas (eds), *Constructing World Culture: International Nongovernmental Organizations Since 1875*, Stanford: Stanford University Press, 1999, p. 230.

26 Ford Foundation, http://www.fordfound.org/about/financial.cfm, accessed 18 March, 2002.

27 Ford Foundation, http://www.fordfound.org/about/mission.html, accessed 11 August, 1998.

28 Thomas Carothers, *Aiding Democracy Abroad: The Learning Curve*, Washington DC: Carnegie Endowment for International Peace, 1999, p. 20.

29 Park Tae-jin, The Asia Foundation Program Officer in Seoul, 17 August, 2000.

30 For an analysis of the applicability of the democratic peace thesis to East Asia see Edward Friedman, 'Immanuel Kant's Relevance to an Enduring Asia-Pacific Peace', in Edward Friedman and Barrett L. McCormick (eds), *What if China Doesn't Democratize? Implications for War and Peace*, Armonk, New York: M. E. Sharpe, 2000, pp. 224–258; and Barrett L. McCormick, 'U.S.–PRC Relations and the "Democratic Peace"', in Edward Friedman and Barrett L. McCormick (eds), *What if China Doesn't Democratize? Implications for War and Peace*, Armonk, New York: M. E. Sharpe, 2000, pp. 305–328.

31 Miyume Tanji and Stephanie Lawson, '"Democratic Peace" and "Asian Democracy": A Universalist–Particularist Tension', *Alternatives*, 22, 1997, p. 135.

32 Thomas Carothers, 'Democracy Assistance: The Question of Strategy', *Democratization*, 4, 3, 1997, p. 112 and p. 115.

33 David Martin Jones, 'The Metamorphosis of Tradition: The Idea of Law and Virtue in East Asian Political Thought', *South East Asian Journal of Social Science*, 21, 1, 1993, pp. 18–35.

34 David S. Goodman, 'Can China Change?', in Larry Diamond, Marc F. Plattner, Yun-han Chu and Hung-mao Tien (eds), *Consolidating the Third Wave Democracies: Regional Challenges*, Baltimore: The Johns Hopkins University Press, 1997, p. 250.

35 Ford Foundation, *The Ford Foundation in China*, undated publication, p. 5.

36 Chabbott, 'Development INGOs', p. 388.

37 Carothers, *Aiding Democracy*, p. 21.

38 It was only after Roh Tae Woo's democratization declaration in 29 June 1987 that Kim was reinstated as an editorial writer, Cho Tong-jae, 'The Asia Foundation', p. 45.

39 Rex Wang, Program Officer and Officer in Charge of The Asia Foundation's Taipei office between 1972–1998, 24 August, 2000.
40 The Asia Foundation, *20 Years in China*, San Francisco: The Asia Foundation, 1999, p. 7.
41 Ibid.
42 Sunny Ho, Program Officer, Asia Foundation in Taiwan, 24 August, 2000.
43 Rex Wang, Program Officer and Officer in Charge of The Asia Foundation's Taipei office between 1972–1998, 24 August, 2000.
44 Rex Wang, Program Officer and Officer in Charge of The Asia Foundation's Taipei office between 1972–1998, 24 August, 2000.
45 CNA, News Releases, http://web/oop/gov/tw/web/enews.nst, accessed 30 June, 2000.
46 Choate, 'Legal Aid', p. 25.
47 Ibid.
48 Ford Foundation, *The Ford Foundation in China*, p. 7.
49 Although there is a large body of literature assessing the significance of village elections, only limited consideration has been given to the role of international NGO activity. See Becky Shelley, 'Political Globalization and the Politics of International Non-governmental Organizations: The Case of Village Democracy in China', *Australian Journal of Political Science*, 35, 2, July, 2000, pp. 225–238; Tianjin Shi, 'Village Committee Elections in China: Institutionalist Tactics for Democracy', *World Politics* 51, 3 April, 1999, pp. 385–412; Robert Pastor, 'Mediating Elections', *Journal of Democracy*, 9, 1, 1998, pp. 154–163; Daniel Kelliher, 'The Chinese Debate Over Village Self-government', *The China Journal*, 37, January, 1997, pp. 63–86.
50 Carter Center, *The Carter Center Delegation Report: Village Elections in China and Agreement on Cooperation with the Ministry of Civil Affairs People's Republic of China March 2–15 1998*, Atlanta: Carter Center, 1998, attachment 1.
51 Ibid., p. 4.
52 Carter Center, *Report of The Carter Center's Fourth Observation of Chinese Village Elections January 4–13, 2000*, http://www.cartercenter.org/CHINA/dox/reports/2000.htm, accessed 14 July, 2000.
53 Tianjin Shi, 'Village Committee Elections in China', p. 408. However, Shi only mentions Kevin O'Brien's involvement but O'Brien himself recalls that White's contribution was significant, email from Kevin O'Brien, 3 May 1998.
54 Ibid.
55 International Republican Institute, *People's Republic of China: Election Observation Report May 15–31, 1994*, Washington, DC: International Republican Institute, 1995, p. 12.
56 For further information on the conference see Carter Center, *The Carter Center Report on Chinese Elections in Fujian and the Conference to Revise the National Procedures on Villager Committee Elections*, Atlanta: Carter Center, 2001.
57 International Republican Institute, *People's Republic of China*, pp. 34–37.
58 Carter Center, *Carter Center Delegation to Observe Village Elections in China March 4–16, 1997*, Atlanta: Carter Center, 1997, p. 12.
59 Carter Center, *Report of the Fifth Mission on Chinese Village Elections by the Carter Center June 20–July 3, 1998*, Atlanta: Carter Center, 1998, p. 4.
60 International Republican Institute, *Election Observation Report Fujian*, p. 5.
61 International Republican Institute, *People's Republic of China*, p. 2.
62 International Republican Institute, *Election Observation Report Fujian, People's Republic of China May 1997: An Update to 1994 Election Observation Report*, Washington DC: International Republican Institute, p. 2.
63 Carter Center, *Carter Center Delegation to Observe*, p. 4.
64 Carter Center, *Carter Center Delegation Report*, p. 3.

65 The experts included the Chair of the California Fair Political Practises Commission, a lecturer on local elections, an election attorney and former elections officer, and a Superintendent of Elections.

66 The March 1997 Carter Center mission included Dr R. Pastor, Dr M. Brown Bullock, Dr D. Carroll, Dr A. Choate, Mr I. McKinnon, Dr Q. Tan and Dr A. Thurston. The March 1998 mission included Dr R. Pastor, Mr J. Aaronson, Ms S. Baker, Mr T. Crick, Dr L. Diamond, Mr P. Dieckmann, Dr Y. Liu, Dr J. Oi, Dr Q. Tan.

67 Carter Center, *Carter Center Delegation Report*, p. 9.

68 Jones, 'Metamorphosis of Tradition', p. 23.

69 Carter Center, *Report of the Fifth Mission*, p. 8.

70 Harry Harding, 'The Halting Advance of Pluralism', *Journal of Democracy*, 9, 1, 1998, p. 11; and Shi, 'Village Committee Elections', p. 339.

71 Carothers, *Aiding Democracy*, p. 333.

72 Cerny, 'Paradoxes of the Competition State', p. 253.

73 Philip G. Cerny, 'Globalization and the Changing Logic of Collective Action', *International Organization*, 49, 4, Autumn, 1995, pp. 595–597.

74 Kelliher, 'The Chinese Debate', p. 76. Andrew J. Nathan concurs that international observers have enhanced the prospects for fair village elections in China, though not by a large amount. He argues that they have done so by serving as an information channel for higher levels of government to learn about problems. Andrew J. Nathan, 'Village Elections'. Email, 7 June, 1998.

75 *Washington Post*, 26 January, 1995.

76 Kelliher, 'The Chinese Debate', p. 76.

77 Carter Center, *Report of the Fifth Mission*, p. 8.

78 *People's Daily*, 19 October, 1998.

79 Carter Center, *Report of the Fifth Mission*, Appendix 8.

80 Andrew J. Nathan, 'Village Elections'. Email, 7 June, 1998.

81 Kelliher, 'The Chinese Debate', p. 77.

82 Liang Chao, 'U.S. Guests to Watch Elections', *China Daily*, 6 March, 1998 p. 3; Xinhua, 'Rural Votes More Democratic', *China Daily*, 13 March, 1998, p. 4.

83 Xinhua, ibid.

84 Xu Haitao, 'Grassroots Committees Made Accountable to Villagers', *China Daily*, 22 June, 1998, p. 9; Xinhua, 'Computer System Helps Rural Elections', *China Daily*, 30 June, 1998, p. 3; He Shang, 'Local Elections Take Democracy to Countryside', *China Daily*, 22 June, 1998, p. 3; Qingshan Tan, 'Village Elections Democratic', *China Daily*, 22 June, 1998, p. 8.

85 Robert Pastor, 'Seems Legit: A Thumbs Up for China's Electoral Experiment', *Time Magazine*, 151, 1, 1998, p. 38; Robert Pastor, 'Mediating Elections'; Robert Pastor, 'China is Climbing Democracy's Learning Curve', *Asian Wall Street Journal*, 8 September, 1998; Robert Pastor, 'Village Elections a Sign of Progress', *The Atlanta Journal*, 30 March, 1997.

86 Carter Center, *Carter Center Delegation Report*, p. 3.

87 Jason, 'The Role of International Nongovernmental Organizations', p. 1802.

88 Carter Center, *Carter Center Delegation*, p. 2.

89 Transcript from a press conference held by Vice President Al Gore, China World Hotel, Beijing, People's Republic of China, 26 March, 1997.

90 Carothers, *Aiding Democracy*, p. 313.

Conclusion

1 Andrew J. Nathan, 'Even Our Caution Must Be Hedged', *Journal of Democracy* 9, 1, 1998, p. 62.

2 Philippe C. Schmitter, 'The Influence of the International Context upon the Choice of National Institutions and Policies in Neo-Democracies', in Laurence Whitehead (ed.) *The International Dimensions of Democratization: Europe and the Americas*, New York: Oxford University Press, 1998, p. 35.
3 Atul Kohli, Peter Evans, Peter Katzenstein, Peter J. Przeworksi, Rudolph Adam, Susanne Hoeber, James C. Scott and Theda Skocpol, 'The Role of Theory in Comparative Politics: A Symposium', *World Politics*, 48, October, 1995, p. 6.
4 Dietrich Reuschemeyer, Evelyne Huber Stephens and John D. Stephens, *Capitalist Development and Democracy*, Oxford: Polity Press, 1992, p. 9.
5 Ibid., p. 73.

Bibliography

Acharya, Amitav, 'Southeast Asia's Democratic Moment', *Asian Survey*, 39, 3 May–June, 1999, pp. 418–432.

Acheson, Dean, *The Korean War*, New York: W. W. Norton and Co, 1971.

Afanasiev, Evgeny V., 'Vladimir Putin's New Foreign Policy and Russian Views of the Situation on the Korean Peninsula', *The Korean Journal of Defense Analysis*, 12, 2, Winter, 2000, pp. 7–17.

Ahn Byung-Joon, 'Korea's International Environment', in Thomas W. Robinson (ed.), *Democracy and Development in East Asia: Taiwan, South Korea and the Philippines*, Washington DC: The AEI Press, 1991, pp. 155–168.

Ahn Chung-Si, 'Democratization and Political Reform in Korea: Development, Culture, Leadership and Institutional Change', in Doh Chull Shin, Myeong-Han Zoh and Myung Chey (eds), *Korea in the Global Wave of Democratization*, Seoul: Seoul National University Press, 1993, pp. 161–178.

Almond, Gabriel and Powell, G. Bingham Jr., *Comparative Politics: A Developmental Approach*, Boston: Little Brown and Co, 1966.

Amnesty International, *Political Imprisonment in the People's Republic of China*, London: Amnesty International, 1978.

Amsden, Alice H., *Asia's New Giant: South Korea and Late Industrialization*, New York: Oxford University Press, 1989.

Angell, Alan, 'International Support for the Chilean Opposition', in Laurence Whitehead (ed.), *The International Dimensions of Democratization: Europe and the Americas*, New York: Oxford University Press, 1998, pp. 175–200.

Archer, Clive, *International Organizations*, second edition, London, New York: Routledge, 1995.

Archibugi, Daniele; Balduini, Sveva and Donati, Marco, 'The United Nations as an Agency of Global Democracy', in Barry Holden (ed.), *Global Democracy: Key Debates*, London, New York: Routledge, 2000, pp. 125–142.

Asia–Europe Foundation Monograph, *The Third Informal ASEM Seminar on Human Rights*, Paris, France, 19–20 June, 2000.

Asia Foundation in Taiwan, 'Taiwan', undated publication.

Bakken, Børge, 'Principled and Unprincipled Democracy: The Chinese Approach to Evaluation and Election', in Hans Antlöv and Ngo Tak-Wing, (eds), *The Cultural Construction of Politics in Asia*, Surrey: Curzon Press, 2000, pp. 107–130.

Barmié, Geremie, 'A Day in the Death of China', *Far Eastern Economic Review*, 146, 9 November, 1989, pp. 45–47.

Barrett, Richard E. and Chin, Soomi, 'Export-oriented States in the Capitalist World

System: Similarities and Differences', in Frederic C. Deyo (ed.), *The Political Economy of New Asian Industrialism*, Ithaca, New York: Cornell University Press, 1987, pp. 12–23.

Beetham, David, *The Legitimation of Power*, London: Macmillan, 1991.

Bell, Daniel A., *East Meets West: Human Rights and Democracy in East Asia*, Princeton: Princeton University Press, 2000.

Bell, Daniel A. and Jayasuriya, Kanishka, 'Understanding Illiberal Democracy: A Framework', in Daniel A. Bell, David Brown, Kanishka Jayasuriya and David Martin Jones, *Towards Illiberal Democracy in Pacific Asia*, London: Macmillan, 1995, pp. 1–16.

Berger, Carl, *The Korea Knot: A Military Political History*, revised edition, Philadelphia: University of Pennsylvania Press, 1968.

Berger, Mark T., 'Mythologies: The East Asian Miracle and Post-Cold War Capitalism', *positions*, 4, 1, 1996, pp. 90–126.

Bernholz, Peter, 'Democracy and Capitalism: Are they compatible in the long-run?', *Journal of Evolutionary Economics*, 10, 2000, pp. 3–16.

Bickers, Charles; Goad, G. Pierre; Dawson, Chester and Lee, Charles S., 'China's Challenge', *Far Eastern Economic Review*, 162, 23 September, 1999, pp. 43–44.

Blondel, Jean and Marsh, Ian, 'Conclusion', in Ian Marsh, Jean Blondel and Takashi Inoguchi (eds), *Democracy, Governance and Economic Performance: East and Southeast Asia*, Tokyo: United Nations University Press, 1999, pp. 333–356.

Bosco, Joseph, 'Factions versus Ideology: Mobilization Strategies in Taiwan's Elections', *The China Quarterly*, 137, March, 1994, pp. 28–63.

—— 'Taiwan Factions: Guanxi, Patronage and the State in Local Politics', in Murray A. Rubinstein (ed.), *The Other Taiwan: 1945 to the Present*, Armonk, New York: M. E. Sharpe, 1994, pp. 114–144.

Brown, David, 'Democratization and the Renegotiation of Ethnicity', in Daniel A. Bell, David Brown, Kanishka Jayasuriya and David Martin Jones, *Towards Illiberal Democracy in Pacific Asia*, New York: St. Martin's Press, 1995, pp. 134–164.

Bullard, Nicola; Bello, Walden and Malhotra, Kamal, *Taming the Tigers: The IMF and the Asian Crisis*, Bangkok: Focus on the Global South, Chulalongkorn University, 1998.

Byung Chul Koh, 'The Foreign and Unification Policies of the Republic of Korea', in Soong Hoom Kil and Chung-in Moon (eds), *Understanding Korean Politics: An Introduction*, New York: State University of New York Press, 2001, pp. 231–268.

Cai, Kevin G., 'The Political Economy of Economic Regionalism in Northeast Asia: A Unique and Dynamic Pattern', *East Asia: An International Quarterly*, 17, 2, 1999, pp. 6–46.

Calhoun, Craig, 'Tiananmen, Television, and the Public Sphere: Internationalization of Culture and the Beijing Spring of 1989', *Public Culture*, 2, 1, Fall, 1989, pp. 54–71.

Carothers, Thomas, 'Democracy and Human Rights: Policy Allies or Rivals', *The Washington Quarterly*, 17, 3, Summer, 1994, pp. 109–120.

—— 'The NED at 10', *Foreign Policy*, 95, Summer, 1994, pp. 123–138.

—— 'Democracy Assistance: The Question of Strategy', *Democratization*, 4, 3, 1997, pp. 109–132.

—— 'The Resurgence of United States Political Development Assistance to Latin America in the 1980s', in Laurence Whitehead (ed.), *The International Dimensions of Democratization: Europe and the Americas*, New York: Oxford University Press, 1998, pp. 125–145.

—— *Aiding Democracy Abroad: The Learning Curve*, Washington DC: Carnegie Endowment for International Peace, 1999.

—— 'The End of the Transition Paradigm', *Journal of Democracy*, 13, 1, 2002, pp. 5–21.

Carter Center, *Carter Center Delegation to Observe Village Elections in China March 4–16, 1997*, Atlanta: Carter Center, 1997.

—— *Report of the Fifth Mission on Chinese Village Elections by the Carter Center June 20–July 3, 1998*, Atlanta: Carter Center. 1998.

—— *The Carter Center Delegation Report: Village Elections in China and Agreement on Cooperation with the Ministry of Civil Affairs People's Republic of China March 2–15 1998*, Atlanta: Carter Center, 1998.

—— http://www.emory.edu/CARTER_CENTER/homepage.htm, accessed 21 April, 1998.

—— *Report of The Carter Center's Fourth Observation of Chinese Village Elections January 4–13, 2000*, http://www.cartercenter.org/CHINA/dox/reports/2000.htm, accessed 14 July, 2000.

—— *The Carter Center Report on Chinese Elections in Fujian and the Conference to Revise the National Procedures on Villager Committee Elections*, Atlanta: Carter Center, 2001.

Carter, Jimmy, 'It's Wrong to Demonize China', *Carter Center: Reports and Speeches*, 1998, http://www.emory.edu/CARTER_CENTER/OPEDS/chinaop.htm, accessed 3 May, 1998.

Cerna, Christina M., 'Universality of Human Rights and Cultural Diversity: Implementation of Human Rights in Different Socio-Cultural Contexts', *Human Rights Quarterly*, 16, 1994, pp. 740–752.

Cerny, Philip G., 'Globalization and the Changing Logic of Collective Action', *International Organization*, 49, 4, Autumn, 1995, pp. 595–625.

—— 'Paradoxes of the Competition State: The Dynamics of Political Globalization', *Government and Opposition*, 32, 2, 1997, pp. 251–274.

Chabbott, Colette, 'Development INGOs', in John Boli and George M. Thomas (eds), *Constructing World Culture: International Nongovernmental Organizations Since 1875*, Stanford: Stanford University Press, 1999, pp. 222–248.

Chan, Steve, 'Cores and Peripheries: Interaction Patterns in Asia', *Comparative Political Studies*, 15, 3, October, 1992, pp. 314–340.

—— 'Peace by Pieces? Mainland–Taiwan Transaction Flows', in Steve Chan, Cal Clark and Danny Lam (eds), *Beyond the Developmental State: East Asia's Political Economies Reconsidered*, Hampshire: Macmillan Press, 1998, pp. 60–70.

Chan, Yuen Ying and Kwong, Peter, 'Trashing the Hopes of Tiananmen?', *The Nation*, April, 1990, pp. 559–564.

Chand, Vikram K., 'Democratization from the Outside In: NGOs and International Efforts to Promote Open Elections', in Thomas G. Weiss (ed.), *Beyond UN Subcontracting: Task-Sharing with Regional Security Arrangements and Service Providing NGOs*, London: Macmillan; New York: St. Martin's Press, 1998, pp. 160–183.

Chao, Liang, 'U.S. Guests to Watch Elections', *China Daily*, 6 March, 1998, p. 3.

Chao, Linda and Myers, Ramon H., *The First Chinese Democracy: Political Life in the Republic of China on Taiwan*, Baltimore: The Johns Hopkins University Press, 1988.

—— 'How Elections Promoted Democracy in Taiwan Under Martial Law', *China Quarterly*, 162, June, 2000, pp. 387–409.

Chen, Jian, *China's Road to the Korean War: The Making of the Sino-American Confrontation*, New York: Columbia University Press, 1994.

Chen, Jianfu, 'Market Economy and the Internationalization of Civil and Commercial Law in the People's Republic of China', in Kanishka Jayasuriya (ed.), *Law, Capitalism and Power in Asia: The Rule of Law and Legal Institutions*, London, New York: Routledge, 1999, pp. 69–93.

Chen, Ming-tong, 'Local Factions and Elections in Taiwan's Democratization', in Hung-mao Tien and Charles Chi-hiang Chang (eds), *Taiwan's Electoral Politics and Democratic Transition: Riding the Third Wave*, Armonk, New York: M. E. Sharpe, 1996, pp. 174–192.

Chen Shui-bian, *The Son of Taiwan: The Life of Chen Shui-bian and his Dreams for Taiwan*, trans. David J. Toman, Taipei: Taiwan Publishing Co. Ltd, 2000.

Cheng, Tun-jen, 'Democratizing the Quasi-Leninist Regime', *World Politics*, 41, 4, 1989, pp. 471–499.

—— 'Is the Dog Barking? The Middleclass and Democratic Movements in the East Asian NICs', *International Studies Notes: Research Paper*, 89–105, Spring, 1990.

Ching, Frank, 'Toward Colonial Sunset: The Wilson Regime 1987–1992', in Ming K. Chan (ed.), *Precarious Balance: Hong Kong Between China and Britain 1842–1992*, Armonk, New York: M. E. Sharpe, 1994, pp. 161–192.

Chiou, C. L., *Democratizing Oriental Despotism: China from 4 May 1919 to 4 June 1989 and Taiwan from 28 February 1947 to 28 June 1990*, New York: St. Martin's Press, 1995.

Cho Tong-jae, 'The Asia Foundation: Korea Office History 1951–1970', unpublished paper, available from Seoul office, The Asia Foundation.

Choate, Allen, 'Legal Aid in China', *The Asia Foundation: Working Paper Series*, 12, San Francisco: The Asia Foundation, 2000.

Chossodovsky, Michel, *Korea Web Weekly*, 1997, http://www.kimsoft.com/1997/sk/imfc.htm, accessed 24 March, 1999.

Chou, Yangsun and Nathan, Andrew J., 'Democratizing Transition in Taiwan', *Asian Survey*, 27, 3, March, 1987, pp. 277–297.

Choung, Haechang, 'The Philosophical Turn and Creative Progress in Korean Philosophy', *The Review of Korean Studies*, 2, September, 1999, pp. 71–94.

Chu, Yun-han, *Crafting Democracy in Taiwan*, Taipei: Institute for National Policy Research, 1992.

Chu, Yun-han and Diamond, Larry, 'Taiwan's 1998 Elections: Implications for Democratic Consolidation', *Asian Survey*, 39, 5, September–October, 1999, pp. 808–822.

Chung, Pei-chi, 'The Cultural Other and National Identity in the Taiwanese and South Korean Media', *Gazette*, 62, 2, 2000, pp. 99–115.

Clark, David, 'The Many Meanings of Rule of Law', in Kanishka Jayasuriya (ed.), *Law, Capitalism and Power in Asia: The Rule of Law and Legal Institutions*, London, New York: Routledge, 1999, pp. 28–44.

Clark, Donald N., 'Introduction', in Donald N. Clark (ed.), *The Kwangju Uprising: Shadows Over the Regime in South Korea*, Boulder: Westview Press, 1988, pp. 1–14.

Clough, Ralph, *Island China*, Cambridge, Massachusetts: Harvard University Press, 1978.

CNA, News Releases, http://web/oop/gov/tw/web/enews.nst, accessed 30 June, 2000.

Cohen, Marc J., *Taiwan at the Crossroads: Human Rights, Political Development and Social Change on the Beautiful Island*, Washington DC: Asia Resource Centre, 1991.

Collier, David and Mahon, James E. Jr., 'Conceptual "Stretching" Revisited: Adapting Categories in Comparative Analysis', *American Political Science Review*, 87, 4, December, 1993, pp. 845–856.

Collier, Ruth Berins, *Paths Toward Democracy: The Working Class and Elites in Western Europe and South America*, Cambridge: Cambridge University Press, 1999.

Compton, Robert, *East Asian Democratization: Impact of Globalization, Culture and Economy*, Westport: Praeger, 2000.

Cooney, Sean, 'A Community Changes: Taiwan's Council of Grand Justices and Liberal Democratic Reform', in Kanishka Jayasuriya (ed.), *Law, Capitalism and Power in Asia: The Rule of Law and Legal Institutions*, London, New York: Routledge, 1999, pp. 253–280.

Cooper, Robert, *The Post-Modern State and the World Order*, London: Demos, 1996.

Copper, John F., 'Taiwan's Recent Election: Progress Toward a Democratic System', in James C. Hsiung (ed.), *Contemporary Republic of China: The Taiwan Experience 1950–1980*, Westport: Praeger, 1981, pp. 374–380.

—— 'Taiwan's 2000 Presidential and Vice Presidential Election: Consolidating Democracy and Creating a New Era of Politics', *Maryland Series in Contemporary Asian Studies*, 157, 2, 2000.

Cossa, Ralph A., 'US–ROK–Japan: Why a "Virtual Alliance" Makes Sense', *The Korean Journal of Defense Analysis*, 12, 1, Summer, 2000, pp. 67–86.

Cotton, James, 'Understanding the State in South Korea: Bureaucratic-Authoritarian or State Autonomy Theory', *Comparative Political Studies*, 24, 4, January, 1992, pp. 512–531.

—— 'From Authoritarianism to Democracy in South Korea', in James Cotton (ed.), *Korea Under Roh Tae Woo: Northern Policy and Inter-Korean Relations*, Sydney: Allen and Unwin, 1993, pp. 22–41.

—— 'Korea in Comparative Perspective', in James Cotton (ed.), *Politics and Policy in the New Korean State: From Roh Tae-woo to Kim Young-sam*, Melbourne: Longman, 1995, pp. 227–242.

—— 'The Koreas in 1999: Between Confrontation and Engagement', Parliamentary Library of Australia Research Paper, 14, 1999, http://www.aph.gov.au/library/pubs/rp/1998–99/99rp14.htm, accessed 5 February, 2002.

Cumings, Bruce, 'The Origins and Development of the Northeast Asian Political Economy: Industrial Sectors, Product Cycles, and Political Consequences', *International Organization*, 38, 1, Winter, 1984, pp. 1–40.

—— 'World System and Authoritarian Regimes in Korea, 1948–1984', in E. A. Winckler and S. Greenhalgh (eds), *Contending Approaches to the Political Economy of Taiwan*, Armonk, New York: M. E. Sharpe, 1989, pp. 249–269.

—— *The Origins of the Korean War: Liberation and the Emergence of Separate Regime 1945–1947*, vol. 1, 3rd edition, Princeton: Princeton University Press, 1989.

—— *The Origins of the Korean War: The Roaring of the Cataract 1947–1950*, vol. 2, Princeton: Princeton University Press, 1990.

—— *Korea's Place in the Sun: A Modern History*, New York: W. W. Norton and Co., 1997.

—— 'The Korean Crisis and the End of "Late" Development', *New Left Review*, 231, September–October, 1998, pp. 43–73.

Curran, James and Gurevitch, Michael, *Mass Media and Society*, London: Edward Arnold, 1991.

Damrosch, Lori Fisler, 'Politics Across Borders: Non-intervention and Non-forcible Influence over Domestic Affairs', *American Journal of International Law*, 83, 1, 1989, pp. 1–50.

Davis, M. C., *Human Rights and Chinese Values: Legal, Philosophical and Political Perspectives*, New York: Oxford University Press, 1995.

Dawisha, Karen and Turner, Michael, 'The Interaction Between Internal and External Agency in Post-Communist Transitions', in Bruce Parrot and Karen Dawisha (eds), *The International Dimension of Post-Communist Transitions in Russia and the New States of Eurasia*, Armonk, New York: M. E. Sharpe, 1997, pp. 398–424.

de Bary, Wm. Theodore, 'Confucianism and Human Rights in China', in Larry Diamond and Marc F. Plattner (eds), *Democracy in East Asia*, Baltimore, London: The Johns Hopkins University Press, 1998, pp. 42–56.

Delfs, Robert, 'The People's Republic', *Far Eastern Economic Review*, 144, 1 June, 1989, pp. 12–15.

Deng, Yong and Gray, Sherry, 'Introduction: Growing Pains – China Debates its International Future', *Journal of Contemporary China*, 10, 26, 2001, pp. 5–16.

Dent, Christopher M., 'ASEM and the "Cinderella Complex" of EU–East Asia Economic Relations', *Pacific Affairs*, Spring, 2001, pp. 25–52.

Deyo, Frederic C., 'State and Labour: Modes of Political Exclusion in East Asian Development', in Frederic C. Deyo (ed.), *The Political Economy of New Asian Industrialism*, Ithaca, New York: Cornell University Press, 1987, pp. 182–202.

Diamond, Larry, *Developing Democracy: Toward Consolidation*, Baltimore: The Johns Hopkins University Press, 1999.

Diamond, Larry and Myers, Ramon H., 'Introduction: Elections and Democracy in Greater China', *The China Quarterly*, 162, June, 2000, pp. 365–386.

Donnelly, Jack, 'Human Rights: A New Standard of Civilization?', *International Affairs*, 74, 1, 1998, pp. 1–24.

—— 'Human Rights, Democracy and Development', *Human Rights Quarterly*, 21, 1999, pp. 608–632.

—— 'The Social Construction of International Human Rights', in Tim Dunne and Nicholas J. Wheeler (eds), *Human Rights in Global Politics*, Cambridge: Cambridge University Press, 1999, pp. 71–102.

Doyle, Michael W., *Ways of War and Peace*, New York: W. W. Norton and Co, 1997.

—— 'Liberalism and World Politics', *American Political Science Review*, 80, 4, December, 1986, pp. 1151–1169.

du Mars, Roger, 'South Korea: Fear is a Hard Habit to Break', in Louise Williams and Roland Rich (eds), *Losing Control: Freedom of the Press in Asia*, Canberra: Asia Pacific Press, 2000, pp. 190–207.

Dunn, John, *Western Political Theory in the Face of the Future*, Cambridge: Cambridge University Press, 1979.

Eckert, Carter J.; Lee, Ki-baik; Young, Ick Lew; Robinson, Michael and Wagner, Edward W., *Korea Old and New: A History*, Seoul: Published for the Korea Institute, Harvard University by Ilchokak, 1990.

Eldridge, Philip J., *The Politics of Human Rights in Southeast Asia*, London: Routledge, 2002.

Fairbank, John K. and Reischauer, Edwin O., *China: Tradition and Transformation*, revised edition, Sydney: Allen and Unwin, 1990.

Falk, Richard, 'The World Order between Inter-State Law and the Law of Humanity: The Role of Civil Society Institutions', in Daniele Archibugi and David Held (eds), *Cosmopolitan Democracy: An Agenda for a New World Order*, Cambridge: Polity Press, 1995, pp. 163–179.

Far Eastern Economic Review, 'South Korea Focus '80', 108, 30 May, 1980, pp. 40–60.

—— 'Britain's Obligation', editorial, 144, 22 June, 1989, pp. 12–13.

—— 'Evolution or Revolution', editorial, 161, 5 February, 1998, p. 6.

Fenton, James, *All the Wrong Places: Adrift in the Politics of Asia*, London: Viking, 1988.

Foot, Rosemary, *The Practice of Power: US Relations with China since 1949*, Oxford: Oxford University Press, 1995.

—— *Rights Beyond Borders: The Global Community and the Struggle Over Human Rights in China*, Oxford: Oxford University Press, 2000.

Ford Foundation, http://www.fordfound.org/about/mission.html, accessed 11 August, 1998.

—— http://www.fordfound.org/about/financial.cfm, accessed 18 March, 2002.

—— *The Ford Foundation in China*, undated publication.

Franck, Thomas M., 'The Emerging Right to Democratic Governance', *American Journal of International Law*, 86, 1, January, 1992, pp. 46–91.

Free China Review, 'From the Stage to the Page', 49, 7 July, 1999, pp. 32–43.

Friedman, Edward, 'Immanuel Kant's Relevance to an Enduring Asia-Pacific Peace', in Edward Friedman and Barrett L. McCormick (eds), *What if China Doesn't Democratize? Implications for War and Peace*, Armonk, New York: M. E. Sharpe, 2000, pp. 224–258.

Fukuyama, Francis, *The End of History and the Last Man*, London: Penguin, 1992.

—— 'Asian Values in the Wake of the Asian Crisis', *The Review of Korean Studies*, 2, September, 1999, pp. 5–22.

Fung, Edmund S. K. and Chen Jie, 'Changing Perceptions: The Attitudes of the PRC Chinese Towards Australia and China, 1989–1996', *Australia–Asia Paper*, 78, November, 1996.

Gayn, Mark, 'What Price Rhee? Profile of a Despot', *The Nation*, 13 March, 1954, pp. 214–217.

Gereffi, Gary, 'More than the Market, More than the State: Global Commodity Chains and Industrial Upgrading in East Asia', in Steve Chan, Cal Clark and Danny Lam (eds), *Beyond the Developmental State: East Asia's Political Economies Reconsidered*, Hampshire: Macmillan Press, 1998, pp. 38–59.

Gilpin, Robert, *The Political Economy of International Relations*, Princeton: Princeton University Press, 1987.

Golding, Peter and Elliot, Philip, *Making the News*, London: Longman, 1979.

Goodman, David S., 'Can China Change?', in Larry Diamond, Marc F. Plattner, Yun-han Chu and Hung-mao Tien (eds), *Consolidating the Third Wave*

Democracies: Regional Challenges, Baltimore: The Johns Hopkins University Press, 1997, pp. 250–257.

Gordenker, Leon and Weiss, Thomas G., 'Devolving Responsibilities: A Framework for Analyzing NGOs and Services', in Thomas G. Weiss (ed.), *Beyond UN Subcontracting: Task-Sharing with Regional Security Arrangements and Service-Providing NGOs*, Hampshire: Macmillan; New York: St. Martin's Press, 1998, pp. 30–48.

Gu, Edward Xin, 'Foreign Direct Investment and the Restructuring of Chinese State-Owned Enterprises (1992–1995): A New Institutionalist Perspective', *China Information*, 12, 3, Winter, 1997–1998, pp. 46–71.

Gu, Xuewu, 'China's Policy Towards Russia', *Aussenpolitik*, 111, 1993, pp. 288–297.

Ha, Yong-Chool, 'South Korea in 2000: A Summit and the Search for New Institutional Identity', *Asian Survey*, 41, 1, January–February, 2001, pp. 30–39.

Haggard, Stephan, 'The Newly Industrializing Countries in the International System', *World Politics*, 38, 2, January, 1986, pp. 343–371.

—— *Pathways from the Periphery*, Ithaca, New York: Cornell University Press, 1990.

—— 'Business, Politics and Policy in Northeast and Southeast Asia', in Andrew MacIntyre (ed.), *Business and Government in Industrializing Asia*, Sydney: Allen and Unwin, 1994, pp. 268–301.

Haggard, Stephan and Kaufman, Robert, *The Political Economy of Democratic Transitions*, Princeton: Princeton University Press, 1995.

Haggard, Stephan and Moon, Chung-in, *Pacific Dynamics: The International Politics of Industrial Change*, Boulder: Westview Press, 1989.

Hale, David, 'The IMF, Now More Than Ever: The Case for Financial Peace-keeping', *Foreign Affairs*, 77, 6, November–December, 1998, pp. 7–14.

Hall, Stuart; Critcher, Chas; Jefferson, Tony; Clarke, John and Robert, Brian, *Policing the Crisis: Mugging, the State and Law and Order*, Basingstoke: Macmillan Education Ltd, 1978.

Halliday, Fred, *Rethinking International Relations*, Basingstoke: Macmillan, 1994.

Han, Sung-Joo, 'South Korean Politics in Transition', in Larry Diamond, Juan Linz and Seymour Martin Lipset (eds), *Democracy in Developing Countries*, vol. 3, Boulder: Lynne Rienner, 1989, pp. 267–299.

Harding, Harry, 'Breaking the Impasse Over Human Rights', in Ezra Vogel (ed.), *Living with China: U.S./China Relations in the Twenty-first Century*, New York: W. W. Norton and Co., 1998, pp. 165–184.

—— 'The Halting Advance of Pluralism', *Journal of Democracy*, 9, 1, 1998, pp. 11–18.

Haynes, Jeff, *Democracy in the Developing World: Africa, Asia, Latin America and the Middle East*, Cambridge: Polity Press, 2001.

He, Baogang, *The Democratization of China*, London: Routledge, 1996.

—— *Democratic Implications of Civil Society in China*, London: Macmillan, 1997.

—— 'Power, Responsibility and Sovereignty: China's Policy towards Taiwan's Bid for a UN Seat', in Yongjin Zhang and Greg Austin (eds), *Power and Responsibility in Chinese Foreign Policy*, Canberra: Asia Pacific Press, 2001, pp. 196–218.

—— 'Are Village Elections Competitive?: The Case Study of Zhejiang', in J. Chen (ed.), *China's Challenge in the Twenty-first Century*, Hong Kong: City University of Hong Kong Press, 2002.

He, Baogang and Zhang, Jing, 'Evaluation Report of CPR/96/503 – Rural Official

Training', Evaluation Conducted for United Nations Development Programme, 2–11 August, 2001.

He Shang, 'Local Elections Take Democracy to Countryside', *China Daily*, 22 June, 1998, p. 3.

Held, David, 'Anything but a dog's life? Further comments on Fukuyama, Callinicos, and Giddens', *Theory and Society*, 22, 1993, pp. 293–304.

—— *Democracy and the Global Order: From the Modern State to Cosmopolitan Governance*, London: Polity Press, 1996.

—— *Models of Democracy*, 2nd edition, Cambridge: Polity Press, 1996.

Held, David and McGrew, Andrew, 'Globalization and the Liberal Democratic State', *Government and Opposition*, 28, 2, 1993, pp. 261–288.

Hewson, Martin and Sinclair, Timothy J., 'The Emergence of Global Governance Theory', in Martin Hewson and Timothy J. Sinclair (eds), *Approaches to Global Governance Theory*, New York: State University of New York Press, 1999, pp. 3–22.

Hinzpeter, Jurgen, 'I Bow My Head', in Henry Scott-Stokes and Lee Jai Eui (eds), *The Kwangju Uprising: Eyewitness Press Accounts of Korea's Tiananmen*, Armonk, New York: M. E. Sharpe, 2000, pp. 63–76.

Hobart, Mark (ed.), *An Anthropological Critique of Development: The Growth of Ignorance*, London, New York: Routledge, 1993.

Hoon, Shim Jae, 'Chun's Hand Can Stay the Noose', *Far Eastern Economic Review*, 109, 19 September, 1980, p. 13.

Hoon, Shim Jae and Sherry, Andrew, 'Cutting the Knot', *Far Eastern Economic Review*, 158, 30 November, 1995, pp. 66–72.

Hsiao, Hsin-Huang Michael and Hsiao-shi, Chen, 'Taiwan', in Ian Marsh, Jean Blondel and Takashi Inoguchi (eds), *Democracy, Governance and Economic Performance: East and Southeast Asia*, Tokyo: United Nations University Press, 1999, pp. 109–136.

Huang, Teh-fu, 'Elections and the Evolution of the Kuomintang', in Hung-mao Tien and Charles Chi-hsiang Chang (eds), *Taiwan's Electoral Politics and Democratic Transition: Riding the Third Wave*, Armonk, New York: M. E. Sharpe, 1996, pp. 105–136.

Huang, Yasheng, *Selling China: Foreign Direct Investment During the Reform Era*, Cambridge: Cambridge University Press, 2003.

Huntington, Samuel P., 'The Clash of Civilisations?', *Foreign Affairs*, 72, 3, Summer, 1993, pp. 22–49.

—— *The Clash of Civilisations and the Remaking of World Order*, London: Simon and Schuster, 1997.

Hurrell, Andrew, 'Power, Principles and Prudence: Protecting Human Rights in a Deeply Divided World', in Tim Dunne and Nicholas J. Wheeler (eds), *Human Rights in Global Politics*, Cambridge: Cambridge University Press, 1999, pp. 277–302.

Ikenberry, G. John, 'America's Liberal Grand Strategy: Democracy and National Security in the Post-War Era', in Michael Cox, John G. Ikenberry, Takashi Inoguchi (eds), *American Democracy Promotion: Impulses, Strategies and Impacts*, Oxford: Oxford University Press, 2000, pp. 103–126.

Inoguchi, Takashi, 'Three Frameworks in Search of a Policy: US Democracy Promotion in Asia Pacific', in Michael Cox, John G. Ikenberry, Takashi Inoguchi (eds),

American Democracy Promotion: Impulses, Strategies and Impacts, Oxford: Oxford University Press, 2000, pp. 267–286.

International Republican Institute, *People's Republic of China: Election Observation Report May 15–31, 1994*, Washington DC: International Republican Institute, 1995.

—— *Election Observation Report Fujian, People's Republic of China May 1997: An Update to 1994 Election Observation Report*, Washington DC: International Republican Institute, 1997.

—— http://www.iri.org.aboutiri/iri.html, accessed 21 April, 1998.

Jacobs, J. Bruce, 'Political Opposition and Taiwan's Political Future', *The Australian Journal of Chinese Affairs*, 6, 1981, pp. 21–44.

Jacobs, Norman, *The Korean Road to Modernization and Development*, Urbana: University of Illinois Press, 1985.

Jan, Hun Yi, 'Interaction Between Mainland China and the UN Human Rights Regime', *Issues and Studies*, 24, 4, November–December, 1998, p. 76.

Jason, Karen, 'The Role of International Non-governmental Organizations in International Election Observing', *New York University Journal of International Law and Politics*, 24, 4, 1991–1992, pp. 1795–1843.

Jayasuriya, Kanishka, 'Political Economy of Democratization in East Asia', *Asian Perspective*, 18, 2, Fall–Winter, 1994, pp. 141–180.

—— 'Introduction: A framework for the analysis of legal institutions in East Asia', in Kanishka Jayasuriya (ed.), *Law, Capitalism and Power in Asia: The Rule of Law and Legal Institutions*, London, New York: Routledge, 1999, pp. 1–27.

—— 'Corporatism and Judicial Independence within Statist Legal Institutions in East Asia', in Kanishka Jayasuriya (ed.), *Law, Capitalism and Power in Asia: The Rule of Law and Legal Institutions*, London, New York: Routledge, 1999, pp. 173–201.

Jin Canrong, 'The US Global Strategy in the Post-Cold War Era and Its Implications for China–United States Relations: A Chinese Perspective', *Journal of Contemporary China*, 10, 27, 2001, pp. 309–315.

Johnson, Chalmers, *MITI and the Japanese Miracle: The Growth of Industrial Policy 1925–1975*, Stanford: Stanford University Press, 1982.

—— 'Political Institutions and Economic Performance: The Government–Business Relationship in Japan, South Korea and Taiwan', in Frederic C. Deyo (ed.), *The Political Economy of New Asian Industrialism*, Ithaca, New York: Cornell University Press, 1987, pp. 136–165.

—— 'South Korean Democratization: the Role of Economic Development', in James Cotton (ed.), *Korea Under Roh Tae Woo: Democratization, Northern Policy and Inter-Korean Relations*, Sydney: Allen and Unwin, 1993, pp. 82–107.

Johnston, Alastair Iain, 'Learning Versus Adaptation: Explaining Change in China's Arms Control Policy in the 1980s and 1990s', *The China Journal*, 35, January, 1996, pp. 27–62.

—— 'Is China a Status Quo Power?', *International Security*, 27, 4, Spring, 2003, pp. 5–56.

Jones, David Martin, 'The Metamorphosis of Tradition: The Idea of Law and Virtue in East Asian Political Thought', *South East Asian Journal of Social Science*, 21, 1, 1993, pp. 18–35.

—— *Political Development in Pacific Asia*, Cambridge: Polity Press, 1997.

—— 'Democratization, Civil Society, and Illiberal Middle Class Culture in Pacific Asia', *Comparative Politics*, 30, 2 January, 1998, pp. 147–169.

—— 'Myths of the Meltdown: The Curious Case of the Developmental State in the Asia Pacific', *London Defence Studies*, 48, 1999, pp. 1–62.

Jones, David Martin and Smith, Mike, 'Tigers Ready to Roar', *The World Today*, 55, 10, October, 1999, pp. 17–19.

Kaldor, Mary, 'Transnational Civil Society', in Tim Dunne and Nicholas J. Wheeler (eds), *Human Rights in Global Politics*, Cambridge: Cambridge University Press, 1999, pp. 195–213.

Kamm, Henry, 'South Korea Troops Recapture Kwangju in Pre-dawn Strike', *The New York Times*, 27 May, 1980, pp. 1–6.

Kant, Immanuel, *Perpetual Peace, and Other Essays On Politics, History and Morals*, trans. by Ted Murphy, Indianapolis: Hackett Publishing Co, 1983.

Kapur, Devesh, 'The IMF: A Cure or a Curse', *Foreign Policy*, 111, 4, Summer, 1998, pp. 114–132.

Karatnycky, Adrian, 'The 1998 Freedom House Survey: The Decline of Illiberal Democracy', *Journal of Democracy*, 10, 1, 1999, pp. 112–125.

Kaslow, Amy, 'Pacific Rim Beckons European Business', *Christian Science Monitor*, December–January, 1994–1995, pp. 21–22.

Kataoka, Tetsuya, *The Price of a Constitution: The Origin of Japan's Post-war Politics*, New York: Crane Russak, 1991.

Katzenstein, Peter J.; Keohane, Robert O. and Krasner, Stephen D., 'International Organization and the Study of World Politics', *International Organization*, 52, 4, Autumn, 1999, pp. 645–685.

Kaufman, Michael T., 'Moynihan Jeered at China Protest', *The New York Times*, 10 June, 1989, p. 6.

Kausikan, Bilahari, 'The "Asian Values" Debate: A View From Singapore', in Larry Diamond and Marc F. Plattner (eds), *Democracy in East Asia*, Baltimore, London: The Johns Hopkins University Press, 1998, pp. 17–27.

Keller, Bill, 'Eager Not to Offend, Soviet Congress Criticizes Outside Pressure on China', *The New York Times*, 7 June, 1989, p. 10.

Kelliher, Daniel, 'The Chinese Debate Over Village Self-government', *The China Journal*, 37, January, 1997, pp. 63–86.

Kelly, David, 'The Search for Freedom as a Universal Value', in David Kelly and Anthony Reid (eds), *Asian Freedoms: The Idea of Freedom in East and Southeast Asia*, Cambridge: Cambridge University Press, 1998, pp. 93–120.

Kent, Ann, *Between Freedom and Subsistence: China and Human Rights*, New York: Oxford University Press, 1993.

—— *China, the United Nations and Human Rights: The Limits of Compliance*, Philadelphia: University of Pennsylvania Press, 1999.

Keohane, Robert O., 'The Demand for International Regimes', *International Organization*, 36, 2, Spring, 1982, pp. 325–356.

Keohane, Robert O. and Nye, Joseph S., *Power and Interdependence,* 3rd edition, New York: Longman, 2001.

Kersten, Rikki, *Democracy in Postwar Japan: Maruyama Masao and the Search for Autonomy*, London: Routledge, 1996.

Kil, Soong Hoom, 'Development of Korean Politics: A Historical Profile', in Soong Hoom Kil and Chung-in Moon (eds), *Understanding Korean Politics: An Introduction*, New York: State University of New York Press, 2001, pp. 33–70.

Kim, Byung-Kook, 'Politics of Democratic Consolidation in Korea', paper presented at the 16th World Congress of the International Political Science Association, Berlin, August 21–25, 1994.

—— 'Korea's Crisis of Success', in Larry Diamond and Marc F. Plattner (eds), *Democracy in East Asia*, Baltimore, London: The Johns Hopkins University Press, 1998, pp. 114–132.

Kim Chum-kon, *The Korean War 1950–1953*, Seoul: Kwangmyong, 1980.

Kim Chung Keun, 'Days and Nights on the Street', in Henry Scott-Stokes and Lee Jai Eui (eds), *The Kwangju Uprising: Eyewitness Press Accounts of Korea's Tiananmen*, Armonk, New York: M. E. Sharpe, 2000, pp. 3–19.

Kim Dae Jung, 'A Response to Lee Kuan Yew: Is Culture Destiny? The Myth of Asia's Anti-Democratic Values', *Foreign Affairs*, 73, November–December, 1994, pp. 189–194.

Kim, Samuel S., *China, the United Nations and World Order*, Princeton: Princeton University Press, 1979.

—— 'China's International Organizational Behaviour', in Thomas W. Robinson and David Shambaugh (eds), *Chinese Foreign Policy in Theory and Practice*, Oxford: Clarendon Press, 1994, pp. 401–434.

—— 'Human Rights in China's International Relations', in Edward Friedman and Barrett L. McCormick (eds), *What if China Doesn't Democratize? Implications for War and Peace*, Armonk, New York: M. E. Sharpe, 2000, pp. 129–162.

Kim, Sunhyuk, 'Patronage Politics as an Obstacle to Democracy in South Korea: Regional Networks and Democratic Consolidation', in Howard Handelman and Mark Tessler (eds), *Democracy and Its Limits: Lessons from Asia, Latin America and the Middle East*, Notre Dame: University of Notre Dame Press, 1999, pp. 115–129.

Kohli, Atul; Evans, Peter; Katzenstein, Peter J.; Przeworski, Adam; Rudolph, Susanne Hoeber; Scott, James C. and Skocpol, Theda, 'The Role of Theory in Comparative Politics: A Symposium', *World Politics*, 48, October, 1995, pp. 1–49.

Kong, Qingjiang, 'China's WTO Accession: Commitments and Implications', *Journal of International Economic Law*, 3, 4, 2000, pp. 655–690.

Koo, Hagan, 'From Farm to Factory: Proletarianisation in Korea', *American Sociological Review*, 55, October, 1990, pp. 669–691.

Kristof, Nicholas D., 'Beijing Residents Block Army Move Near City Centre', *The New York Times*, 3 June, 1989, p. 1.

Krugman, Paul, 'The Myth of Asia's Miracle', *Foreign Affairs*, 73, 6, November–December 1994, pp. 62–78.

Kuo, Cheng-tian, 'Privatization *within* the Chinese State', in Steve Chan, Cal Clark and Danny Lam (eds), *Beyond the Developmental State: East Asia's Political Economies Reconsidered*, Hampshire: Macmillan Press, 1998, pp. 71–83.

Kurata, Phil, 'Violence in the Name of Reason', *Far Eastern Economic Review*, 106, 28 December, 1979, p. 27.

—— 'Soft-line Prosecution', *Far Eastern Economic Review*, 107, 7 March, 1980, p. 22.

—— 'Democracy Goes on Trial With the Dissidents', *Far Eastern Economic Review*, 108, 4 April, 1980, pp. 10–11.

—— 'The Sound of Silence', *Far Eastern Economic Review*, 108, 13 June, 1980, p. 16.

Kwang Suk-kim and Foemer, Michael, *Growth and Structural Transformation*, Cambridge, Massachusetts: Council on East Asian Studies, Harvard, 1981.

Lampton, David, 'America's China Policy in the Age of the Finance Minister: Clinton Ends Linkage', *The China Quarterly*, 139, September, 1994, pp. 597–621.

Lardy, Nicholas R., 'Comments', *Brookings Papers on Economic Activity*, 2, 1996, pp. 338–340.

Lasater, Martin L., 'Taiwan's International Environment', in Thomas W. Robinson (ed.), *Democracy and Development in East Asia: Taiwan, South Korea and the Philippines*, Washington DC: The AEI Press, 1991, pp. 91–104.

Lau, Emily, 'Mourning the Dead', *Far Eastern Economic Review*, 144, 27 April, 1989, pp. 11–12.

Lee, Chae-Jin, 'The United States and Korea: Dynamics of Changing Relations', in Young Whan Kihl (ed.), *Korea and the World: Beyond the Cold War*, Boulder: Westview Press, 1994, pp. 69–82.

Lee, Chyungly, 'Impact of the East Asian Financial Crisis on the Asia–Pacific Regional Order: A Geo-Economic Perspective', *Issues and Studies*, 35, 4, July–August, 1999, pp. 109–132.

Lee, Eliza, 'Human Rights and Non-Western Values', in Michael Davis (ed.), *Human Rights and Chinese Values: Legal, Philosophical and Political Perspectives*, New York: Oxford University Press, 1995, pp. 72–86.

Lee, Jung Bock, 'The Political Process in Korea', in Soon Hoom Kil and Chung-in Moon (eds), *Understanding Korean Politics: An Introduction*, New York: State University of New York Press, 2001, pp. 140–174.

Lee, Su-Hoon, 'Transitional Politics of Korea, 1987–1992: Activation of Civil Society', *Pacific Affairs*, 66, 3, 1993–1994, pp. 351–367.

Lee Teng-hui, 'Chinese Culture and Political Renewal', *Journal of Democracy*, 6, 4, 1995, pp. 3–8.

Lewis, John, 'In Search of a Moderate Image', *Far Eastern Economic Review*, 103, 5 January, 1979, pp. 12–13.

Lewis, Linda, 'The "Kwangju Incident" Observed: An Anthropological Perspective on Civil Uprisings', in Donald Clark (ed.), *The Kwangju Uprising: Shadows Over the Regime in South Korea*, Boulder: Westview Press, 1988, pp. 15–28.

Lie, John, *Han Unbound: The Political Economy of South Korea*, Stanford: Stanford University Press, 1998.

Lijphart, Arend, 'Comparative Politics and the Comparative Method', *The American Political Science Review*, 65, September, 1971, pp. 682–693.

Lipset, Seymour Martin, 'Some Social Requisites of Democracy: Economic Development and Political Legitimacy', *American Political Science Review*, 53, March, 1959, pp. 69–105.

Liu Binyan, 'Civilization Grafting: No Culture is an Island', *Foreign Affairs*, 72, 1, September–October, 1993, pp. 19–21.

Liu, I-chou, 'The Development of the Opposition', in Steve Tsang and Hung-mao Tien (eds), *Democratization in Taiwan: Implications for China*, Hong Kong: Hong Kong University Press, 1999, pp. 67–85.

Lovell, John P., 'The Military and Politics in Postwar Korea', in Edward Reynolds Wright (ed.), *Korean Politics in Transition*, Seattle: University of Washington Press, 1975.

Luard, Evan, *Britain and China*, London: Chatto and Windus, 1962.

Lull, James, *China Turned On: Television, Reform and Resistance*, London: Routledge, 1991.

Lynch, Cecilia, 'The Promise and Problems of Internationalism', *Global Governance*, 5, 1, January–March, 1999, pp. 83–102.

MacDonald, Donald Stone, *The Koreans: Contemporary Politics and Society*, 2nd edition, Boulder: Westview Press, 1990.

Mackerras, Colin (ed.), *Asia Since 1945: History Through Documents*, Melbourne: Longman Cheshire, 1992.

Mahbubani, Kishore, 'The Pacific Way', *Foreign Affairs*, 74, 1, January–February, 1995, pp. 100–111.

Mainwaring, Scott, 'Transitions to Democracy and Democratic Consolidation: Theoretical and Comparative Issues', in Scott Mainwaring, Guillermo O'Donnell and J. Samuel Valenzuela (eds), *Issues in Democratic Consolidation: The New South American Democracies in Comparative Perspective*, Notre Dame, Indiana: University of Notre Dame Press, 1992, pp. 294–342.

Mandelbaum, Michael, 'Westernizing Russia and China', *Foreign Affairs*, 76, 3, May–June, 1997, pp. 80–95.

McCormick, Barrett L., 'U.S.–PRC Relations and the "Democratic Peace"', in Edward Friedman and Barrett L. McCormick (eds), *What if China Doesn't Democratize? Implications for War and Peace*, Armonk, New York: M. E. Sharpe, 2000, pp. 305–328.

McLuhan, Marshall, *Understanding the Media: The Extensions of Man*, London: Routledge, Kegan and Paul, 1964.

McQuail, Denis, 'The Influence and Effects of Mass Media', in James Curran, Michael Gurevitch and Janet Woollacott (eds), *Mass Communication and Society*, London: Edward Arnold, 1977, pp. 70–94.

Mengin, François, 'State and Identity', in Steve Tsang and Hung-mao Tien (eds), *Democratization in Taiwan: Implications for China*, London: Macmillan, 1999, pp. 116–130.

Moore, Barrington Jr., *Social Origins of Dictatorship and Democracy: Lord and Peasant in the Making of the Modern World*, Harmondsworth: Penguin, 1973.

Morlino, Leonardo, 'Democratic Establishments: A Dimensional Analysis', in Enrique Baloyra (ed.), *Comparing New Democracies: Transition and Consolidation in Mediterranean Europe and the Southern Cone*, Boulder: Westview Press, 1987, pp. 53–78.

Munro, Robin, 'Who Died in Beijing and Why', *The Nation*, June, 1990, pp. 811–822.

Munro, Ross H., 'Giving Taipei a Place at the Table', *Foreign Affairs*, 73, 6, November–December, 1994, pp. 109–122.

Nathan, Andrew J., *China's Crisis: Dilemmas of Reform and Prospects for Democracy*, New York: Columbia University Press, 1990.

—— 'Historical Perspectives on Chinese Democracy: The Overseas Democracy Movement Today', in R. Jeans (ed.), *Roads Not Taken: The Struggle of Opposition Parties in Twentieth Century China*, Boulder: Westview Press, 1992, pp. 313–327.

—— 'Human Rights in Chinese Foreign Policy', *The China Quarterly*, 139, September, 1994, pp. 622–643.

—— 'Even Our Caution Must Be Hedged', *Journal of Democracy*, 9, 1, 1998, pp. 60–65.

—— 'What's Wrong with American Taiwan Policy', *Washington Quarterly*, 23, 2, Spring, 2000, pp. 93–106.

Nathan, Andrew J. and Link, Perry, *The Tiananmen Papers*, London: Little, Brown and Co, 2001.

National Endowment for Democracy, http://www.ned.org/page_3/asia.html, 1999, accessed 15 October, 1999.

Naughton, Barry, 'China's Emergence and Prospects as a Trading Nation', *Brookings Papers on Economic Activity*, 2, 1996, pp. 273–337.

—— 'The Dangers of Economic Complacency', *Current History*, 95, 602, 1996, pp. 260–265.

Neary, Ian, 'Political Culture and Human Rights in Japan, Korea and Taiwan', *Nissan Occasional Paper Series*, 28, Oxford: Nissan Institute of Japanese Studies, 1998.

Ngo Tak-wing, 'Civil Society and Political Liberalization in Taiwan', *Bulletin of Concerned Asian Scholars*, 25, 1, 1993, pp. 3–15.

Nossal, Kim Richard, *The Beijing Massacre: Australian Responses*, Canberra: Australian Foreign Policy Papers, Australian National University, 1993.

O'Brien, Kevin J. and Li, Lianjiang, 'Accommodating "Democracy" in a One Party State: Introducing Village Elections in China', *The China Quarterly*, 162, June, 2000, pp. 465–489.

O'Donnell, Guillermo and Schmitter, Philippe C., *Transitions from Authoritarian Rule: Tentative Conclusions about Uncertain Democracies*, fourth impression, Baltimore, London: The Johns Hopkins University Press, 1993.

Odom, William O., 'The US Military in Unified Korea', *The Korean Journal of Defense Analysis*, 12, 1, Summer, 2000, pp. 7–28.

Ogden, Suzanne, 'The Conflict Escalates as the Students Defend their Patriotism', in Suzanne Ogden, Kathleen Hartford, Lawrence Sullivan and David Zweig (eds), *China's Search for Democracy: The Student and Mass Movement of 1989*, Armonk, New York: M. E. Sharpe, 1992, pp. 121–134.

Ohmae, Kenichi, 'The Rise of the Region State', *Foreign Affairs*, 72, Spring, 1993, pp. 78–88.

Oi, Jean C., 'Fiscal Reform and the Economic Foundations of Local State Corporatism in China', *World Politics*, 45, October, 1992, pp. 99–126.

Oi, Jean C. and Rozelle, Scott, 'Elections and Power: The Locus of Decision-Making in Chinese Villages', *The China Quarterly*, 162, June, 2000, pp. 513–539.

Oksenberg, Michel; Sullivan, Lawrence R. and Lambert, Marc (eds), *Beijing Spring, 1989: Confrontation and Conflict: The Basic Documents*, New York: M. E. Sharpe, 1990.

Oxman, Stephen; Triffterer, Otto and Cruz, Francisco, *South Korea: Human Rights in Emerging Politics*, Switzerland: International Commission of Jurists, 1987.

Palais, James, *Human Rights in Korea*, Washington DC: Asia Watch, 1986.

Pan, Chengxin, 'Understanding Chinese Identity in International Relations: A Critique of Western Approaches', *Political Science*, 51, 2, December, 1999, pp. 135–148.

Pann, Lynn; Balakrishnan, N. and Paul Handley, 'Stirring the Blood', *Far Eastern Economic Review*, 145, 24 August, 1989, pp. 16–17.

Parekh, Bhikhu, 'The Cultural Particularity of Liberal Democracy', in David Held (ed.), *Prospects for Democracy: North, South, East, West*, Cambridge: Polity Press, 1993, pp. 156–177.

Parrot, Bruce and Dawisha, Karen, *The International Dimension of Post-Communist Transitions in Russia and the New States of Eurasia*, Armonk, New York: M. E. Sharpe, 1997.

Pastor, Robert, 'Village Elections a Sign of Progress', *The Atlanta Journal*, 30 March, 1997.

—— 'China is Climbing Democracy's Learning Curve', *Asian Wall Street Journal*, 8 September, 1998.

—— 'Seems Legit: A Thumbs Up for China's Electoral Experiment', *Time Magazine*, 151, 1, 1998, p. 38.

—— 'Mediating Elections', *Journal of Democracy*, 9, 1, 1998, pp. 154–163.

Pear, Robert, 'President Assails Shootings in China', *The New York Times*, 4 June, 1989, p. 21.

Pei, Minxen, 'Creeping Democratization in China', *Journal of Democracy*, 6, 4, 1995, pp. 65–79.

People's Daily, 19 October, 1998.

Peterson, Mark, 'Americans and the Kwangju Incident', in Donald Clark (ed.), *The Kwangju Uprising: Shadows Over the Regime in South Korea*, Boulder: Westview Press, 1988, pp. 52–65.

Pieterse, Jan Nederveen, 'Globalization as Hybridization', *International Sociology*, 9, 2, June, 1994, pp. 161–184.

Pinder, John, 'The European Community and Democracy in Central and Eastern Europe', in Geoffrey Pridham, Eric Herring and George Sanford (eds), *Building Democracy? The International Dimension of Democratization in Eastern Europe*, London: Leicester University Press, 1997, pp. 110–132.

Pridham, Geoffrey (1991), 'Democratic Transition and the International Environment: A Research Agenda', *Centre for Mediterranean Studies-Occasional Paper*, 1, February, 1991.

—— 'The International Dimension of Democratization: Theory, Practice and Inter-regional Comparisons', in Geoffrey Pridham, Eric Herring and George Sanford (eds), *Building Democracy? The International Dimension of Democratization in Eastern Europe*, London: Leicester University Press, 1997, pp. 7–29.

Pridham, Geoffrey; Herring, Eric and Sanford, George (eds), *Building Democracy? The International Dimension of Democratization in Eastern Europe*, London: Leicester University Press, 1997.

Pridham, Geoffrey and Vanhanen, Tatu (eds), *Democratization in Eastern Europe: Domestic and International Perspectives,* London, New York: Routledge, 1994.

Przeworski, Adam, 'Minimalist Conception of Democracy: A Defense', in Ian Shapiro and Casiano Hacker-Córdon (eds), *Democracy's Value*, Cambridge: Cambridge University Press, 1999, pp. 23–55.

Pye, Lucian W., 'Introduction: Political Culture and Political Development', in Lucian W. Pye and Sidney Verba (eds), *Political Culture and Political Development*, Princeton: Princeton University Press, 1965, pp. 3–26.

—— *Asian Power and Politics: The Cultural Dimensions of Authority*, Cambridge, Massachusetts: Belknap Press of Harvard University Press, 1985.

Rawnsley, Gary D. and Rawnsley, Ming-Yeh T., 'Regime Transition and the Media in Taiwan', *Democratization*, 5, 2, Summer, 1998, pp. 106–124.

Reuschemeyer, Dietrich; Stephens, Evelyne Huber and Stephens, John D., *Capitalist Development and Democracy*, Oxford: Polity Press, 1992.

Ro, Young-chan, 'Korean World View and Values: Economic Implications', *The Review of Korean Studies*, 2, September, 1999, pp. 45–54.

Rodrik, Dani, *The New Global Economy and Developing Countries: Making Openness Work*, Baltimore: The Johns Hopkins University Press, 1999.

Roett, Riordan and Crandell, Russell, 'The Global Economic Crisis, Contagion and Institutions: New Realities in Latin America and Asia', *International Political Science Review*, 20, 3, 1999, pp. 271–283.

Rosecrance, Richard, *The Rise of the Trading State*, New York: Basic Books, 1986.

Rosett, Claudia, 'Mapping the New World Markets', in Brian T. Johnson, Kim R. Holmes, Melanie Kirkpatrick (eds), *1999 Index of Economic Freedom*, New York: The Heritage Foundation and Dow Jones and Co. Inc, 1999, pp. 35–39.

Rostow, Walt, *The Stages of Economic Growth: A Non-Communist Manifesto*, 3rd edition, Cambridge: Cambridge University Press, 1990.

Russett, Bruce with Antholis, W.; Ember, E.; Ember M. and Maos, Z., *Grasping the Democratic Peace: Principles for a Post-Cold War World*, Princeton: Princeton University Press, 1993.

Sachs, Wolfgang (ed.), *The Development Dictionary: A Guide to Knowledge as Power*, London, New Jersey: Zed, 1992.

Schmitter, Philippe C., 'Dangers and Dilemmas of Democracy', *Journal of Democracy*, 5, 2, 1994, pp. 57–74.

—— 'On Civil Society and the Consolidation of Democracy: Ten General Propositions and Nine Speculations about their Relation in Asian Democracies', paper presented at the International Conference on Consolidating the Third Wave Democracies: Trends and Challenges, Taipei, Taiwan, 1995.

—— 'The Influence of the International Context upon the Choice of National Institutions and Policies in Neo-Democracies', in Laurence Whitehead (ed.), *The International Dimensions of Democratization: Europe and the Americas*, New York: Oxford University Press, 1998, pp. 26–54.

Schumpeter, Joseph A., *Capitalism, Socialism and Democracy*, 3rd edition, New York: Harper and Row, 1976.

Scott-Stokes, Henry and Lee, Jai Eui (eds), *The Kwangju Uprising: Eyewitness Press Accounts of Korea's Tiananmen*, Armonk, New York: M. E. Sharpe, 2000.

Sen, Amartya K., *Development as Freedom*, New York: Knopf, 1999.

Seymour, James D., 'Human Rights and the World Response to the Crackdown in China', *China Information*, 4, 4, Spring, 1990, pp. 1–14.

Shelley, Becky, 'Political Globalization and the Politics of International Non-governmental Organizations: The Case of Village Democracy in China', *Australian Journal of Political Science*, 35, 2, July, 2000, pp. 225–238.

—— 'Protest and Globalization: Media, Symbols and Audience in the Drama of Democratization', *Democratization*, 8, 4, Winter, 2001, pp. 155–174.

Sheng, Lijun, 'China Eyes Taiwan: Why a Breakthrough is so Difficult', *The Journal of Strategic Studies*, 21, 1, March, 1998, pp. 65–78.

Shi, Tianjin, 'Village Committee Elections in China: Institutionalist Tactics for Democracy', *World Politics*, 51, 3, April, 1999, pp. 385–412.

Shin, Doh C., *Mass Politics and Culture in Democratizing Korea*, Cambridge: Cambridge University Press, 1999.

Sikkink, Kathryn, 'The Effectiveness of US Human Rights Policy 1973–1980', in Laurence Whitehead (ed.), *The International Dimensions of Democratization: Europe and the Americas*, New York: Oxford University Press, 1998, 93–124.

Simons, Geoff, *Korea: The Search for Sovereignty*, London: Macmillan, 1995.

Skocpol, Theda, *States and Social Revolutions: A Comparative Analysis of France, Russia and China*, Cambridge: Cambridge University Press, 1979.

Sohn, Donald, 'Chun Doo Hwan's Manipulation of the Kwangju Popular Uprising', unpublished M.A thesis, Cornell University, 1998.

Song Qiang, Zhang Zangang and Qiao Bian, *China Can Say No* [*Zhongguo keyi shuo bu*], Beijing: *Zhonghua gongshang lianhe chubanshe*, 1996.

Steinberg, David, 'Korea: Triumph and Turmoil', *Journal of Democracy*, 9, 2, 1998, pp. 76–90.

—— 'The Role of the US Press in Improving Inter-Korean Relations', *The Korea Times*, 3 November, 2001, p. 3 and p. 11.

Steinbruner, John D., *Principles of Global Security*, Washington DC: Brookings Institution, 2000.

Stepan, Alfred, 'Religion, Democracy and the "Twin Tolerations"', *Journal of Democracy*, 11, 4, 2000, pp. 37–570.

Strange, Susan, *The Retreat of the State: The Diffusion of Power in the World Economy*, Cambridge: Cambridge University Press, 1996.

Svensson, Marina, *The Chinese Conception of Human Rights: The Debate on Human Rights in China 1898–1949*, Lund: Studentlitteratur, 1996.

Tai, M. C., 'Face Healing', *Far Eastern Economic Review*, 145, 27 July, 1989, pp. 11–12.

Tan, Qingshan, 'Village Elections Democratic', *China Daily*, 22 June, 1998, p. 8.

Tanji, Miyume and Lawson, Stephanie, '"Democratic Peace" and "Asian Democracy": A Universalist–Particularist Tension', *Alternatives*, 22, 1997, pp. 135–155.

Tatsuo, Inoue, 'Liberal Democracy and Asian Orientalism', in Joanne R. Bauer and Daniel A. Bell (eds), *The East Asian Challenge for Human Rights*, Cambridge: Cambridge University Press, 1999, pp. 27–59.

Taylor, Charles, 'Conditions of An Unforced Consensus on Human Rights', in Joanne R. Bauer and Daniel A. Bell (eds), *The East Asian Challenge for Human Rights*, Cambridge: Cambridge University Press, 1999, pp. 124–146.

Taylor, William J. Jr., *Great Power Interests in Korean Unification*, Washington DC: Centre for Strategic and International Studies, 1998.

Tenney, Warren John, 'U.S. Responses to the Tiananmen and Kwangju Incidents: American Relations with China and Korea', *Journal of North East Asian Studies*, 11, 4, 1992, pp. 58–76.

The 5.18 History Compilation Committee of Kwangju City, trans. Lee Kyung-soon and Ellen Bishop, City of Kwangju, 1988.

The Asia Foundation, *20 Years in China*, San Francisco: The Asia Foundation, 1999.

—— *The Asia Foundation Annual Report 2000*, San Francisco: The Asia Foundation, 2000.

——   http://www.asiafoundation.org/programs/prog-asia-kore.html,   accessed   7 March, 2002.

Tien, Hung-mao, *The Great Transition: Political and Social Change in the Republic of China*, Stanford: Hoover Institution Press, 1989.

—— 'Elections and Taiwan's Democratic Development', in Hung-mao Tien and Charles Chi-hsiang Chang (eds), *Taiwan's Electoral Politics and Democratic Transition: Riding the Third Wave*, Armonk, New York: M. E. Sharpe, 1996, pp. 3–26.

Time, 24 June, 1974, p. 46.

Tsang, Steve and Tien, Hung-mao, 'Introduction', in Steve Tsang and Hung-mao Tien (eds), *Democratization in Taiwan: Implications for China*, Hong Kong: Hong Kong University Press, 1999, pp. 1–28.

Tsingos, Basilios, 'Underwriting Democracy: The European Community and

Greece', in Laurence Whitehead (ed.), *The International Dimensions of Democratization: Europe and the Americas*, New York: Oxford University Press, 1998, pp. 285–314.

Tu, Weiming, 'A Confucian Perspective on the Core Values of the Global Community', *The Review of Korean Studies*, 2, September, 1999, pp. 55–70.

Underhill, Geoffrey R. D, 'State, Market and Global Political Economy: A Genealogy of an (inter-?) Discipline', *International Affairs*, 76, 4, 2000, pp. 805–824.

United Nations, http://www.un.org.Depts/dpa/ead/website5.htm, accessed 8 February, 2002.

—— http://www.un.org/Overview/growth/htm, accessed 8 February, 2002.

United Nations Development Programme, *Human Development Report*, New York: United Nations Development Programme, 1993.

—— United Nations Development Programme CPR/96/503.

Verba, Sidney, 'Comparative Political Culture', in Lucian W. Pye and Sidney Verba (eds), *Political Culture and Political Development*, Princeton: Princeton University Press, 1965, pp. 512–560.

Wade, Robert, *Governing the Market: Economic Theory and the Role of Government in East Asian Industrialization,* Princeton: Princeton University Press, 1990.

Wan, Ming, 'Policies, Resource Commitments and Values: A Comparison of United States and Japanese Approaches to Human Rights in China', in John D. Montgomery (ed.), *Human Rights: Positive Policies in Asia and the Pacific Rim*, Hollis: Hollis Publishing Co, 1998, p. 44.

Wang Chaohua, Wang Dan and Li Minqi, 'Dialogue on the Future of China', *New Left Review*, 235, 1999, pp. 32–107.

Wang, Shujen, 'Ideology and Foreign News Coverage: Propaganda Model Re-examined', *Asian Journal of Communications*, 5, 1, 1995, pp. 110–125.

Ward, Robert E., 'Reflections on the Allied Occupation and Planned Political Change in Japan', in Robert E. Ward (ed.), *Political Development in Modern Japan*, Princeton: Princeton University Press, 1969, pp. 477–537.

Washington Post, 26 January, 1995.

Watson, James L., 'Introduction', in James L. Watson (ed.), *Golden Arches East: McDonald's In East Asia*, California: Stanford University Press, 1997, pp. 1–38.

Weiner, Myron and Huntington, Samuel P. (eds), *Understanding Political Development*, Boston: Little and Brown, 1987.

Weinraub, Bernard, 'President Spurns other Sanctions', *The New York Times*, 6 June 1989, p. 14.

Weisman, Steven R., 'Japan, China's Main Foreign Benefactor Puts Billions in Aid in Doubt', *The New York Times*, 7 June, 1989, p. 10.

Weiss, Linda, *The Myth of the Powerless State*, Ithaca, New York: Cornell University Press, 1998.

West, James M., 'South Korea's Entry Into the International Labour Organization: Perspectives on Corporatist Labour Law During a Late Industrial Revolution', *Stanford Journal of International Law*, 23, 2, Summer, 1987, pp. 477–547.

White, Gordon, 'Civil Society, Democratization and Development (I): Clearing the Analytical Ground', *Democratization*, 1, 3, 1994, pp. 375–390.

Whitehead, Laurence, 'Three International Dimensions of Democratization', in Laurence Whitehead (ed.), *The International Dimensions of Democratization: Europe and the Americas*, New York: Oxford University Press, 1998, pp. 3–25.

—— 'The Democratization of Taiwan: A Comparative Perspective', in Steve Tsang and Hung-mao Tien (eds), *The Democratization of Taiwan: Implications for China*, London: Macmillan, 1999, pp. 168–185.

—— 'The Drama of Democratization', *Journal of Democracy*, 10, 4, 1999, pp. 84–98.

—— 'Stirrings of Mutual Recognition', *Journal of Democracy*, 11, 4, 2000, pp. 65–79.

—— *Democratization: Theory and Experience*, Oxford: Oxford University Press, 2002.

Whiting, Allen S., *China Crosses the Yalu: The Decision to Enter the Korean War*, New York: Macmillan, 1960.

Wickham, John, *Korea on the Brink: From the '12/12 Incident' to the Kwangju Uprising*, Washington DC: National Defense University Press, 1999, pp. 203–204.

Winckler, Edwin A., 'Taiwan Transition?', in Tun-jen Cheng and Stephan Haggard (eds), *Political Change in Taiwan*, Boulder: Lynne Rienner, 1992, pp. 221–257.

Woodiwiss, Anthony, *Globalization, Human Rights, and Labour Law in Pacific Asia*, Cambridge: Cambridge University Press, 1998.

World Bank, *World Development Report*, Washington: World Bank, 1996.

Wu Dunn, Sheryl, 'A Portrait of a Young Man as a Beijing Student Leader', *The New York Times*, 3 June, 1989, p. 4.

Wu Xinbo, 'Four Contradictions Constraining China's Foreign Policy Behaviour', *Journal of Contemporary China*, 10, 27, 2001, pp. 293–301.

Xinhua, 'Rural Votes More Democratic', *China Daily*, 13 March, 1998, p. 4.

—— 'Computer System Helps Rural Elections', *China Daily*, 30 June, 1998, p. 3.

Xu Haitao, 'Grassroots Committees Made Accountable to Villagers', *China Daily*, 22 June, 1998, p. 9.

Yang, Kun, 'Judicial Review and Social Change in the Korean Democratizing Process', *The American Journal of Comparative Law*, 41, 1993, pp. 1–8.

Yang, Ma-li and Engbarth, Dennis, 'Taiwan: All Politics, No Privacy', in Louise Williams and Roland Rich (eds), *Losing Control: Freedom of the Press in Asia*, Canberra: Asia Pacific Press, 2000, pp. 208–218.

Yang, Mayfair Mei-Hui, 'The Gift Economy and State Power in China', *Comparative Studies in Society and History*, 31, 1, 1989, pp. 25–54.

Yasuaki, Onuma, 'Toward an Intercivilizational Approach to Human Rights', in Joanne R. Bauer and Daniel A. Bell (eds), *The East Asian Challenge for Human Rights*, Cambridge: Cambridge University Press, 1999, pp. 103–123.

You, Ji, 'Zhao Ziyang and the Politics of Inflation', *The Australian Journal of Chinese Affairs*, 25, January, 1991, pp. 69–91.

—— 'China and North Korea: A Fragile Relationship of Strategic Convenience', *Journal of Contemporary China*, 10, 28, 2001, pp. 387–398.

Young, Oran R., 'Regime Dynamics: The Rise and Fall of International Regimes', *International Organization*, 36, 2, Spring, 1982, pp. 277–298.

Young, Robert J. C., *Colonial Desire: Hybridity in Theory, Culture and Race*, London: Routledge, 1995.

Young, Whan Kihl, 'Democratization and Foreign Policy', in James Cotton (ed.), *Politics and Policy in the New Korean State: From Roh Tae-woo to Kim Young-sam*, Melbourne: Longman, 1995, pp. 109–140.

Yuan, Jing-dong 'Sanctions, Domestic Politics and US–China Policy', *Issues and Studies*, 33, 10 October, 1997, p. 95.

Zakaria, Fareed, 'The Rise of Illiberal Democracy', *Foreign Affairs*, 76, 6, November–December, 1997, pp. 22–43.

Zha, Daojiong, 'Chinese Perspectives on International Political Economy', *Political Science*, 49, 1, July, 1997, pp. 62–80.

Zhang, Yongjin, *China in International Society Since 1949: Alienation and Beyond*, London: Macmillan; New York: St. Martin's Press, 1998.

Zhao, Quansheng and Press, Barry, 'The U.S. Promotion of Human Rights and China's Response', *Issues and Studies*, 34, 8, August, 1998, pp. 30–62.

Zhao, Suisheng, *Power by Design: Constitution-Making in Nationalist China*, Honolulu: University of Hawai'i Press, 1996.

Zhao, Yuezhi, *Media, Market, and Democracy in China: Between the Party and the Bottom Line*, Urbana and Chicago: University of Illinois Press, 1998.

Zheng Yongnian and Lai Hongyi, 'Rule By Virtue: Jiang Zemin's New Moral Order for the Party', *East Asian Institute Background Brief*, 83, March, 2001.

Zhu, Wenli, 'International Political Economy from a Chinese Angle', *Journal of Contemporary China*, 10, 26, 2001, pp. 45–54.

Zou, Keyuan, 'Reforming China's Judicial System: New Endeavours Toward Rule of Law', paper presented at the East Asian Institute Conference on The Challenges To China's Fourth Generation Leadership, Singapore, 8–9 November, 2001.

Zweig, David, *Internationalizing China: Domestic Interests and Global Linkages*, Ithaca and London: Cornell University, 2002.

Index

www.ingramcontent.com/pod-product-compliance
Ingram Content Group UK Ltd.
Pitfield, Milton Keynes, MK11 3LW, UK
UKHW020353010325
455677UK00021B/432

9 780415 649032